...D DICE

ALASKA 1897-1930

By

EDWARD E. P. MORGAN, 1870?-193?

IN COLLABORATION WITH

HENRY F. WOODS

"The dice of God are always loaded."
GREEK PROVERB

THE CAXTON PRINTERS, LTD.

CALDWELL, IDAHO

1948

Printed, lithographed, and bound in the United States of America by
The CAXTON PRINTERS, Ltd.
Caldwell, Idaho
60898

CONTENTS

Book 1

GOLD, THE MAGNET

9

Book 2

MUSHING AND MINING

85

Book 3

THE UNSINKABLE MARINER

191

ILLUSTRATIONS

	Facing Page
Alaska's Sawtooth Range	38
Lynn Canal and Sprawling Skagway	42
Loading Supplies for Prospectors	43
The Toilsome Ascent of White Pass	48
Heavy Traffic to White Pass Summit	52
Lake Bennett in its Mountain Frame	60
The Swirling Waters of Whitehorse River	64
Five Finger Rapids of the Yukon	80
Dawson Town at the Peak of the Stampede	81
Dawson Water Front in 1899	96
Dawson's Original Hostelry	97
Bonanza Creek Where the Rush Originated	100
El Dorado Creek of the Golden Gravel	108
Morgan Driving Sleigh	144
A Husky Poses for the Camera	145
Husky Mother and Family	160
Rest Period for the Dog-Sled Team	161
A Reposeful Moment for Prospector and Dogs	164
Canadian Troopers Before a Northwest Station	172
They "Always Get Their Men"	173
Placer Miner Panning Gold	180
A Kodiak Bear, Biggest of 'Em All	228
The Famed Inhabitant of Kodiak Island	236
Morgan Before Totem Pole at Wrangel	260
Alaskan Natives	261
The Wreck of the *Mariposa*	268
Dock at Valdez	296

Book 1

GOLD, THE MAGNET

CHAPTER I

FROM A SPOT FAR UP TOWARD the top of the world late in the summer of 1896 came tidings that quickened the pulses of venturesome men in every quarter of the globe. From Victoria, from Seattle, from San Francisco, telegraph dispatches, meager at first, told of the discovery on August 16, in a little tributary of the Klondike River, of rich deposits of gold.

The gold strike in the Yukon was heavy with destiny for me. As daily reports added to the importance of the discovery on Bonanza, the world knew that the first announcements, far from exaggerating the richness of the find, had understated it. It was soon realized that not since the days of '49 had anything like it been known. Before long the stampede was on.

From palace and hovel, from farm and ranch, from the mountains and the plains, from great cities and humble crossroads villages, men and women by the thousands joined the great rush to the Klondike. From desks and forges, from counting rooms, factories and shops, from the pulpit, legislative halls, the sombre atmosphere of courtrooms, the gay make-believe of the theaters, the quiet of studios and ateliers, the feverish activity of newspaper offices, from everywhere they came seeking fortune. And other thousands came from the barrooms and brothels and haunts of the underworld to batten on those who joined in the greatest gold rush the world has ever known.

I was in it, among the first, and the spell of Alaska and the great North was to hold me there for thirty years. Even today I have not shaken it off completely. My quest of gold, like a fata morgana, led me a long, hazardous chase through frozen wilds, riches many times within my grasp, but always eluding me. Although it has left me today with no more wealth than when I started, I count myself far richer for the experience.

In musing over happy Arctic days, days not less full of hopes than of hardships, I live again in the crystalline air of Alaska, I breathe deep of its tonic qualities, hear the metallic song of sled runners on the trail, feel the crunch of hard-packed snow under foot, see its deep, swift, clear rivers and creeks, the entrancing loveliness of the Inside Channel, the icy majesty of its great glaciers and the gorgeous patterns of its summer fields in colors shaming Solomon in all his glory.

Again I live over the days of the stampede from Skagway, of the heartbreaking struggle through White Pass, of the weary climb to the summit, exhausted and spent under a backbreaking load; of a long and bitter trail at the end of which human endurance seemed at the breaking point; of days and nights passed unsheltered in unbelievable cold. Once more I am one in the motley company of gentle and simple, rich and poor, merchants, lawyers, preachers, writers, artists, artisans, farmers, sailors, cowboys, gamblers, harlots, thieves, murderers, cheats, chamberers, pariahs, and—yes, saints—all now seeming like ghosts whirling in a dance of death to the rhythmic tinkle of the gold that lured them—to what? Disappointment, too often. Or death. And to some, even that, at the end, seemed good.

CHAPTER II

I left New York for the Klondike on January 10, 1897. I was in far higher spirits than any of the numerous friends and relatives who were at the old New York Central Station to see me off and bid me Godspeed. Most of them considered my venture harebrained and doomed to failure. I was undertaking it against the advice of my father, in whose mineral water plant I was employed at the time. He tried to dissuade me from what he regarded as a wild and foolhardy project born of the restlessness of youth.

He made a final effort just before my train pulled out to head me off from the trip.

"You still have time, Ed, to change your mind. Why so set on Alaska, that Godforsaken waste of ice and snow that nobody knows anything about?"

I shook my head without answering. We had gone all over this many times before.

"You've got money enough for a trip around the world. It's yours for that purpose if you want to do it."

He had generously staked me to $5,000 for the Alaskan venture, besides providing my outfit of clothes and my railroad and Pullman fare to Seattle. Still I was silent, and he sighed, resigned in the face of my stubbornness.

"All right, my boy, go with my blessing and best wishes, but remember, Ed, there are no telegraph wires in Alaska and if you go broke there you'll surely be up against it. I'm told the walking there is none too good."

Dad was a good sport. He smiled as he spoke, but I knew that his smile masked a great uneasiness. It was a final parting. For the fraction of a second I wavered in my determination, but it was the most transitory indecision.

I was free, white, just twenty-four, and footloose. Better, I thought, to live dangerously, experience the thrills of derring-do, and hazard all on a single desperate throw for fortune than to go on in the treadmill of a clerk's existence, however sheltered and safe. Of what advantage to be well fed and clothed, if one had to pay for it by a deadly routine passed in a setting of bricks and mortar in the daily company of others as bored and dull as myself?

So, heedless of all advice and urgings to the contrary, I went. The only way I could have been stopped would have been to break both my legs. None of those who advised against my going was willing to go to that extent to keep me at home.

On the train which bore me to Chicago, whence I was to go on to Seattle over the Great Northern, I soon met others bound for the Alaskan gold fields. I had been out of New York hardly an hour when I fell in with a party of four, consisting of Dr. Isidor McWilliam Burke; his son, John; his brother, Thomas; and Julius Ullmann, a young Bavarian artist whom Dr. Burke had met on the steamer crossing the Atlantic and whom he had induced to accompany him to the gold fields. As the members of this little party will reappear in this narrative, I shall here devote a little space to introducing them.

Dr. Burke, then about sixty years of age, was a former officer in the British Army, retired with the rank of surgeon major. He had seen years of service in India, South Africa, and Australia, and he possessed the urbane air of a cosmopolite and citizen of the world that characterized some retired army officers. His family was of the landed gentry in Ireland and has figured, in a minor

way, in its history. One of his brothers, Thomas Henry
Burke, was that undersecretary to the Lord Lieutenant of
Ireland who, with Lord Cavendish, Chief Secretary, was
assassinated by Fenians on May 6, 1882, in Phoenix Park,
Dublin.

Although Dr. Burke had had experience in early gold
rushes in Coolgardie, Australia, I somehow had difficulty in
picturing this dignified, cultured and really likable gentleman mushing over Alaskan trails. It seemed much more in
character to envision him as a sahib, white-clad, pith-
helmeted, monocle in eye, seated at ease in a bungalow in
the tropics, enjoying the breeze of a swaying punka, with
a brandy and soda at hand.

It was not difficult, however, to get acquainted with
Dr. Burke, for all his army swank. Almost at the outset
a bond was established between us, for I learned that he
had another brother living in New York, Dr. Gregory
Burke, then head of the medical staff of St. Vincent's
Hospital. I knew Dr. Gregory Burke very well, for he was
at that time our family physician as well as our neighbor,
his country home at Sayville, Long Island, being about two
miles distant from our Bayport home.

John Burke was a frank and friendly lad of about twenty,
who had seen much of the world with his father. Although
by no means a souse, he was as two-fisted and expert a
drinker for his age and weight as I have ever met. He could
down a tumbler of whisky neat without turning a hair,
batting an eye, or pausing for breath.

Thomas Burke, the doctor's brother, had conducted a
retail grocery in West Twelfth Street and had sold it out
to join his brother in the gold-hunting expedition. The
fourth member of the party, Ullmann, at that time could
not speak a word of English, but had a fluent command of
Italian, Spanish, French, and, of course, German. His
lack of English, however did not shut him out of all con-

versation, for both the doctor and John spoke French with as much ease as English, and they conversed in that language with the young Bavarian.

Dr. Burke was most cordial and urgent in suggesting that I cast my lot with his party on the journey to the Yukon. I was quite willing, for they were seasoned travelers, regular fellows, and in every way good company. We were, accordingly, a party of five bound for the gold fields when we arrived in Seattle after an uneventful journey.

SEATTLE'S NORMAL POPULATION, at that time about eighty thousand, was considerably augmented by transients outfitting there for the Alaskan journey. I speak of the population as "normal," but there was nothing normal about it early in 1897, for the city was innoculated with the gold fever and its temperature was abnormal. Those of its citizens who were not planning to join the Klondike stampede were just as eager in some way to profit by it. Hotels, boardinghouses, saloons, bawdy houses, stores, and restaurants were reaping a rich harvest from the hordes of strangers who tarried there until they should start upon their quest for gold.

Dr. Burke advised that we remain in Seattle three or four days to get our bearings and acquire what information we might about the journey ahead of us, the outfit required, and other data of value to prospectors. We put up at the Hotel Northern, then a pretentious hostelry, but since gone into decay. Like every place in the city, it seethed and bubbled with talk and anticipation of the great adventure into the Far North, and of the fabulous wealth there that awaited those who sought it.

It was the sort of talk further to inflame the gold fever that possessed us, but we obtained little information which was of real use, for all the guests at the hotel were fellow

Argonauts who knew as little as we did about what lay ahead of us in the Yukon. We fared no better at the hands of residents. Although on all sides we met persons who professed to know all about Alaska, particularly of the gold fields, and who were prodigal of advice, my subsequent experience convinced me that none of them had ever seen the country.

We were no more successful when we called at the offices of the Seattle Chamber of Commerce, which had a standing invitation to prospectors to come there and get information at firsthand. After a couple of hours spent there, we went down to the docks to look over one of the two or three steamers that were carrying prospectors to Skagway, the starting point for the gold fields. The boat we inspected was a small converted lumber schooner of about eight hundred tons. We were not very well impressed by the dingy little craft.

"She may have been converted," Dr. Burke remarked, "but it's jolly well evident she hasn't been reformed."

It was an opinion in which we all concurred. We were not more favorably impressed with Seattle as a springboard into Alaska, and we readily fell in with Dr. Burke's suggestion that we go on to Victoria, eighty miles distant by steamer, to seek further and, we hoped, more reliable information.

It was better in Victoria and we decided to outfit there and make it our port of embarkation for Skagway. We were staying at the Old Dominion Hotel, run by Ralph Jones. Here we became acquainted with Edward Hamilton, who had just come from the gold fields in western Australia and was outfitting now for a prospecting adventure in the Klondike. At Dr. Burke's invitation Hamilton joined our party for the Alaskan expedition.

Although not as large a town as Seattle, Victoria had
its full quota of transient prospectors. Also it had its
quota, and more, of talk about the Klondike gold strike.
Like Seattle, the town was in a ferment over the newly
discovered Golconda, and it seethed with advice, much
of it conflicting, but all of it guaranteed, to those about to
set out for the Yukon. We were good listeners and took
it all in, exchanging what we had heard when we met
each evening in Dr. Burke's room. After several such
meetings Dr. Burke proposed that we remain in Victoria
until about the first of June, or until the opening of
navigation on the Yukon, which was due at about that
time of the year.

This was counsel not entirely agreeable to Hamilton,
who was for an immediate start which would get us, without delay, into Yukon Territory, and over the ice to
Dawson. At first, I was undecided. I was confused by
the conflicting advice and information of those who, for
all their pretense, knew no more about it than I did.
But I was young, unheedful of dangers that might lie
ahead, eager to reach the gold fields, and as impatient of
avoidable delay as Hamilton was. He saw that while I
felt bound in a way to remain with the Burke party, I
was averse to cooling my heels in Victoria, waiting for
the ice in the Yukon River to break. He continually urged
that we two pull out immediately and make the journey
on our own.

"There isn't an even chance that Burke can get by the
Northwest Mounted Police at the international boundary,"
he declared.

"Why?" I asked in surprise.

"Because he only wants to get to Dawson to open an
office and practice, and in his outfit he has more than two

tons of instruments, medicines and drugs—and not enough food supplies."

I knew that was so. It was a clincher and decided the question for me.

In the modicum of reliable information we had collected was the fact that everyone entering the Yukon bound for Dawson would be required to have in his or her possession not less than fifteen hundred pounds of assorted food, for there was a shortage of provisions in Dawson and the Klondike. This regulation was enforced by Mounties (as the police were popularly known) stationed at the international border between Alaska and Yukon Territory, and they relentlessly turned back everyone who did not have the required food supplies.

Hamilton and I decided to get the first steamer out of Victoria for Skagway, and immediately we began purchasing our outfits at the Hudson's Bay Company store which handled every imaginable kind of food, clothing, machinery, and utensils. We confined our food supply to only the bare necessities: flour, 300 pounds each, double-sacked in fifty-pound sacks; slab bacon, 250 pounds; dried beef, 100 pounds; coffee, 50 pounds; tea, 10 pounds; butter, 50 pounds in one-pound tins packed in sacks; salt, 25 pounds; sugar, 100 pounds; canned milk, 4 cases. Miscellaneous items included 100 pounds of rolled oats, dried potatoes, and dried fruit. Nothing for a Lucullus to get excited about, but good chow for a hungry musher.

This small commissary made up the required fifteen hundred pounds each and cost us about $285 apiece. Upon the advice of the clerk who sold us the bill of goods we had everything double-sacked in stout canvas bags, and then these sacks packed in cases of three hundred pounds each. This proved to be just about the most valuable counsel we had received in either Seattle or Victoria. Subsequent experience convinced us that this clerk knew his outfits, and a thousand times on the trail I blessed his good horse sense. I never knew his name, but he has ever been revered by me as the Unknown Friend.

In addition to the food supplies, I bought an outfit of clothing consisting of two canvas coats, three pairs of trousers, a cap, and two pairs of heavy, hobnailed, laced boots. Coats, trousers, and cap were heavily lined with good-quality wool. At the hotel I donned my trail attire and stowed away my city clothes in the big trunk I had brought with me from New York. In Victoria I was advised to leave all this behind on setting out for the Yukon. I took the advice, which proved to be as worthless as most I had garnered there, for three years later, when I returned to Victoria and claimed my wardrobe, I found that moths had held high carnival with it. My finery was riddled and useless.

It took Hamilton and myself a solid day to obtain our outfits. Early the next day with our packs we were aboard the *Amur* of the Canadian Pacific Steamship Company, bound for Skagway.

CHAPTER IV

AS LONG AS I LIVE AND RETAIN my mental faculties I shall remember the *Amur*. My memories of her will not be altogether pleasant, but they will not be wholly ungrateful, for all that, for I learned about ships from her. What I endured on that abominable little craft gave me a foretaste of the discomforts and the hardships that lay ahead of me, and the experience proved the first step in the hardening process without which I could not have stood up under the greater stresses of the trail. Many times later, on icy paths, in camp, and working a claim, I have looked back on my twelve days aboard the *Amur* and wondered at what I considered hardship. In retrospect, existence aboard the *Amur* seemed all beer and skittles.

Nevertheless, the *Amur* was a floating bedlam, pandemonium let loose, the Black Hole of Calcutta in an Arctic setting. Her passengers, a company of free men and women, for the twelve days of their voyage lived under conditions that would rival those on the prison ships of earlier times.

She was a steamer of less than a thousand tons burden, with accommodations for about sixty cabin and one hundred steerage passengers. She actually had aboard more than five hundred passengers, and nearly that many dogs.

Hamilton and I had engaged first-class passage, for

which we had paid seventy-five dollars each, and which
called for separate berths in a stateroom. When we went
to install ourselves in our quarters we found the room to
contain three wall berths. We also discovered that at
least ten persons held tickets calling for accommodations
in this same room. When the *Amur* cast off for the
voyage, the assemblage of ticket holders in this little
stateroom made one think of an Elks' convention being
held in a telephone booth. The same condition applied to
every other stateroom on the ship.

It was impossible to sleep or rest in our stateroom
except by special arrangement among the ticket holders.
A candidate for slumber or repose had to watch for some
berth occupant to show signs of awakening, and the moment the berth was vacated pounce upon it. He did not
dare remove his clothing, for while he was in the act of
doing so, someone less fastidious would beat him to the
bunk.

Fortunately my prospector's getup was new and clean,
also strictly *de rigueur*, for all the men aboard were similarly attired, and it was the costume for twenty-four
hours of the day. The duds were not handsome, but they
were tough and durable; they kept you warm and dry.
After wearing them for days on end without change, they
seemed to be a part of you. You became attached to them,
and regarded taking them off pretty much as unthinkable
as stripping off your skin. Of course they soon lost their
pristine purity, but keeping clean was the least of our
worries; indeed, it was out of consideration, for it was not
possible in any case.

Providing for cleanliness was not on the ship's program.
On that voyage I was never able to find any fresh water
for washing purposes. There was a salt-water tap near

the toilet and a cake of salt-water soap beside it—the sole concession to hygiene by the steamship company. I tried this arrangement, but found it a delusion and a snare. I gave it up after demonstrating that the soap was no more effective in raising a lather than a piece of wood would have been.

Naturally the passengers were indignant at these conditions and they complained loudly, and bitterly. That is, they did for the first twenty-four hours or so. After that, they concluded it was a waste of time and effort. There was no one to give a sympathetic hearing to their complaints, except fellow passengers, and they were literally in the same boat. The officers were indifferent to the protests and referred all complaining passengers to the captain. The captain was inaccessible; he had retired to his quarters early on the voyage and remained there in serene aloofness. During my twelve days aboard the *Amur* I never saw him. As far as any visual evidence of his existence was concerned, he was as much a myth as the skipper of the *Flying Dutchman*.

The attitude of the ship's officers was that the complaining passengers were unreasonable in expecting ordinary decencies aboard ship. At that time in the Alaska trade anything went. When the gold stampede to the Yukon was at its height, the steamship companies operating in these waters went to the marine bone yard to resurrect any old hulk that might be made to float in order to handle the eager throngs of gold seekers. Discarded wrecks, although they never could be made seaworthy and were utterly unfit for any waters, not to speak of the hazardous waters of Alaska, were nevertheless, put in service to carry their thousands of passengers. It was a God's mercy that there were so few marine disasters during the gold rush, considering the dilapidated vessels, the rakehell crews that manned them, and the unlighted and uncharted waters they navigated.

Every man aboard one of them knew that every moment of the voyage he was in peril, that death rode in the rigging, and that the next hour might be his last. Perhaps the thought was responsible for the decorum, sobriety, and comparative gravity of the Argonauts who traveled on these ships in the early days of the stampede. For there was then a singular absence of merrymaking and hell-raising on these Alaska-bound vessels. Later it was different, but of that, something anon.

I was not disposed to be too critical of the ship's accommodations. Undeniably, they were deficient and crude, but all of us aboard were setting out for adventures, unrevealed to us, which we certainly knew were to prove rough and full of hardships. However little we knew of prospecting or of the region to which we were going, we knew that it was not a place for weaklings, or even for the strong who were not content to forego the soft comforts of civilized existence.

My fellow passengers, I am bound to say from my observations of them, seemed to realize this quite as well as I did. Uncouth and rough as they appeared in their rude prospectors' apparel, they were a sober, earnest lot, purposed to get to the Klondike, be the discomforts of getting there what they might. They included lawyers, merchants, clerks—most of them, I judged, from the same station in life as myself, others perhaps more prosperous. There were also some half-dozen clergymen—"sky pilots" in the terminology of the Northwest—among the passengers, 90 per cent of whom were Americans.

In contrast to this respectable element of the ship's

passenger list there were about fifty sporting women,
some of them young and comely, but most of them mature,
experienced, hard, bold-faced, strident-voiced harpies of
morals looser than ashes. They were the vanguard of the
steady stream of bawds that flowed northward to garner
gold in the dance halls and bagnios that were among the
first enterprises to spring up in the mushroom towns of
the gold fields.

They were a fractious and unhappy lot who were not
maintaining their character of *filles de joie*. Disappointed
that under such crowded conditions as prevailed aboard it
was not possible for them to ply their trade, they railed
bitterly and obscenely at the discomforts of the voyage,
cursed the steamship line, the *Amur's* captain, officers, and
crew, and their progenitors, even to the fifth generation,
and altogether piled confusion upon the existing pandemonium.

One of the sky pilots, a venerable and kindly preacher,
on the first day out, when the women's clamor was at its
highest, sought to pour oil on the troubled waters.

"Yes, yes," he tried to soothe Big Annie, one of the most
vocal of them and a veteran in her calling, "things aboard
are terrible, and it's indeed shameful. But try to bear it.
We'll be in Skagway in little more than a week, and once
there you'll see that things will be a whole lot better for
you and the other girls."

Big Annie was either too surprised to say anything, or
else the preacher's words brought her comfort. At any
rate her complainings from then on diminished.

On our part, amused as we were, we never could be
sure whether the dominie spoke in earnest in a well-meant
effort to bring peace and quiet to the harassed ship, or
whether he was consciously perpetrating a bit of sly irony.

Strangely enough, in all that assorted half thousand or
more of Argonauts, there did not seem to be among us any
notorious gangsters or desperadoes of the half-horse-half-
alligator breed, and certainly not a hobo or tramp. After
all, it was not surprising that the latter were absent. They
are not pioneers, but parasites, who come in the wake of
the sturdy trail breakers and builders. Besides, it must be
remembered, every man and woman aboard had to have
a minimum grubstake of fifteen hundred pounds, in addition to a good outfit of clothing and some tools, possession
of which presupposed funds in the first place. Then, too,
he needed money for his passage and some few hundreds
in cash, at the very least, to keep him going until he should
strike pay dirt, if ever. This, of course, would bar the
Weary Willies, although it would not keep out the
gamblers. They always seemed to have funds.

By the second day out, the grumbling and complaints
of passengers began to quiet down. It was not because
conditions aboard had improved, for they were worse, if
anything. More probably it was because most of us were
rendered docile by sleeplessness. Also, in a measure, we
were starved into submission. For although the price of
our passage included meals, getting something to eat on
the *Amur* was an adventure that was successful only part
of the time.

The dining room was a cubicle aft, below the main
deck, with a maximum capacity of twenty-six persons.
By crowding, twelve passengers could be seated at each of
the two tables. By crowding a little harder, an additional
two diners could be accommodated. As even the most
expert wolfer can do a little better than ten minutes flat in
gulping a meal, and the average is perhaps twenty minutes,
it will be appreciated that it took more than four hundred

minutes, or something less than seven hours, to accommo-
date the *Amur's* five hundred passengers for a single meal
each day at its far-from-bounteous board. The answer
was, of course, that the great majority of the passengers
did not even attempt, after the first few efforts, to eat at
the tables. Even those who had accomplished that feat
were not assured of being fed, for the few waiters, or those
who were not agile dodgers, were intercepted on their way
to the tables with food and their trays despoiled by hungry
passengers, some of whom had stood in line for hours for
a chance to satisfy their hunger.

The tired, sullen waiters naturally resented these on-
slaughts and in the ensuing melees the spilled food added
yet more stains to their jackets, as well as to the soiled
tablecloths, the dining-room floor, and even its walls. The
protests of the waiters, however, were of no avail. They
were hopelessly outnumbered by hungry passengers who
had paid for food, were not getting it, and were determined
they would get it somehow. Some of the good-hearted
passengers even grabbed an extra portion to feed scraps to
the horde of ravenous dogs aboard, who were quite as
hungry as any of us.

The sporting women, led by Big Annie, had been the
first to loot the food trays. At the first protest by the out-
raged servitor whom Annie waylaid, she had knocked him
flat with a mighty wallop, accompanied by a flood of
billingsgate and vile oaths such as the most versatile swearer among the male passengers could not hope to match.
Thereafter, the women were accorded right of way to the
tables, and the men adopted their direct-action tactics in
order to obtain food.

I was a lusty trencherman, and young and strong besides, and had had not too much difficulty in edging into

a place at the table. After the first day, however, I tired
of the effort, and, moreover, the stained tablecloths, the
greasy waiters, and the sight of half-starved passengers
audibly wolfing their food repelled me. I did not propose
to be starved, but I had an idea for satisfying my hunger
under more appetizing conditions. I got it from observing
Big Annie in action.

The second day out I approached this harridan privately,
took a dollar bill from my wallet and held it in her sight.

"Annie," I asked, "how would you like to make an
occasional dollar easy?"

The gentle irony of the question did not then occur to
me. If it did to her, she gave no sign of it. She only
grinned expansively, displaying at least three gold molars.

"How, I'd like to know, in this mob?" she countered.

"Easy. For every meal you get me on this damned ship,
there's one of these in it for you. Are you on?"

"Sure, kid, I'm on."

She was as good as her word. She never failed to produce,
for the waiters all feared her and her vile tongue even as
the wrath of doom, and would meekly allow her to com-
mandeer the trays of food they were carrying to the tables.
I never missed a meal thereafter on that trip. And though
I paid twice for every meal—to the steamship company
and to Annie—I lived like a fighting cock for the rest of
the voyage.

It was not by any means a bad enterprise for Big Annie
either. She did a thriving business filling the food orders
of other male passengers who profited by my example.

CHAPTER V

THE LITTLE *Amur* LUMBERED ahead through the calm,
deep waters of the Inside Passage on its leisurely progress
over the twelve hundred miles to Skagway. I have made
this same voyage countless times since then, but never so
often as to tire of the matchless scenery it affords. Even the
superlative discomforts of my first trip through these
waters could not make me indifferent to the natural
grandeur and beauty that unfolded in a constant procession of ever-changing vistas. The passage today is one dear
to the heart of every world traveler who has made the
voyage. Splendid liners now go from Victoria to Skagway,
with stops, in three days; and with all the safety, ease, and
comfort of a trip up the Hudson. Thanks to the Canadian
and United States governments, the passage has every aid
to navigation. At night every one of its thousand miles is
illuminated almost like the roads in Central Park.

There were no such aids at the time I made my first
voyage aboard the *Amur*. The hardiest skipper then sailing those waters would not have dreamed of running at
night, and, at dark, the *Amur* was tied up like a Mississippi
side-wheeler in the old days.

None of the steamers then operating in the Alaskan
trade had any speed to brag of, least of all the *Amur*. Her
best gait under the most favorable conditions was not

better than seven knots. In places the channel is very narrow, frequently less than a quarter mile wide, all deep water with sheer rock walls on either side, and beaches a rarity. Throughout the thousand-mile length of the passage there is a rise and fall in the tide of twenty-six feet, so that the consequent strong current, which in places raced at ten to twelve miles an hour, was always a handicap on speed.

It was the season of short days and long Arctic nights, and the *Amur* had not more than six hours of daylight for running. There was betting among the passengers that she would not make it to Skagway in her maximum schedule of twelve days.

It was a dismal prospect to the *Amur's* passengers, already fed up with the uncomfortable voyage. By now we had become inured to the culinary shortcomings of the vessel. "Hunger is the best sauce" and we could do with the *Amur's* food without too much complaining. But short rations on sleep was another thing, and sleep, under the best conditions, was next to impossible aboard that misbegotten craft. Above the noise and tumult on the tiny, overcrowded vessel was the ceaseless snarling, fighting, yelping, barking, yapping, snapping, and growling of a pack of dogs that for variety of breed, mendicancy, orneriness, and ubiquity rivalled the canine population of Constantinople in its palmiest days.

They were unnumbered, for no reliable census existed. They were omnipresent, on the decks, in the staterooms and cabins, the steerage, the cook's galleys, the lifeboats, everywhere but the rigging. Some were tied, but most were running loose and always under foot. They were of every conceivable breed—except the right one for the purpose for which they were intended. For they were "outside dogs," that is, dogs not native to the Arctic regions.

There were among them great Danes, English mastiffs, collies, sheep dogs, Saint Bernards, Newfoundlands, wolf-hounds, crosses, and just dogs. But not in the lot a Husky or a Malamute—the only breed of the slightest use in Alaska. For all the good they were to prove to their owners they might just as well have been shot. Indeed, it would have been a merciful act that would have saved them from the abuse, the stupid cruelty, and the dire suffering they were doomed to experience at the hands of their owners, and from the rigors of a climate for which they were utterly unfitted. But I shall reserve till later in this narrative my further observations on the subject of dogs in Alaska.

During the slow progress of the *Amur* I had plenty of opportunity to observe my fellow passengers. They were an intensely serious lot, who had no time either for philandering or drinking on this voyage. They were full of the great adventure and could talk of nothing else. Hamilton and I, in Seattle and Victoria, had absorbed advice and information about the Alaskan terrain, the lore of the trail, and the ways of prospectors. We were pretty well fed up on it and were convinced that little of it was authentic. On the *Amur* we had to listen to much that was no more authoritative than what we were already crammed full of, for it came from men as inexperienced as ourselves, men who knew no more—perhaps not as much—as we did.

In particular, one talkative little chap was so unwearying in conversation, so boastful of what he would do on the trail and in prospecting, that we were amused, rather than bored, by his incessant chatter. He owned twenty-two of the dogs aboard, had been a druggist in San Francisco, and carried in his outfit the full equipment for a drugstore. He might have served as the 1897 model "Drugstore Prospector," for, palpably, he was city-bred, had never had an experience more thrilling than that of rolling pills or compounding prescriptions, and was wholly unfitted, either in the way of physique or stamina, for the hardships of the Arctic trail. We dubbed him Doctor Apothecary, and ever after on the voyage that was the only name I knew for him.

The windy little pharmacist held forth for hour after hour, like the Ancient Mariner, to any passenger who would listen, declaring that with the aid of his twenty-two mutts he would be the first of all the ship's company to make Dawson.

"Hell, Pardner," he would say, throwing out his chest, "the seven hundred miles from Skagway to Dawson will be just a jaunt for me and my dogs. Just a jaunt, I'm telling you."

Then he would strut a bit, like most men of little stature, and add, "North of sixty-four or bust, Pardner."

This became the derisive slogan of all of us, and I was to hear it months later on the Yukon trail. Perhaps in just such a manner were born other slogans which have become identified with the conquest of the great West, such as "From the Isthmus to the Ice," "Fifty-four Forty or Fight," and "Pikes Peak or Bust!"

Then there was the Fat Boy aboard the *Amur*. He was about twenty years old, and it always amused me to reckon that his weight averaged around fifteen pounds for each year of his life, for he toted more than three hundred pounds of none-too-solid flesh. He was six feet, two inches in height, ate like a horse—he had to, I'll admit, to support his poundage—and exuded good nature from every pore of his enormous bulk. He was less talkative than Doctor Apothecary, but quite as much a ship's character. I was to meet both these men later in greatly different locale and circumstances.

It was on this trip that I first witnessed the glory of the aurora borealis. I had often heard of this glowing spectacle, and now the unearthly beauty and eerie mystery of the northern lights filled me with an awe I had never before experienced. I am sure it had the same effect upon most of the other passengers who beheld it for the first time. But not on all of them. One of the passengers, a swaggering, silly fellow, regarded the splendor for a moment, then asked of no one in particular:

"Now, what in hell do you suppose that is?"

A quiet, middle-aged passenger who had been enjoying the spectacle with a rapt sort of expression, now turned with a look of thinly veiled disgust at the interruption.

"Do you really mean to say you don't know what it is?" he asked.

"I sure enough don't know."

"That," the quiet passenger told him gravely, "is the reflection of the gold in the Klondike."

The *Amur's* first stop after crossing the international boundary between British Columbia and Alaska in Dixon Entrance was at Mary Island, a small island on the extreme southern tip of Alaska. Here the United States Customs Office was then located. There was then no wharf at which to land and the *Amur* came to anchor, sending a ship's officer in a lifeboat to report and clear for Wrangell, about eighty miles north. Wrangell is the oldest seaport town in Alaska, for it was there that, in 1867, the American flag was first unfurled when the United States took formal possession of the great domain that "Seward's

Folly" had acquired by purchase from Russia. By the late seventies and eighties it had become a flourishing town of several hundred inhabitants where prospectors outfitted for the stampede up the Stikine River, whose mouth is near Wrangell, on to Telegraph Creek at the head of the Stikine, to the old Cassiar gold diggings. After the mines in the Cassiar Range were worked out, Wrangell settled down to a long somnolence. Its deserted cabins fell into decay. When I first saw the little town, its water front was marked by the rotting hulks of two old vessels that had served as boardinghouses in the flush days. These flush days were temporarily back, now that the rush to the Klondike was on. After the terrible hardships of the trail to Dawson over White Pass and Chilkoot Pass had become well advertised, many had learned that there was another way of reaching Dawson. This was by crossing the divide from Wrangell into the Cassiar Range. The perils of this trail were greater even than those of White and Chilkoot passes, and none attempting it ever got to Dawson. So once more Wrangell lapsed into slumber.

We knew that gold, much of it, had been taken out of the country around Wrangell, but we were not interested in Telegraph Creek, Dease Lake, or the Cassiar Range. Wrangell itself served only to mark definite progress on our long voyage to the new El Dorado.

From Wrangell the *Amur* steamed slowly, all too slowly for her eager passengers, through Wrangell Narrows to Frederick Sound, into Stephens Passage, Taku Inlet, into Gastineau Channel, and thence to Juneau, named for Joseph Juneau, who outfitted at Sitka, two hundred miles distant, for the prospecting venture that was to end in a fortune for himself and his partner, Harris. Joe Juneau's gold strike became the famous Treadwell Mine, but the

CHAPTER VI

THERE IS MORE OF BEAUTY IN the locale of Skagway than in its name or climate. The Indian word "Skagus," meaning "the home of the North Wind," is not a misnomer for the town, as anyone who has experienced its winter rigors will agree. I have no firsthand acquaintance with the weather of Medicine Hat, but I fancy Skagway is a fair contender for the distinction of originating winter storms.

The town lies in a canyon, enclosed on three sides by lofty snow-capped mountains, in the valleys of which are many Alpine glaciers with foaming cascades dashing down their sides into the waters thousands of feet below. Two of the strikingly beautiful peaks visible from Skagway are the Arctic Brotherhood, on which snow-filled crevices in its side form the perfectly outlined letters A B; and the Grecian Lady, whose classic profile is turned heavenward. Probably hers is the face that launches a thousand storms, for there are plenty of them here.

Yet this snowy waste in the home of the North Wind is transformed in summer from its monochrome into something lovely and warm and colorful. I have seen the valley in which the town nestles a flaming carpet of every variety of wild flower, and I have seen berries growing here which are the delight of picnickers.

There was no luxuriant vegetation or color to gladden the eyes now, only an unending sweep of snow. Our jubilation at having finally arrived in Skagway was so great, however, that any sort of weather would have been forgiven. Now that we were at the real starting point of our journey to the gold fields, I could look back upon the voyage aboard the *Amur* as one so filled with delight for the eye as to make me forget the abominable conditions on the vessel. For nine hundred miles before entering Alaskan waters the voyage was through British Columbia, and all the way was superlatively beautiful, the shores on either side an ever-changing vista of highlands, some of the peaks rising to a height of five or six thousand feet. The lofty hills were heavily timbered and many of the summits were sharply saw-toothed, grim, but with a stark beauty about them. For miles the mountains sloped gently to the water's edge. Some steep hillsides showed scars left by avalanches that had cut wide swaths through the timber. Scattered clearings denoted the presence of prospectors delving for gold in this awesome solitude.

Passing through Johnstone Strait, Queen Charlotte Strait, Fitz Hugh Sound, McKay Reach, Wright Sound, Grenville Channel, and Chatham Strait, we came at length to Dixon Entrance, and through it to Cape Fox, the northernmost point of British Columbia, where we had our first view of Alaska.

It was terrific in its grandeur. Even the most raffish among the passengers were impressed. For a time the ship's noise and confusion ceased, while all crowded to the rails to gaze on the land they fondly hoped would yield them gold. For days we had steamed through waters within sight of a tamer beauty. Now we were come to a land not less beautiful, but one on a far grander scale. For the

Courtesy Canadian National Railways

Alaska's Sawtooth Range

dominant note of Alaska is its magnificence. It is a land of great mountains, splendid rivers, vast forests, huge glaciers, and an all-pervading solitude.

Our first view of it was of a great mountain range whose tops were lost in cloud, trailing into mist through which great bulks were only outlined. As the *Amur* steamed north these huge upheavals of nature seemed to march along with us. They were never out of sight.

The last lap of our voyage, through Lynn Canal, was the culmination of a scenic spree which had begun with our entrance upon it. The canal is about one hundred miles long, and through its entire length its shores are lined with lofty mountains, snow-clad the year round. High up in canyons between pinnacles lost in vapor are many dead and living glaciers, huge masses of crystal in fantastic and beautiful shapes that no mortal architect could ever hope to match. Always we could see the foaming white of cascades tumbling down the mountainsides. Men who had viewed the fjords and mountains of Scandinavia told me the North countries had no scenery to equal this in wild beauty.

CHAPTER VII

As the *Amur* docked at Skagway's only wharf her passengers all crowded to the rail for their first view of the town. It was merely a huddle of rude buildings, tents, stores, unpaved streets and footpaths in the hard-packed snow. In the midwinter of 1897 the rush to the Klondike had not yet attained momentum—the stampede did not really begin until the summer of 1898—and Skagway was just becoming known as the starting point for the voyage through the wilderness to Dawson.

Into the little town a year later steamships from ports to the south were pouring thousands of gold seekers; most of them tarried only briefly before plunging forward upon the trail. The great majority of those who stayed were of the worth-while breed of men who build cities, but there were also the weaklings, the physically, mentally, and morally unfit—the parasitic company of crooks, gamblers, rakes, and trulls who seek fortune the easiest way. By the summer of 1898 Skagway, although still a town mostly of tents, was doing business and was developing a civic consciousness that in time was to flower into a really fine community.

It was then that the devil's crew of men and women parasites saw their opportunity. The leading spirit in this band was a pitchman, one "Soapy" Smith. He organized a gang of kindred spirits, known to Skagway as the "Pallid Pimps," and for a time they had things their own way. They robbed, slugged, drugged, sometimes killed, and always cheated and swindled. They operated crooked gambling joints, fleeced the suckers, and, if they protested, slugged them—but always from behind. They had their fancy women lure victims, whom they drugged and robbed and threw into the snow to die or become maimed for life. They created a reign of terror in Skagway, without interference from the United States Marshal, a barrel-chested, pot-bellied hulk who regularly received his cut out of the gang's ill-gotten gains.

A company of United States colored infantry troops was stationed in Skagway, but their presence was no protection to the citizens, for they were commanded by a spineless officer who refused to take any action to relieve Skagway from the depredations of "Soapy" and his gang. At length, when their protests went unheeded, the decent element in Skagway acted, firmly and relentlessly.

Led by Frank E. Burns, who in the early days of the gold rush had quit his clerk's job in Seattle, chartered several barges and towed them, loaded with coal, to Skagway, the long-suffering citizens organized a vigilance committee to clean out the crooks. Burns was doing a thriving retail coal business in the tented town, had visions of a law-abiding, thriving city, and did not propose to have the lives of good citizens and their plans for Skagway upset by the operations of the scourings of humanity. He was a small, wiry chap, vital, fearless, and full of the energy that was later to move him to the vice-presidency and general managership of the Alaska Steamship Company, and still later to the presidency of the Tower Savings Bank, Seattle, which he had organized.

Under his leadership the vigilantes took charge. Frank Reed, one of their number, was ordered to arrest "Soapy" Smith. As Reed approached the gang leader, Smith, without warning, shot him through the stomach with a rifle he held at his side. From the ground, Reed shot the gangster through the heart. Reed died twenty-four hours later, and the vigilantes arose in wrath. They routed out every member of "Soapy's" gang, dragging the cowering, whimpering wretches from under beds where they hid in homes in the "dead line," flogged them, and sent them in droves aboard steamers returning to the States. Then they removed the marshal, and served notice that from that moment Skagway had ceased to be a wide-open town and a haven for crooks.

Skagway today is a beautiful little city with well-paved streets, fine buildings, modern hotels and stores, and pretty homes with flower gardens resplendent in summer with a great variety of cultivated blooms, particularly gorgeous dahlias, and sweet peas of extraordinary size and color.

At the ocean terminal of the White Pass and Yukon Railroad, and as the gateway to the Upper Yukon country, it is a tourist city. Perhaps for this reason the local Babbitts have thought it necessary to glorify the memory of "Soapy" Smith and create a saga about him that will satisfy the traveler's yen for romance. At any rate, one large painting in Skagway depicts the gangster mounted on a splendid black horse, the rider an impressive figure in picturesque costume, with six-shooters strapped to his side and a rifle at the pommel, his eyes piercing, his whole appearance the perfect movie ideal of a border bad man.

Those who knew the Skagway of '98 know well how different was the real "Soapy," cowardly leader of the

Lynn Canal and Sprawling Skagway

Landing Supplies for Prospectors

Courtesy Canadian National Railways

"Pallid Pimps." But tourists love the fiction. After getting their fill of the idealized picture, women have been known to visit his grave in the cemetery ten miles up the canyon and there lay their tribute of flowers. A hundred feet distant a solid shaft of marble sunk in a granite base marks the resting place of Frank Reed, the gangster's victim. Few tourists ever pause at his tomb.

There were no hotels or bunkhouses in Skagway when the *Amur* docked, and for the first twenty-four hours after our arrival our domicile was on the wharf or aboard the *Amur*. The vessel's management was true to form in discharging its cargo, which consisted almost entirely of the outfits of her passengers. These were unloaded in great slings, from which the sacks, boxes, bales, and bundles were dumped helter-skelter on the dock, where every man claimed his own, for there were no sheds or warehouses for proper sorting. The confusion and tumult on the dock were even greater than they had been aboard ship during the voyage.

Hamilton and I took turns at watching for our property and by hard work, aided by good luck, we were able to assemble all the cases containing our outfits. Thanks to the advice of the clerk who had sold us the goods in Victoria, nothing was missing. We were more fortunate than many prospectors whose goods were not packed as were ours. Some of them never did get their property, and others got only what they could grab or what was left unclaimed.

We had a teamster haul our stuff off the dock to a spot about a quarter mile back from high tide and here we pitched our tent, unpacked our food supplies, and began light housekeeping. Thirteen days after leaving Victoria we were established in our first location in Alaska. We were agreed that it should be a brief stay, for we both were eager to take the trail and be on our way to Dawson.

Neither of us knew the best way there. Later we learned there was no best way. All we certainly knew at that time was that there were two routes open to get through the mountain range that was the forbidding barrier between us and the headwaters of the Yukon, on the banks of which, seven hundred miles distant, was our objective, Dawson. We knew that whatever route we chose, whether White Pass or Chilkoot, there was only one means of transportation for ourselves and our packs, and that was by shanks' mare.

"Well, we can do it," Hamilton asserted philosophically. "If the worst comes to the worst, we have sturdy legs and good strong backs."

"Even if we have weak minds," I agreed.

I was not dismayed at the prospect, but I was beginning to realize that we, like most of the prospectors, had undertaken this expedition perhaps heedlessly, without a proper conception of the difficulties attending it.

No one we inquired of in Skagway had any firsthand knowledge of either White Pass or Chilkoot Pass. No one we met had ever been through either. All they knew was that by general reports both were terrible.

"And," they added, "whichever one you take, you'll wish you'd taken the other."

Hamilton was a practical soul. He suggested that before we definitely set out for Dawson we reconnoiter each pass in turn. So we closed our tent and set out afoot, traveling light, without even blankets, and with just enough grub for a couple of days. We explored White Pass first for about ten miles and agreed that all we had heard in disparagement of it was too conservative.

Returning to our tent, we replenished our food supply and set out for a look see at Chilkoot. Whatever our bad opinion of White Pass, three days spent in reconnoitering Chilkoot convinced us it was hopeless. Trudging over its boulder-strewn, icy trail and observing its sheer granite walls, in some places one hundred feet up, where only a block and tackle could lift our outfits, we concluded that it was a route fit only for Titans. And we were not Titans. So White Pass won the decision, and we returned to Skagway to begin the journey.

The deciding factor for White Pass was the discovery that, as far as we had gone, there was a gradual ascent to the summit and a route for a horse-drawn or dog-team sled. In Skagway, seeking to buy a horse, some feed, and two Yukon sleds, we met Ed Burrows, an Australian who had landed in the town a few days prior to our arrival. He had four horses, and several stout sleds and he offered to haul our outfits over White Pass to Lake Bennett, on the other side, for twelve cents a pound. We snapped him up on the spot, for it was a bargain price, as even we realized.

So, five days after landing in Skagway, in the early morning, we set out on the fifty-mile trail to Lake Bennett on the first leg of the long journey to Dawson. Burrows, his helper Williams, a young lad, Hamilton, and I each drove a sled which carried nine hundred pounds containing our outfits in four equal parts. The first three or four miles out were comparatively easy—too easy, it seemed— and I began to wonder why the terrors of the trail had been painted by everyone in such somber colors. Although we saw many prospectors ahead of us and to the rear, and passed others, we did not recognize any of them as having been fellow passengers on the *Amur*. In the next three years in the Klondike I met only two that had been on that voyage.

This set me to thinking of Doctor Apothecary, the boastful little druggist who had sworn a mighty oath to be the first of the ship's company to reach Dawson. I was wondering what luck he was having, if he had taken the trail. Then, coming up over a rise, I met him.

He was standing in the open flap of his tent on the bank of Skagway River, which at this point skirted the trail. He was a forlorn- and dejected-looking object. Gone were the bravado, the gusty talk, the strut, and the boastfulness. Gone, too, were most of the twenty-two dogs in his original entourage. On the wall of his tent, facing the trail, was a sign with the legend in letters of great size:

COMPLETE DRUG STORE OUTFIT
FOR SALE CHEAP

"Hello, Doc," I hailed him. " 'Sixty-four North or Bust.' Well, I see you made it."

He recognized me, but neither the recognition nor the heartiness of my greeting served to chase away the gloom that enveloped him.

"The Klondike be damned," he exploded without returning my greeting. And he continued with deep feeling, "Say, if all the mountains and valleys in the Yukon were lined with gold and studded with diamonds, I wouldn't go a step further. To hell with the Klondike."

In the face of such epochal disillusionment and burst of feeling there was nothing to be said. So, with a "Good luck to you," I passed on. I never saw him again, but I hope he returned safely to his pills and pestles in San Francisco.

CHAPTER VIII

THERE IS NO TRUER TEST OF A man's qualities than trial by difficulties. I would ask no better means of reading character than the chance to observe him on a trail such as White Pass was when I first knew it. Every one of my three companions in that toilsome climb, Hamilton, Burrows, and his helper Williams, under the gruelling six-days' journey to Lake Bennett stood up to the hardships like a real he-man. I soon realized they had the stuff in them that was needed for such going.

Hamilton and I had supposed that we had discounted the hardships of the trail which had been so eloquently pictured for us in Skagway. We had known very well it would prove no holiday jaunt, but at the end of the first day, when we ate our supper of coffee, dried beef, dried fruits, and crackers, we admitted to each other that it was even worse than we had expected. I found myself comparing the day on the trail to a day on the *Amur,* and thinking a little less ill of that vessel.

We had made ten miles on our first day, which was good traveling on that trail. It was perhaps too good for a start, for we were all pretty stiff in our muscles when we set out on the second day. My own soreness was greater because of indiscretion, due to my ignorance of how to take care of myself on the trail. When I retired that first night I spread my blankets on the ground, curled up in them, and almost immediately fell asleep. Some four hours later I awoke chilled to the marrow. The heat from my body had thawed the ice on which the blankets were spread. I should have placed them on a canvas tarpaulin instead of directly on the frozen ground. I never again made that error.

As we climbed the grade to the summit we found the going ever harder. Often the inclines were so steep that we had to divide our loads, leaving part behind while we went forward with the lighter burden, repeating this until the full load had been carried. This of course delayed us and increased the day's stint of work. Burrows and his helper were hard workers, who never seemed to tire, whatever the task, and who were willing always to take on their full share, or more, of labor. Hamilton also, although taciturn almost to the point of sullenness, was a glutton for work, which he disposed of capably and uncomplainingly. I considered myself fortunate to have as trail companions three men who showed no yellow streak under the most trying difficulties and dismaying obstacles.

As the trail wound up the slope, or just as often scaled it, we began to see on all sides evidences of the terrific toll it was taking of those attempting it. We passed hundreds of prospectors moving forward singly and in small parties, some staggering under packs loaded on their backs, others drawing or pushing small sleds laden with their outfits, and still others driving sleds moving, sometimes, under dog power. Whatever our own hardships, those of most of the men we encountered were terrific. Many of the prospectors appeared to me to be men who had never before done a day's manual labor in their lives. They had not undergone any hardening process to fit them for the

Courtesy Canadian National Railways
The Toilsome Ascent of White Pass

trail after lives spent in offices or in white-collar jobs and
were wholly unfitted for the backbreaking experience of
the trail. Many of them seemed at the point of utter exhaustion and barely able to stagger forward. Resting
meant only greater difficulties for them, for during the
few minutes they halted for renewed strength the sled
runners would freeze to the ice. This meant that they
would have to get down on all fours to give them a better
purchase to start the sled going again.

Quite as pitiable in their misery were the ill-chosen dogs
that drew the sleds. No outside dog, no matter what his
breed or stamina, is equal to the task of making the Arctic
trail. I have a wholesome respect for the usefulness, if not
for the character, of the trained Alaskan dog team, but
even the best of them cannot compare for efficiency in
this work with the horse. A thousand times on this journey
I blessed the luck—it was just that, for we knew nothing
about them—that moved us to choose horses instead of
dogs for this trek. I am convinced that one good horse
will pull more in one day than forty of the best-trained
dogs in Alaska—for later I learned about dogs.

The poor brutes we saw drawing sleds on this journey
were not only untrained, but they were underfed, over-
worked, and in every way shockingly used by their owners
or drivers who, to a man, were either ignorant or cruel, or
both. Some of the dogs, scrawny, half-starved, weak, and
numbed by the bitter, unaccustomed cold, unable to drag
their heavy loads on steep grades, lay down in the traces.
This was the signal, always, for the driver, himself half
maddened by the rigors of the weather and the trail, to
beat and kick them.

I had seen so much of this senseless brutality that my
first sensation of anger was turning to a sort of callous

disgust. After all, there was nothing I could do about it. At a turn in the trail late in the afternoon of the second day we came upon one of these stalled sleds. It was piled high with a load for which a dozen dogs would not have been too many. Actually, six were harnessed to the sled, and one of the dogs had dropped to the ground from exhaustion. As we came up, the driver, a great hulking figure, was kicking the exhausted dog with his heavy, hobnailed boots. Insensate to the feeble yelps of the tortured beast, he continued in a blind rage to kick it, shouting as he did so.

"Now, damn you, will you pull?"

It was too much for me. A feeling of nausea seized me. I tried to look away, but the cries of the dog, becoming ever feebler, could not be shut out.

"Here, for God's sake, lay off that," I shouted to the prospector.

He stopped kicking the dog, surprised. Then with a scowl at us, he grabbed the poor creature by the tail, swung it aloft and brought the emaciated body down hard upon the frozen ground.

Hamilton and I started for him simultaneously.

"I saw him first, Hamilton," I said. He paused and I leaped forward.

I think I must have caught the fellow unprepared, for certainly he had the advantage of me in weight and I was no more than the garden variety of boxer. At any rate, I caught him a powerful wallop in the midriff which sent him sprawling. He was up with an alacrity surprising in a man of his bulk, and had grabbed a tent pole from the sled.

"Come on, you ——— buttinsky," he bellowed, "and I'll give you what I gave that mutt just now."

He brandished the club in wide circles, but did not offer to advance on me. This gave me the fellow's measure, but coward though I knew him to be, I didn't dare take a chance of having my skull bashed in while he flourished the tent pole. I felt pretty equal to tackling him if he would discard it, for it seemed to me he had gone down under the first blow almost too readily.

"Drop your club and let's settle it with fists," I invited him.

"Like hell I will. You started this, now finish it."

At that moment Hamilton, who had been standing quietly by to see fair play, with a well-simulated expression of alarm on his face and pointing in the bully's direction, yelled, "Look out there, behind you!"

It was an old schoolboy trick, but it worked perfectly. The tent-pole wielder turned in alarm to face the new danger, and in that instant I was on him in a single leap. Wresting the pole from him, I kicked it away, whirled him around, and rained blows on his face. I went into action in the approved berserk manner. Certainly I know that never before or since in any fight—and I have had my share—did my blows have the steam I put into them on that occasion. He put up a rotten fight, only attempting to cover his face with his hands. When the first enthusiasm of my rage had abated, I gave him a final crack on the point of the jaw and he dropped like an ox.

At first I thought I had killed him, and later feared I had not. Hamilton rubbed snow, none too gently, on the fallen dog-beater's face. In a minute or so he came to, and lay there blinking, trying to remember what had happened.

"You rotten blighter," Hamilton said, looking down at him with a world of cold contempt in his expression, "I hope when you die and go to hell that dogs will tear you to pieces for all eternity."

It was quite the longest speech I remember ever to have heard Hamilton make. We left the fellow sitting on the ground, rubbing his jaw.

"That was a good day's work, Morgan," was Hamilton's laconic comment as we went on.

Courtesy Canadian National Railways

Heavy Traffic to White Pass Summit

CHAPTER IX

THERE IS SOMETHING exhilarating, even to a pacific soul, in a good lively scrap. My bout with the dog-beater had a tonic effect on me, for I felt that the terrific strain of the trail had had no disintegrating effects, on my moral fibre at least, certainly not to the point where I could be indifferent to the brutality I witnessed. I really believe I should have been content to take a good licking from the bully, satisfied that I had done my best to stop his brutal treatment of his dogs.

However, I was pleased to have come off victor and without a scratch. It made me feel that I had become seasoned, that I could row my weight and hold up my end in the arduous tasks of the trail. When I started out from Skagway I weighed 192 pounds. I had no way of knowing how much of this I had left on the trail, but I was pretty certain I was scaling down to fighting trim. I felt that my muscles had hardened, for I could stand up to any task, and the increasing altitude did not distress me in the least, nor did the cold—about twenty degrees below zero, surely enough to freeze the traditional brass monkey—nor did the occasional icy blasts which whistled through the canyon make me want to cry quits. I sprang to my meals with the voracious appetite of the traditional hired man, slept a full eight hours every night without turning, and awoke each morning refreshed, with a clear head, easy muscles, a keen appetite, and an eagerness to hit the trail.

The procession of toiling humanity thinned out as we climbed ever nearer the summit. That is, many of them had ceased all attempts to go on and had pulled their outfits to one side, seated themselves on their belongings, and hung up signs advertising:

OUTFIT FOR SALE CHEAP

We saw many such signs lining the trail clear to the summit, and even on the summit itself. They did not misrepresent either, for on inquiry we found that it would have been possible to buy a good outfit for less than half of what it would have cost in Victoria or Seattle. Most of the prospectors who gave up did so because they were worn out, physically exhausted, or daunted in spirit by the difficulties they had so far encountered. But not all of them. Some of them belatedly realized that even if they reached the summit, there was an obstacle there which they could not hope to surmount.

The summit marked the international boundary between the United States and the Northwest Territories of the Dominion of Canada, and here the Canadian Government had established a customs office administered by the Mounties. Any prospector whose outfit contained food under the prescribed limit was turned back. Any who had supplies bought in the United States had to pay duty on them before he was allowed to enter the promised land. Many of those in the latter situation either did not have the funds to pay the duty, or were unwilling to deliver to the Canadian Government, and chose to sell out instead.

The consequences of the fatigue and surrender of the prospectors that we observed at every mile of the trail were beneficial, in a way, to the poor, spent dogs drawing the sleds. We saw that they received less abuse at the hands of their masters. The bodies of hundreds of them were strewn along the trail. As far as I was concerned, their condition evoked more pity than one felt for their drivers. After all, their owners undertook this gruelling adventure of their own free will and whatever woes afflicted them were of their own seeking.

Half a day's distance from the summit we came upon a sight that would have been ludicrous if it had not been so unbelievably heartless. A prospector, more imaginative than knowing, had conceived the bright idea that oxen were the perfect beasts of burden for the Arctic trail. Mixed with his imagination was a practical instinct, for he intended to sell his beasts for beef after they had hauled his outfit to Dawson. When we overtook him it was obvious that he was beginning to doubt his own wisdom. The oxen were rooted in their tracks and not all the oaths in their driver's repertory—and he was a versatile swearer —could budge them. The poor beasts were physically unequal to the task of pulling the heavy sled up the steep trail, their owner having brought along an inadequate supply of feed for them.

In desperation he had built a fire under them, probably having heard that this was effective in starting a balky animal. It was no use; the oxen strained feebly at the load, but could not move it, and the prospector began to prod the poor beasts with burning brands. Still without moving them, he seemed likely to have roast beef before his eyes if he persisted. We spoke to the distraught driver and dissuaded him from going on with the senseless business. He was not so cruel as he was stupid and half maddened by his experiences. We left him undecided what to do next. How long he had been on the trail, I did not know, but at the rate of progress he was making when we saw him, it must have been weeks. If he ever got to Dawson, which I doubt, I am very sure that he did not bring his beef in on the hoof.

We reached the summit at about noon of that day, four and a half days after setting out from Skagway. Our outfits were intact, our horses in good condition, and we ourselves physically fit, although our clothes and our hides showed some ravages of the trail. Reviewing our experiences during the ascent, I found myself wondering that we had come through alive. Never at any place was the trail easy. Mostly it was perpendicular, and our progress was almost similar to that of the monkey climbing the greased pole—slipping back some for every foot advanced. In places the trail was so steep that it seemed to bend forward, its great rocks jutting out in sharp angles and many times necessitating our unloading the sleds, lifting them over the steep places, and toting our outfits up in many toilsome trips. Then we had to push, pull, and sometimes partly lift our horses over the barriers. Our escapes from falling over cliffs to certain death were many, narrow, and miraculous.

During our progress up the trail I do not believe that any of our fellow voyagers met death, but later it was quite different. When the stampede was at its height a year afterward, hundreds of gold seekers were maimed for life in falls on the trail, and many others killed. In that year, it was estimated that, of the many thousands who started from Skagway for the Klondike, less than 10 per cent ever reached the summit of White Pass, and only half of those reached Dawson.

I find it easy to understand the dismay of the engineers, stouthearted men accustomed to solving the toughest

problems, who were called in a few years later to survey a
route over the Coastal Range through White Pass for the
projected railroad from Skagway to Whitehorse, 120
miles distant.

"This is an aeronaut's job, not an engineer's," they declared, after a preliminary observation of the pass. "The
only way passengers and freight can cross those mountains
is by balloon."

But they tackled the job, and today the White Pass and
Yukon Railroad, with its ocean terminal at Skagway, is
one of the engineering marvels of the world.

We halted at the summit just long enough to show the
invoice for our outfits to the customs officers and have
them cleared, then began the descent to Lake Bennett.
"Easy is the descent," and it was sometimes too easy, for
often we had to rough-lock our sleds to prevent them from
careening down the slope like Hannibal's soldiers coasting
the Alps on their shields.

We made Bennett on the sixth day out from Skagway
and here we parted with Burrows and his helpers, who immediately set out with their horses for the return journey.
That was our last sight of them. They were grand workers
and square shooters.

CHAPTER X

SEVERAL HUNDRED PROSPECTORS were already camped at Lake Bennett when we arrived for a couple of days' rest there. Many of them were busy cutting timber and whip-sawing it in order to have boats ready by the time the thaw set in, hoping to reach Dawson by open water. Others were leaving daily, hauling by dog or horse team. Some had heard at Victoria or Seattle that from Lake Bennett on, a loaded sled rigged with sails would skim over the ice with fair winds. We had heard the same fantastic yarn ourselves at Victoria, but were skeptical. It proved to be beautiful in theory, but pure bunk in practice, and we profited by the example of those who tried it unsuccessfully.

As everywhere else we had been in this region, this lake colony of prospectors hummed and vibrated with information and advice. We were told by men who were as new to this country as ourselves, particularly by the boat builders, that it was foolhardy to go forward in winter, that as we got further north we would encounter temperatures as low as seventy degrees below zero. By waiting until the thaw, then proceeding by boat, they advised us, we could make Dawson, locate a claim, build a cabin, and be all ready for work by the time of the coming of the next winter.

We were deaf to this advice. We would stick by the sleds. We agreed to strike out over the ice for Dawson without delay. From two of the prospectors who intended to remain at Bennett we bought a small, sturdy horse, two stoutly built Yukon sleds, and some feed. The horse cost us $300 and the sleds $50 each. We paid $100 for a bale of hay and the same amount for two sacks of oats. Even at stampede prices, I am inclined to think that that nag of ours cost more to feed than Man o' War ever cost his owner.

We were well pleased with our bargain nevertheless; and fully equipped, well rested, fit and eager, we left Lake Bennett on the fourth day after our arrival there. It was a small settlement then, but by the following summer it had grown to a community of a thousand tents, with five thousand camped there, and a sawmill operating and selling lumber to prospectors at $250 a thousand feet.

We lashed the two sleds together tandem and drove on over the frozen lake. It was easy going and we made fifteen miles the first day, camping that night in a small sheltered cove on the shore. We cooked turn and turn about, Hamilton one day, I the next. There were always plenty of chores to do—putting up and taking down the tent, setting up the cookstove, rustling and cutting firewood, packing and unpacking cooking and sleeping gear, and getting water for drinking and cooking. We obtained water by chopping a hole about three feet deep in the ice, then firing a steel-jacketed bullet at an angle through the lowest part of the hole. When we had to leave the water levels and make our way overland, we melted snow in a gold pan.

Our cooking was simple and pretty much the same for breakfast, lunch, and supper. We used three or four slices of bacon or a pound tin of corned or roast beef warmed up, dried sliced potatoes boiled and served with a strip of bacon, coffee and slapjack bread made in the skillet. A simple menu that would have made Oscar of the Waldorf elevate his nose, but we never needed a dry Martini to urge us to it. After tidying up for the night we dropped off to sleep almost immediately, arising eight hours later with heads as clear as a bell, with no last-year's-bird's-nest taste in the mouth, and with renewed appetite for food and travel.

By night of the second day we had made the lower end of the lake, traveling always in a northerly direction, making easy progress over the ice in a temperature that was always bracingly cold but never bitterly so. We had no thermometer, but since we were as comfortable as when we were on the White Pass trail and at the head of Lake Bennett, where the temperature was twenty degrees below, we judged it was no more severe now.

In traveling this country, at such times as we had to take to the land, we were not greatly impeded by snow. Once past the Coast Range, the Alaskan climate changes. West of the range from Ketchikan to Seward Peninsula, nearly two thousand miles, the snowfall is heavy, with plenty of rainy intervals. In Valdez and on the coast in Prince William Sound the average snowfall, in some winters, is ten or twelve feet, with drifts in canyons and gulches twenty or thirty feet deep, or even greater perhaps, if anyone ever troubled to measure them. This snow is heavy and wet, and the climate on the coast generally, especially in winter, is damp, with strong gales prevailing.

In the Lake Bennett region little rain falls during the summer months; and in winter, from the end of September to the end of April, none whatever. There is a light

Courtesy Canadian National Railways

Lake Bennett in its Mountain Frame

snowfall daily, but for the entire winter it does not attain a depth of more than two feet, and is as light and powdery as fine beach sand. In level places with one kick it can be displaced to show the frozen ground. Disappointing stuff it is for a snowball fight, for it lacks the consistency to make a missile equal to the feat of knocking off a shining topper. However, we could bear up under this disappointment, as neither Hamilton nor I was wearing a silk hat on this trek.

After camping at the lower end of the lake we entered, the next morning, on the ice of a small lake, Nares, also known as Caribou Crossing from the vast herds that in the grazing season pass here on their way to the feeding grounds.

From now on the going became slower and more difficult, for the water is swift and shallow and in freezing presents a hummocky surface. From Lake Nares we entered the Fiftymile River, where the way was still more difficult. The freeze in early winter lays the groundwork of terrific obstacles to come, as the swift current breaks the new ice and pushes it forward until it heads up against a rock or other obstruction, where it again freezes. Thereafter, the process in creating ice barriers continues, the ice breaking, moving forward, then piling up in blocks and slabs, tier on tier, and erecting a barrier that cannot be hurdled or scaled. The only way to pass it is to go around it, which we did countless times in the ensuing days, until at length we lost all count of time.

Each day was a repetition, in its increasing difficulties and hardships, of the day that had gone before. There were steep places to go around, necessitating loading and unloading the sleds, moving the outfit forward piecemeal by many wearisome trips, and repeating this dozens of times in a day. Some days we made but a few miles.

At one spot, a bend in the river, jutting rocks caused a particularly swift current, with the usual results when the river froze. We thought it the apotheosis of all the terrors of this trial. I was told later it is even worse in summer. Our opinion of it evidently was shared by some prospector who had encountered it before us, for on a tree near by was a sign, with a finger pointing to the steep incline, and the legend:

THIS WAY TWO DAYS AROUND

And another, pointing to the water, read:

THIS WAY TWO MINUTES

It was here that a prospector, Joe Collins, some months before, had surrendered to fate. He was known throughout the Northwest and Alaska as a stouthearted man of extraordinary endurance. He had need to be, for three times he had crossed Chilkoot Pass, each time losing his outfit and only saving himself from perishing by superhuman effort and after unbelievable hardships. On his final voyage the summer before we passed this way he lost his outfit in the swift current at this point, somehow saving himself and his rifle. With that he blew off the top of his head.

When they found him days later, a note was pinned to his shirt and on it he had scribbled:

"Hell can't be any worse than this trail. I'll chance it."

CHAPTER XI

By dint of hacking and chopping the obstructing ice, going around it by wearisome detours when it made the way impassable, dragging or pushing our loads up and over steep inclines and then easing them down through the tricky, powdery snow, we at length reached Whitehorse, at the end of this devilish canyon.

Because we were fagged out, and because our faithful nag was pretty well spent, we halted here to rest for three days. There was a little settlement at Whitehorse, with a small detachment of Northwest Mounted Police, a store, and a few log cabins. It was good after those toilsome days in the wilderness to see other human beings and the primitive civilization the few rude buildings represented.

Although the temperature here was thirty-two degrees below zero—we had probably been traveling for days in a like temperature—I did not experience any suffering from the cold. In fact, during my entire stay in Alaska the cold did not seriously distress me, although I had never encountered any weather more severe than the blizzard of 1888 in New York. On location in the Yukon I have known the temperature to drop as low as seventy-two degrees below zero, but even then I was able to stand up to it. No weather-wise person in such extremes attempts to travel, but waits until the cold moderates, which it always does in a day or so. Sudden drops in temperature, such as are common on the Atlantic seaboard, are practically unknown in Alaska; rarely does the temperature drop or rise more than five degrees within any twenty-four hours.

About ten miles out from Whitehorse we came to the head of Lake Laberge, where Robert W. Service got the inspiration for "The Cremation of Sam McGee." The lake was thirty-five miles of smooth ice, which we did easily in two days. We were within twenty-five miles of the foot of the lake when, on the second day, we overtook a prospector struggling forward with a small, but heavily loaded sled, drawn by the voyager and a lone dog, of no great size or strength. Between them they were not making much progress and we readily granted permission to the traveler to hook on to the rear of our sleds for a lift for the next half-dozen miles or so.

The prospector was a rather undersized figure, attired in Mackinaw coat and trousers, with the regulation heavy boots and fur-lined cap, and we were surprised to learn that our fellow voyager was a woman. Nellie Cashman was her name, she told us, and she was on her way to Dawson. Although she was not possessed of the required amount of food supplies, she had been able to pass the police barracks at the summit of White Pass, Lake Bennett, and Whitehorse by talking the Mounties into permitting her to go on. I met her many times later in Dawson and could well believe her story of the persuasive power of her tongue, for she had the gift of palaver and was a most convincing talker.

We camped at the foot of Lake Laberge, but Hamilton refused Nellie permission to camp with us on account of her sex, and after supper she moved on. In the morning we emerged upon the ice of Thirtymile River, into which

The Swirling Waters of Whitehorse River

the lake empties. The river's name is meaningless; an appropriate one for it would be Corkscrew River, for over its entire length—which is more than thirty miles—it winds and twists and squirms around and between high terraces and lofty mountains. We grew dizzy from following its meanderings. Then at length we approached its mouth at the Hootalinqua (now the Teslin) River, and this proved a fateful point, for it was here that our sleds were nearly wrecked. And here a friendship certainly was.

As we approached the river's mouth the difficulties of travel became ever greater. We had come to an impassable ice barrier in the river, necessitating a detour around a point on a bluff. Five times we had worked back to pick up loads left behind to lighten the sleds, and we were on our sixth trip forward. The trail was over masses of loose rock and we had to exercise the utmost caution to avoid sliding down the forty-five-degree angle of the bluff to the river bed three hundred feet below.

Hamilton was at the horse's head leading him; I was with the sleds at the lower side of the trail to watch that the runners did not go off the pathway. The least misstep of the horse or slip of the runners would have meant disaster, probably death. We moved by inches, Hamilton stopping the horse at my signals, which were frequent. It was harrowing work, and between the physical exertion and the nervous tension we both were in a deplorable state.

Slowly the faithful horse pulled the sleds, starting, stopping, starting again. Suddenly I heard a rock underfoot slide down the bluff, and another and another. Then the runners of the forward sled sagged gently.

"Stop!" I yelled to Hamilton.

It was too late. Horse, sleds, outfits, Hamilton, and I went off the trail pell-mell in an avalanche of slipping

rocks. Over and over we slid down in a welter of confusion. It seemed to me that we would never stop rolling,
and I dreaded the moment when we would, for I was sure
the end was death for all of us. Surprisingly, we all ended
up on the ice of the river, alive, with no bones broken, no
bloody wounds, but a bit bruised and breathless, and our
dignity considerably upset. When I got my breath, Hamilton had freed the horse from the overturned sleds.

I was in a black mood. Instead of being profoundly
thankful for my escape from death, I was enraged at the
upset. The tremendous efforts of hours on the trail, the
physical exhaustion, and the difficulties generally of this
vile journey, culminating now in our present predicament,
brought me to the limit of my endurance. I cursed Alaska
and the Yukon and the Klondike and all the gold contained therein. I cursed the trail, the sleds, the horse, and
our outfits. With ever-increasing feeling I cursed the day
I left New York, unkind fate, and, I have no doubt,
Hamilton, while I was at it. Not until I had exhausted
my breath and the range of available subjects for male-
diction did I pause.

During the outburst Hamilton had stood looking at me,
silently, and with disgust. In the pause he said:

"Are you quite through?"

His quietly contemptuous manner infuriated me anew.
"No, by God, I am not!" I shouted.

And I started afresh. I do not now know exactly what I
said—I never did know—but whatever it was, this renewed
outburst was of briefer duration than the first. I realized
with a sickening sense of defeat that my vocabulary of invectives was wholly inadequate to do justice to the situation, and I stopped short.

At the first of the renewed flow of profanity, Hamilton

had turned his back on me and quietly set about righting the sleds and their loads. A little ashamed of myself, but still in a smouldering rage, I joined him in the task. Together we unloaded the sleds and, in repeated trips up the bluff, got the last of the outfit, the horse, and the sleds back on the trail. We were at it for hours, neither one uttering a word all the while.

It was late at night before we carried the last load to the spot where we had cached our supplies and equipment. We camped there, both too exhausted for food, and turned in just as we were, without exchanging a word.

A sound, uninterrupted sleep had immensely refreshed me and I was up at daylight. Hamilton was still abed and I set to the task of preparing breakfast. By the time I had worked off some of the stiffness and soreness of my muscles in rustling and cutting firewood and procuring water, I was in great spirits, and put a real enthusiasm into the preparation of a breakfast of slapjack bread, fried bacon, and steaming coffee.

"Breakfast, Hamilton," I called to him when it was all set.

He did not answer or move, and I called a second time. Still no move or answer from him, but I saw that he was awake and steadily observing me.

I turned to, ate breakfast alone—all of it—and then cleared away the cooking gear, fed and watered the horse, and performed the accustomed camp chores. A couple of hours later Hamilton turned out, prepared his own breakfast and ate it. All this time he had not spoken a word to me or given me the slightest heed. It seemed childish to me, but I pocketed my pride.

"Well, how do you feel this morning, old man?" I asked him.

He ignored me and my greeting. My anger flared up.

"What the hell's the matter with you anyhow, Hamilton?" I demanded.

This time he looked at me coldly for a moment, then said:

"Morgan, when we went off the trail last night you called me a God-damned son of a bitch."

I had no recollection of cursing Hamilton directly. I knew I had done some pretty fluent swearing that had embraced a wide variety of persons and things. It might well be that in my blind rage I had called him names. I said I was sorry. And I truly was. My obvious contriteness did not soften him in the least.

"I'll allow no man to call me that," he said. "In Australia——"

"But, Hamilton," I broke in, "I've told you I'm sorry, terribly sorry. Take into consideration the fix we were in, what we had gone through all day, and what happened and might have happened. Damn it, man, I didn't know what I was saying. I don't know yet, but whatever it was, I apologize most sincerely."

He said nothing, and I went on. "Let's forget it, and be thankful we weren't maimed for life or busted up for keeps."

But nothing I could say in the way of an apology mollified him. He told me, coldly and flat-footedly, he would not accept an apology.

"Well, if that's the way you feel," I told him at length, "perhaps you'd prefer to settle it with fists."

I was not suggesting this in anger, although his attitude was getting under my skin. I really thought that in his obstinate state it might serve to clear up the situation, after which we could resume our journey in amity.

"That won't settle anything," he answered coldly.

"Well, for God's sake, what do you suggest then?" I asked in desperation.

"The only way that will satisfy me is to call off our partnership, divide the stuff we own in common, and each one go his own way."

I had not thought of this solution, did not welcome it, and was really dismayed at the thought. I liked Hamilton, admired his capacity for hard work, his silent, uncomplaining endurance under the most appalling conditions, and the entirely unselfish way in which he stood up to the tasks of the trail, never at any time shirking or seeking the easy end of a job. But I saw he was determined upon a parting. Silently I nodded assent, and we agreed on a division of the assets in our outfits, some of which we had bought jointly. He kept the tent, the stove, mining tools, some of the cooking gear, one of the sleds, and $150 in cash for his half ownership of the horse. The remaining feed went with the full ownership of the animal.

When we had sorted out the goods and divided them, it was about the middle of the afternoon. I loaded my possessions on the sled and prepared to set out alone on the trail. I did not have it in my heart to part in enmity with the only fellow man in this desolate waste of snow and ice.

"Good-by and good luck, Hamilton," and I offered him my hand.

"Good-by," he said, but he did not take the hand I offered.

Then I drove on. My path never again crossed Hamilton's. If so be he is living and reads these words, let him know that I never bore him enmity, that I greatly regretted the rupture of our friendship, and its cause, and today bear him in kindly remembrance as a truehearted comrade and honorable man.

CHAPTER XII

FIVE MILES FURTHER ON I made camp in a likely looking cove. That is, I halted there for my supper and night's rest under no shelter other than my blankets and what protection the cove afforded, for I had now no tent—or stove, either—but I was confident I would miss neither. On the trail we frequently had made camp without pitching our tent, sleeping on it instead of under it. Also we had cooked our meals at times over open log fires. I was well upholstered in warm clothes, my blankets (three of them) were of the best wool, and curled up in them and rolled up in a ten-ounce canvas tarpaulin I turned in after supper and slept like a dead man.

In the morning, thoroughly rested and refreshed, I considered my situation. Without any choice in the matter I was—so it seemed to me—alone in Alaska. Reviewing what had happened, it seemed to me that Hamilton had been unreasonably obstinate in refusing to accept my apology. His insistence upon a parting between us appeared to be due to possibly another reason than his resentment at my conduct when we tumbled over the bluff. The more I thought of it, the more it seemed to me that he had seized upon this as a plausible excuse to go it alone.

Prospectors were like that, I knew, and Hamilton's constant gravity and taciturnity indicated that he was normally a lone wolf who, having associated himself with another, later regretted it. I recalled the story I had heard on the *Amur* about the two prospectors working together in the foothills of the Rockies at the headwaters of the Klondike River. They were silent, sturdy men who passed days together in camp without the exchange of any words that were not absolutely necessary.

One day one of them came into the tent and remarked to his partner:

"Seen a dead horse up the gulch jest now."

" 'Tain't no horse. It's a mule," said the other.

That was all. Not another word was spoken by either and after supper they turned in, still as silent as two sphinxes. In the morning the prospector who identified the dead animal in the gulch as a mule discovered that his partner was not in his bunk. Getting up he noticed a note on the table, and read:

"Leaving this camp. Too damned much argument."

Whatever the reason for Hamilton's insistence on our separation, it left me with a big problem which was no nearer solution by the time I had had my breakfast and cleared up things. I felt that I needed to come to some decision before again taking up the trail, but what it ought to be I could not for the life of me figure out. The only thing I was certain about just then was that I needed at least a day's rest and this spot seemed as good as the next for that.

It was desolate enough surely, and being alone was far from agreeable in my state of mind, through which all sorts of imaginable and unimaginable dangers passed in endless procession. Not a sign of life——

At that moment I saw a flicker of movement against the white mass of the landscape. A couple of rabbits were within gunshot. It had been a long time since I had tasted fresh meat—not since leaving the *Amur,* where the quality, God knows, had been none of the best—and this seemed a heaven-sent opportunity to supply the lack. Promptly I knocked the cottontails over with one shot, and soon had them skinned and dressed and all ready for the stew, which I prepared in the horse pail. The recipe was my own, rabbit meat with slices of bacon, slices of dried potatoes, dried onions, and dried carrots, all well seasoned. As the savory odors arose from the simmering mess my spirits rose with them in anticipation of the feast I was preparing for myself. After all, the bottom had not fallen out of my world; what Hamilton could do alone surely I also could do unaided, and—there was the Klondike with its gold awaiting me.

In this better frame of mind I dished out the stew and sat myself down to enjoy a feast. But again the melancholy of my situation came upon me. Here I was, eating alone the first of many similar meals to be eaten in silence and a solitude unbroken by the presence of any human being nearer than a thousand miles, or more perhaps.

Glancing up the trail in the direction of the spot where Hamilton and I had parted, I saw far away, outlined against the snow, a small, solitary figure moving slowly but steadily in my direction. I could see the trail for a distance of perhaps two miles and the object, whatever it was, whether beast or man, was probably a mile and a half away. With pounding heart I watched its gradual approach, until with a great elation I could be sure it was the figure of a man. I think then, for the first time, I appreciated the feelings of Robinson Crusoe at that moment when on his island, he saw human footprints in the sand.

Intently I watched. Could it be Hamilton, relenting and coming to rejoin me? A few minutes later I knew that it was not he, for the figure was that of one smaller in bulk and stature than Hamilton, and with a different gait. Soon the moving figure was near enough for me to make out plainly. It was that of a man, whose youthfulness of figure even his bulky garments could not conceal, dragging a small sled with a light load, and he was singing at the top of his voice "I'm the Man That Broke the Bank at Monte Carlo." I stepped out on the trail and hailed him.

"Hello there, partner, where you bound for all alone? Come on and join me in the finest rabbit stew you ever tasted. It's just ready and your name, whatever it is, is in the pot."

If he was surprised at meeting me in this spot and receiving this prompt invitation to dine, he did not show it. He merely stopped singing and grinned from ear to ear, giving me an instantaneous impression of the best-natured human being I had ever met. And so he proved to be in the years I was to know him. Silently, but still smiling expansively, he drew his sled to the side of the trail and followed me to where the feast awaited. I was as hungry as I have ever been. But my guest was even hungrier than I. We fell to without ceremony or words. We ate, we gormandized, we stuffed, only pausing for renewed effort, and in such intervals our only conversation was in praise of the stew. Then we began anew until at length the horse pail was almost empty. We washed down the food with copious drafts of steaming coffee, lighted our fags, and by conversation proceeded to the work of consolidating a friendship which began then and there and has endured through the lapse of time and separation.

My guest's name, he told me, was Jack Lindsay. He was twenty years old, born in Scotland, and had come to this country at an early age with his parents, who had settled in Pennsylvania, where his father, a coal miner, obtained employment in the mines. Jack followed his father's occupation when he was old enough to become a bread-winner, and it was while working as a miner that he had heard, about six months prior to our meeting, of the gold strike in the Klondike. Inflamed by the gold fever, he left the mines and beat his way across the continent to Seattle where he shipped as one of the crew of the steamer, *City of Topeka,* bound for Alaska.

On the voyage he met up with a Californian, Frank Moran, a shipmate, who also had been inoculated with the gold fever. They jumped ship at Skagway, forfeiting their wages thereby, but "borrowing" a couple of blankets apiece from the ship's stores. Between them they had a total cash fund of twenty-five dollars and, although they well realized the tremendous difficulties before them in making their way to Dawson with such slender resources, being born gamblers they had set out on their travels light-heartedly and undismayed.

They had left Skagway with two fifty-pound sacks of flour, a couple of slabs of bacon, twenty-five pounds of coffee, a skillet, coffeepot, two tin cups, a few tin plates, and two small sleds, the purchase of all of which had meant the outlay of their entire capital. Knowing that they would be stopped and turned back by the North-west Mounted Police wherever stationed, they avoided the barracks, taking to the hills to go around them. They had done so at White Pass barracks, at which point they had become separated. At the time I hailed Lindsay he was hurrying forward on the trail, hoping to overtake Moran, who, he calculated, had gone on ahead of him.

I told him that I had been within sight of the trail since early morning and that no one had passed that way prior to his coming.

"Well, I guess he'll be along any time now," he said, and he added with a wide grin, "And I reckon he'll be as hungry as I was just now, because we both were on short rations."

Then, after the manner of prospectors at their first meeting, I told him about myself and about the parting with Hamilton.

"Yes, I seen him three, four miles back," he said, "and when I seen you I figured you was of the same outfit and had gone on to make camp in advance."

About an hour later Moran appeared and I invited him to set to and finish the rabbit stew, which he did effectively and with evident enthusiasm and appetite. When he had satisfied his hunger I suggested that they throw in with me for the rest of the voyage to Dawson, I to supply all the grub in return for their help and companionship on the trail. They had not to bother about being turned back, for there was not another police barracks to be passed this side of Dawson. They were short of food supplies, and they readily agreed to my proposition.

We got under way early the next day. There followed a succession of days, weeks, and months on the trail, each one a repetition of the dangers, obstacles, and toil that had gone before. But I did not mind them, for my two young companions were stout fellows who tackled the hardest tasks as if they were sport. They were always cheerful, even playful, no matter what the weather or the difficulties of the going. It was a delight to travel with them, particularly Lindsay, who bubbled over with good spirits every hour of the day and every foot of the trail. Usually he was singing at the top of his voice, running through a repertory that was extensive, but always coming back to his favorite, "I'm the Man that Broke the Bank at Monte Carlo," which he was caroling when I first saw him coming down the trail.

After we had left Thirtymile River and entered the Lewes River Valley, the topography of the country changed gradually, the rivers becoming wider, the shores more heavily timbered, the flanking hills not so high, and the great saw-toothed mountain peaks receding into the distance. Although the country was becoming more rolling, the ice of the Lewes River was as rough as any we had encountered, and there were days when we did no more than a few miles.

We lost track of time for we had not seen the sun since leaving Lake Laberge, and then only for a few hours each day. Now we were traveling always in an Arctic dusk and in cold that became increasingly bitter, so that at times we would have to make camp and wait for the weather to moderate. Dawson seemed a long way off and all we knew of its location was that it was somewhere ahead and that by following the river we would reach it eventually, for we had no knowledge of our position and no maps, none being in existence then. There were times when I was sure we would never get to Dawson, that death was just around the next bend, and that it would be a welcome relief from this terrible cold and the blind, stumbling march over the ice in the eternal twilight.

It was at such times that Lindsay's voice would be raised in song and jest and laughter. And it was not simulated, either. The boy had an invincible cheerfulness that no dangers, no hardships, no suffering, no solitude could

overcome. He was a regular Mark Tapley, and for the
first time in my life I conceded that Dickens had not
overdrawn this famous exemplar of optimism and cheerfulness, whose spirits rose inversely to causes for woe. I
hold Lindsay in the most affectionate remembrance, for
I am convinced that if it had not been for his sunny nature
I would have gone mad or else have lain down in the snow
and welcomed death.

At length, after what seemed months of travel, during
which we had met no other fellow human beings, had
crossed mountains of ice, slept in the open while blizzards
raged, always stumbling forward somehow in the direction
of Dawson, we noticed that the drab grey, dawnlike days
were getting longer, and presently we made camp at a
spot we knew later to be the mouth of Stewart River,
where it empties into the Yukon. There were several
prospectors camped here, and from them we learned that
the day was April 16.

CHAPTER XIII

THE YUKON! WE HAD reached the famed river—which, until now, had been no more than a name to us, a name linked with our dreams of wealth. For the first time it seemed that we were truly within striking distance of our goal. Yet Dawson was one hundred and fifty miles farther on, and between it and us there was an unknown trail which threatened daily to become ever more hazardous.

We decided to rest a week in camp at the mouth of the Stewart. Reviewing our journey over the ice of Thirty-mile River, it seemed to us to have been such a journey as few men have ever made, so long, so toilsome, so beset with suffering and peril, and yet——

One bitter cold day in December, 1905, a great blond man drove his team of half-starved wolf dogs into Fort Egbert, the northernmost post of the United States Army and the end of the army telegraph line. Although somewhat gaunt from obvious fatigue, he was evidently physically fit and as rugged as the mountains that loomed on the horizon. Without pausing for rest, he sought the general store where he made several purchases.

The storekeeper, thinking him just another "Swede" prospector (all Scandinavians are "Swedes" in Alaska) asked his customer where he had come from. He answered that he had been cruising in a little sloop "up north," and had put the vessel in winter quarters off King Point, near Herschel Island, on the north coast of Canada. He seemed reluctant to talk about himself or his travels to the storekeeper, but the latter was inquisitive and did not scruple to ask questions. He learned from the "Swede" that he had made the journey afoot every step of the way to the fort, accompanied part of the distance by two natives, and over the whole journey by a companion who was unequal to the hardships of the trail and had had to be carried on the sled.

The storekeeper was astounded at the man's story. Even in Alaska, what the stranger had done was accounted a remarkable feat of traveling. Five hundred miles over the ice, scaling a mountain range nine thousand feet high, traversing an unbroken trail in the Arctic dusk—but, for what? The inquisitive merchant persisted.

Almost brusquely, the Norseman inquired for the telegraph office. There he filed a message to the king. It was addressed simply "Haakon, Christiania, Norway," and signed "Amundsen." The message announced that on August 26, preceding, he had discovered the Northwest Passage and had ample corroborative data to make good his claim. Thus the explorer told of the feat that had been the dream of venturesome men since Columbus.

For several weeks Amundsen rested at Fort Egbert against the return voyage to King Point, then harnessed his dog team and, pipe in mouth, set out on the trail. While the Arctic wilderness once again enveloped him, the world rang with plaudits for his discovery.

At Golden Gate Park, San Francisco, I have seen the *Gjoa,* seventy-two feet long, a shallow-draft vessel in which for the first time in history man sailed by the northern route from the Atlantic to the Pacific.

The prospectors who had preceded us to this camp were convinced that the one hundred and fifty miles to Dawson could not be made over the ice before the thaw set in, that it would be too dangerous for travel on foot. We allowed ourselves to be influenced by their opinion and decided to remain here and build a boat in order to be ready by the time the river opened up, which we were told would be about May 20. Had we persevered in our decision to trust to the ice and gone on immediately we would have reached Dawson a month earlier than we did.

Our horse was showing the severe strain of the journey and our supply of oats and hay was about exhausted, without a chance of replenishing it. In the circumstances I decided that the humane thing would be to shoot the faithful beast that had shared with us so much toil and danger on the trail. My well-meant act was a foolish thing, for after the horse was no more I realized that he could have been kept alive on flour and rolled oats, of which I had plenty, and that I could have sold him for one thousand dollars at Dawson.

We had a wealth of material at hand from which to select the timber for the boat we were to build. Moran had worked in various logging camps in Oregon and Washington and on his advice we selected a site on a fairly steep hill about a thousand feet back from the river, and established a saw pit in which to prepare the spruce logs for our boat timbers, which we rolled down the grade after performing the initial operations on them with a six-foot ripsaw. Felling, sawing, roughdressing, and hauling the logs was a man-sized job for all three of us, and at night we were ravenous for supper at our camp. We had made quite a comfortable and homelike place out of pine boughs constructed into a windproof lean-to, and had

Courtesy Canadian National Railways

Five Finger Rapids of the Yukon

Courtesy Department of Mines and Resources, Ottawa, Canada
Dawson Town at the Peak of the Stampede

installed a good solid flooring. Lindsay and Moran possessed
all the elasticity of spirits of healthy youth and after
supper they enlivened things with music, with remi-
niscences, songs and jokes (some of them Rabelaisian and
salty). Lindsay had a good tenor voice and Moran played
the mouth organ well, and our camp soon became the
rendezvous of evenings for every socially minded prospector in the little settlement.

We finished building our boat—it was, more properly,
a scow—in a little more than a week's time. It was sixteen
feet long by six feet wide, flat-bottomed, with straight
sides and rounded-up ends. When we launched her we
were delighted to see that she was as tight as a drumhead,
and did not leak a drop. Moran had hewed out sweeps for
both ends, these to be used in steering the craft. Although
the boat did not have the lines of a cup-defending yacht,
she was stout and staunch and fit to navigate any river,
no matter how full of rocks and ice floes it might be. She
proved it subsequently.

We were rarin' to go as May was ushered in by a warm
south wind before which the snow began to melt, but the
launching of the boat must await the breakup of the ice
in the river. All the signs of spring were present—the
daily thaw, the rising sap in the trees, the flight of migrating birds—but the season here, as elsewhere, was one
of fits and starts. Until the ice broke we had to use what
patience we could invoke in our eagerness to be on our way.

Not until May was in its second week did the ice in the
Stewart River show signs of breaking up. Even then we
could not launch our boat because the free movement of
the ice downriver could not begin until the Yukon cleared
the way with a seaward discharge of its own ice. Somewhere down the line there was a jam, and until its pressure

was relieved, our way was barred. It was as a block in the
subway. In your stalled train you cannot see the cause of
the halt, but you know that somewhere ahead on the line
there is an obstruction and that, until it moves or is removed, your train cannot proceed.

At length the jam in the Stewart broke and the river
began its flow to the Yukon. We cut a passage through
the shore ice, wide enough to haul our boat through, and
launched it. Then we loaded our supplies and pushed off
for Dawson on May 14.

We were following the tail run of the ice downstream
and our progress was limited to the speed with which the
ice moved. This meant that we had to stop every time
the ice was slowed by a jam somewhere ahead. It was
ticklish work, for every minute of the journey we were in
danger of being crushed by the ice. Even when we tied up
someplace to await the resumption of the ice run, we had
to choose our mooring place very carefully, not only to
avoid stray floes, but also to keep clear of overhanging
masses of rock and ice on the shore, any one of which,
falling on us, would have smashed the boat like an eggshell.

Many times during the journey down the Yukon we
sighed for the dangers of the ice trail we had thought so
malignant, for these new perils seemed far greater than
any we had yet encountered. The Yukon in flood was
truly formidable, and with the flood complicated by
migrating ice, we faced death almost all the way. Grave
as were the dangers, they could not serve to dampen the
spirits of Lindsay, who at one of the most difficult stages
of the journey was reminded of a story.

"There was a guy," he began, "who lived through the
Johnstown flood and who was always tellin' anyone who
would listen all about it. Well, this chap died and went to

glory. In Heaven he buttonholed everyone he could lay his hands on and told 'em about the horrors, the hardships, and deaths he had witnessed in the great Johnstown flood. Every time he told his yarn he noticed that a very old man with long, white whiskers would throw his head back and give him the horselaugh. This finally got the storyteller's goat and he complained to Saint Peter, who told him to point the old guy out to him. When Saint Peter saw those old whiskers, he said to the Johnstown flood feller: 'Why, don't you know who that is?' 'No, I don't,' he answered. 'Why, that's Noah,' Saint Peter told him."

As May drew to a close and the sun grew warmer every day, the ice run was accelerated and the Yukon flowed freer and swifter. We were on the last leg of our journey and were ending it with less exertion and danger.

Two days later, on June 2, about noon, we made fast to a bank a little north of the mouth of the Klondike River, at its junction with the Yukon. There was Dawson. We had reached the new El Dorado.

Book 2

MUSHING AND MINING

CHAPTER I

As a city Dawson was nothing to get excited about. Yet we were tremendously thrilled by our first view of it. I doubt whether Columbus, when he first beheld the shores of the New World, or Balboa, when he looked down from his "peak in Darien" upon the shining waters of the Pacific, could have been more deeply moved than we were as we surveyed the unlovely huddle of huts and tents that was Dawson, for it marked the end of a heartbreaking trail over which we had journeyed for months.

In the summer of 1897 Dawson consisted of some hundreds of tents and log cabins, dwellings, stores, restaurants, saloons, and dance halls spread out on a large flat at the edge of a valley. Its population then was not more than three thousand, mostly men. What few women were there were dance-hall dames who had flocked in from Yukon River points at the first tidings of the gold strike. They were unlovely specimens of femininity, but as the only available representatives of their sex they did not lack for followers, including the loathsome cadets who lived on their earnings.

Our landing was the signal for an outpouring of practically every man, woman, and dog in the little town. If we had any thought that it was a reception committee on hand to welcome us we very soon got over the idea.

They had come to trade, not to palaver. Hardly greeting us, and not asking our names or where we hailed from (that wasn't done those days in the Yukon, lest such questions prove embarrassing), they watched hungrily as we unpacked our stores and scanned each item as it was stacked on the riverbank, trying to determine whether it was something they were in need of.

Apparently they were in need of everything in the outfit, for there was a shortage of foodstuffs and provisions generally in Dawson just then. Long before we had discharged cargo there was a clamor of many voices offering to buy various supplies in my outfit at prices that made me fairly gasp. No offer under a dollar a pound for anything was tendered. Although I did nothing to encourage them, they bid each other up until the figures reached sums so fantastic that I laughed. They misinterpreted this as derision at the size of the offers and immediately raised the bids. I had ten pounds of T and B plug-cut smoking tobacco among the stores, and one slave of Lady Nicotine begged me to sell him the lot at $20 a pound. When I refused, I am sure he thought me avaricious, or crazy, or both. The bidding for my canned milk started at $2.00 a tin and soon skyrocketed to $4.00.

At length I was able to still the clamor by declaring flatly that I would not sell anything at any price. This angered one of the bidders, a huge fellow who radiated health and vigor.

"Won't you sell some of your milk to a sick man?" he demanded.

"No," I told him, "but if you'll show me the sick man I'll give him all he wants."

I think this convinced most of the would-be traders that I was sincere, and not merely holding out for higher prices, for they desisted in their efforts to get me to sell, and left us to our unloading. Later I estimated that, had I disposed of my outfit at the prices offered, the transaction would have brought me more than $3,500. It was tempting, and I was being overcautious in passing up the opportunity. I reasoned that to restock would probably cost me twice as much, but I was wrong. Within the month a steamer arrived at Dawson laden with supplies, and prices for everything dropped immediately. I had overlooked the supply-and-demand feature of the most elementary economics and muffed a chance at fortune. It was one of many muffs.

When we had completed the unloading of the stores and had beached the boat, Lindsay, Moran, and I reconnoitered for a likely place to store the outfit and park our tired bodies until we became settled and ready to set out on the serious business of gold hunting. Even at that early date there was a brisk exchange in Dawson real estate and lots were selling up to five thousand dollars. While we were unloading the boat one man among the crowd of would-be buyers had varied the monotony by offering to sell me a desirable townsite lot at a bargain, but I was not eager just then to become a landed proprietor and I passed up the opportunity, much to his disgust. Until we could locate our diggings, we set up our temporary headquarters at the base of a hill beyond the limits of Dawson, and for one hundred dollars bought a small tent and a second-hand Yukon stove.

On our scouting trip we came to a ramshackle log building on the river front. A sign proclaimed it to be the Klondyke (the original spelling) Hotel, and the bar, of course, was its outstanding entertainment feature. It seemed to be the time and place appropriately to celebrate our arrival, so we entered and lined up at the bar. I ordered Scotch and invited the bartender to join us. He graciously accepted, setting out four diminutive liqueur glasses and the bottle.

The whisky was the most outrageous libel on the nectar of Scotland that it has ever been my misfortune to taste. I laid a ten-dollar bill on the counter in payment and the bartender put it in a drawer behind him and stood at attention, apparently ready to serve another round. He made no movement to return any change.

"What's the price of drinks?" I asked.

"Two-fifty for Scotch," he answered.

I knew nothing about the Dawson scale of prices and thought that extortionate, but it gave me an idea. I knew that booze was included in the shortage of the necessities of life from which Dawson just then was suffering. In my outfit I had six quarts of prime Scotch.

"What is good Scotch worth the quart?" I inquired.

"I'll pay seventy-five dollars a quart for good Scotch," he answered. He emphasized the adjective, smiling with the air of one who challenged, "try and get it."

Four hundred and fifty dollars for a gallon and a half of whisky! I just simply couldn't afford to keep mine at that price. I made a mental note on the spot that I would sell him my six quarts just as soon as I unpacked my outfit. But I delayed, and when, three days later, I got around to it the Scotch had been stolen. I had a pretty good idea about the identity of the thief. I was sure it could not be blamed on any of the predatory dogs that roamed Dawson devouring whatever they could find.

Our first day in Dawson was toilsome. After pitching our tent we were busy for hours transporting our stores from the riverbank, and every pound of it had to be carried on our backs through mud up to our hips. Ever since, I have had a fellow feeling for stevedores and long-shoremen. But we were none the worse for it, for my two companions had been born to toil and I myself was feeling as strong as a grizzly. I was hard as nails, stripped down to fighting weight, having shed fifty of my normal 192 pounds on the gruelling trail from Skagway, and could tote a seventy-five-pound pack on my shoulders all day without undue fatigue.

When the last bundle in the outfit had been stacked in the tent, we were agreed that we were not too tired to look Dawson over. One of my first purchases in the town had been a galvanized iron washtub at a cost of ten dollars. I had not had a bath since leaving Victoria nearly six months before. I could not be sure how long it had been since my two companions had last enjoyed one, but I guessed it was not more recently than mine. So we had our baths in water that cost me fifty cents a pail. The Yukon at Dawson runs swift and its water was little better than mud in solution, unfit for drinking, cooking, or bathing. The only source of potable water was a spring in the hill-side about a mile up the Klondike, and an enterprising public utilities magnate in the bud was hauling it by dog team and selling it as fast as it could be ladled out.

One luxury leads to another. After enjoying our un-accustomed cleanliness we felt that the attentions of a barber were indispensable. On the trail we had trimmed each other's hair and whiskers, not out of vanity or fas-tidiousness, but only sufficiently to keep icicles from forming. The result never was a thing of beauty, and now that we had reached such civilization as Dawson boasted it seemed fitting we should be made more presentable. My beauty treatment at Dawson's finest tonsorial parlor cost

CHAPTER II

IF WE HAD EXPECTED TO FIND the relaxed hours of the little mining camp riotous and fevered we were speedily disabused of the idea. In the first place, night in Dawson in the month of June is only a term. There was no darkness, for the long Arctic days were come and one could read Dawson's only newspaper, the *Klondyke Nugget*, at midnight without difficulty. Of course, this fact made for sleeplessness, more or less, for men new to the Arctic at first found it difficult to retire for slumber with the sun blazing at a period in the day when any self-respecting sun should be well below the horizon. In the circumstances, relaxation was called for, and where better to seek it than in the saloons, dance halls, and gambling hells where joy reigned unrefined?

The lid was off and the little camp was wide open—but not lawless. When I first saw it, it was less than a year since Joseph Ladue, a trader and prospector—it was he who had offered to sell me the lot at a bargain—had staked out the townsite claim which he named for his friend, George M. Dawson, a Canadian engineer who was then making a survey of the route from Lynn Canal to the Klondike. Ladue, who had lived on the Yukon for many years, had hurried from Circle City to the mouth of the Klondike at the first news of the strike. He knew the disappointments and uncertainties of gold quests and he sought a quicker and surer way to wealth. He was cleaning up on his sales of townsite lots in Dawson, and continued to do so.

There was a reason why Dawson's play hours were as sedate as they were. Almost from the beginning of the gold rush to the Klondike the Northwest Mounted Police were on the job at Dawson. At the time of my arrival there was a detachment of eighty men, under command of Major Walsh, engaged in establishing order, and they did it most effectively. They represented all of organized society that Dawson knew. They were not only the police, but the courts, the post office, the marine department, the law and justice. At this time their task was not too difficult, at least as far as crimes of violence were concerned, for only the vanguard of the later hordes of riffraff and of society's offscouring had arrived, and they were hopelessly outnumbered by honest men. Not a great while later, Dawson became a city of ten thousand, and the Mounties had their problems.

On this sunlit June night Dawson's main street, which paralleled the river, was crowded with men, women, and dogs, most of them (including the dogs) just strollers like ourselves. This street was the little camp's Rialto, where were strung along its length the restaurants, barrooms, dance halls, brothels, gambling dens, and the one hotel. The street itself was a morass, bordered by sidewalks of narrow planking on which the promenaders, with more or less effort, kept a footing and averted plunges into the mud.

Our sight-seeing outdoors required not more than a quarter of an hour. We entered the most likely looking dance hall. A large bar and gaming tables occupied the front part of the place, with space for dancing in the rear. The bar, like all the others in Dawson, was doing a lively trade. Customers were lined up there, buying whisky at $2.50 a slug, and beer at $1.00 a glass. There was plenty of play at the tables, with some good-sized bets being made, and the roulette and chuck-a-luck wheels were spinning; faro was dealt and a crap game was running full blast.

The dance hall proper, however, was the most interesting feature of the whole layout. It was my first peek at Dawson society. The dancers, men and women, to anyone not acquainted with the Yukon, might seem to be in masquerade costume. Mackinaws, blue denim shirts, and rough canvas breeches were *de rigueur* for the men. Gingham and calico frocks, little more modish in line than Mother Hubbards, or at best faded and shapeless silk gowns, were the women's ballroom costumes. Men and women danced in moccasins, some of the men in hip gum boots, and several of the dancers of both sexes in their stocking feet. A few of them were splendid dancers, and it was evident that they had learned the steps of the polkas, redowas, schottisches, and waltzes that were favored in that day at routs somewhat politer than those held in a Dawson dance hall.

The men were a rough-looking lot—Berry Wall himself would have looked tough in a sourdough's rig—but they very evidently were not of the bad-man fraternity. Their dancing partners, however, were unmistakably harpies. Without exception they were a homely, even repulsive, collection of painted, coarse-featured, loud-voiced, brazen hussies from mining camps at Eagle and Circle City down the river, and from the stews of Juneau, Douglas City, and the Alaska coast towns. The more notorious of them bore soubriquets playfully bestowed and roughly descriptive of the traits and characteristics for which they were noted.

I recall several of these allusive names, although the personalities of the women themselves long since have faded from my recollection. "The Grizzly Bear," applied to a mountain of a woman whose eye had been gouged out in a fight with another woman, was an acknowledgment of her ferocity in combat and also of her physical amplitude. "Diamond-toothed Lil" earned her name by reason of her advanced ideas as to what constituted recherché denture. No one, especially no one who knew the lady, required any explanation of the simple eloquence of the cognomen, "The Oregon Mare."

The dance-hall women were the advance guard of the bawds that flocked to Dawson hungering for gold. They were getting it, too, without any more digging than was figurative. At the end of each dance the couples retired to tables in stalls or boxes at the edge of the floor, and the men bought drinks. Champagne at thirty dollars the pint was the favorite order, for each girl got a commission of five dollars for every bottle of fizz her partner bought. The women had terrific thirsts out of all proportion to their dancing exertions. A few hours' work in a dance hall paid a girl well, for she had no time for any partner except one with a full poke. When she finished with him much of the gold had found its way from his poke into the house's till, and some of that to the girl's stocking bank. The pity of it was that most of her earnings in turn went to her cadet, that unspeakably vile counterfeit of a man. Yet any girl without one of these parasites lost caste among her sisters as a cheap skate.

The rivalry among the women for the favor of cavaliers was intense, but it was of course purely commercial. They

Dawson Water Front in 1899

Dawson's Original Hostelry

reserved sentiment for their cadets. The more dances a girl had, the more champagne would be ordered and the fatter her commissions. It was amusing to note the excellent timing of the program. The intervals between dances were spaced for the duration of a pint bottle.

The music for this revelry was provided by a young man at a piano which, although obviously more upright than its tormentor, gave forth the tinniest of sounds, eloquent of its want of tuning. Although I am bound to say that the pianist's performance was not on a par with that of the accomplished stranger described by Robert W. Service in "The Shooting of Dan McGrew," it had, at least, rhythm, and apparently it satisfied the dancers. At best they did not expect too much of the dissolute-looking youth who provided the music, for in the rough society of that day the term "piano player" was one of contempt implying a status somewhat akin to that of a cadet. The music was of the ragtime variety, with sentimental waltzes interspersed.

As we watched the couples from the sidelines one impossible blonde woman dancer, whose weight I judged was not less than 170 pounds on the hoof, fascinated me. She had only one eye (later I was to identify her as the "Grizzly Bear"), and she worked it overtime. As this cyclopean Amazon whirled in the arms of her partner to the strains of a waltz, her single orb was directed tenderly on his perspiring features. Round and round they swirled, her glance fixed on him in what was fast becoming an alcoholic glaze. The waltz, I remember, was a lilting melody fresh from the States. Some of the words were:

> "Casey would waltz with a strawberry blonde,
>   And the band played on——
> He'd glide 'cross the floor with the girl he adored,
>   And the band played on——"

The "Grizzly Bear" plainly was overdoing it. Her smile for her partner almost seemed gloating. At least it must have been so considered by one of the women dancers. Without warning she broke away from her partner, rushed at the one-eyed charmer, and in a trice had slapped her face resoundingly several times, clawed her with fingernails, and was enthusiastically engaged in tearing out her blonde hair by the handful.

Immediately the engagement became more or less general. Partisans of the two combatants took sides. The women were furies, who gouged, bit and clawed as they shrieked and screamed out curses. Nor did their partners hold back, and now we witnessed the first of many single combats à la Yukon that we were to see during our stay in the gold fields. No knives or guns were drawn, nor were fists used as freely as one would suppose in the absence of lethal weapons. But the footwork was superb. The men wrestled under no known rules, and the one thrown "got the boot" until he cried quits, passed out, or was rescued. The fracas was lively while it lasted, and was hugely enjoyed by a ring of men from the gaming tables, among whom were the cadets who viewed the melee from a safe distance.

For perhaps five minutes the battle raged. Then one of Major Walsh's men came on the run, and on the instant hostilities ceased. Partners were hastily retrieved, for the music had not stopped all this time, and it was on with the dance. There were no arrests and no casualties, beyond injured feelings and, no doubt, the classic "lacerations, contusions and abrasions" of the police report.

We had enough, for a while, of Dawson's night life. We returned to our tent sufficiently tired to be certain of sleep, even in the bright sunlight.

ALTHOUGH IT WAS LESS than a year since the Klondike gold discovery had been made known to the world, controversy already had arisen as to whom the honor of the discovery rightly belonged. History gives that distinction to George W. Carmack, the one who, on August 16, 1896, first uncovered the rich gold deposits on Bonanza Creek. Technically or literally, perhaps, that is correct, but there were many on the ground at that time who contended that to Robert Henderson really belonged the honor.

Henderson, an American prospector, in 1895 journeyed eight hundred miles up the Yukon from Circle City to the Klondike River, lying to the east of the Yukon near the international boundary, thence traveling up that stream some twelve miles to a small branch afterwards named Hunker Creek. He made his way up this creek for about ten miles to its junction with a smaller creek, which he named Gold Bottom, and there started prospecting in a small gulch. From the beginning the ground showed encouraging colors right at the grass roots and Henderson built himself a cabin, stored his small outfit, and prepared to work the location. He had taken out more than fifty ounces by the time of the first freeze in the fall of 1895. Then he went to Juneau, where he outfitted and set out, without delay, to double back to Gold Bottom Creek.

On the return journey he met Carmack, a squaw man of Circle City, his wife, and her brothers, Tagish Charley and Skookum Jim, who were on their way from Circle City to Juneau to outfit. Carmack had spent fifteen years on the Yukon prospecting without anything much to show for it. Henderson told Carmack of his location in the Klondike Valley and was enthusiastic over its possibilities. He urged its superiority over the Circle City diggings and advised Carmack to stake a claim in the gulch, giving him a rough map of the location.

The Carmacks, on their return from Juneau, went up the Yukon to the Klondike, which they ascended in search of the gulch where they hoped to join Henderson. Instead of leaving the Klondike at Hunker Creek as the map indicated, they mistook for it another stream only a few miles from the mouth of the Klondike. They traveled up this creek about ten miles, but of course saw no sign of Henderson. They made camp there and in the evening Carmack decided to do a little surface prospecting in the creek.

His first test showed coarse gold. Excitedly Carmack called to his companions to join in the testing. Every pan of gravel they tested showed coarse gold. There and then Carmack staked a discovery claim. His brothers-in-law staked the next two claims up the stream, and Carmack's native wife a fourth one, downstream from the discovery claim. Henderson was forgotten. Carmack named the little stream Bonanza Creek, harnessed his dog team, and, traveling light, set out in all haste for Circle City. He left his wife and her brothers in charge of the claims.

From Circle City, where some four hundred miners and prospectors were located and had been working for years, news of Carmack's strike traveled up and down the Yukon

Bonanza Creek, Where the Rush Originated

with greater speed than its current. From Juneau it spread to the outside world. The greatest gold rush in history was on. In its vanguard was every miner, prospector, trapper, and trader along the entire three-thousand-mile length of the Yukon and its hundreds of tributaries. They dropped whatever they were doing and, with hastily assembled outfits, stampeded to the new gold fields.

Feverishly the firstcomers staked claims on Bonanza Creek, from its mouth to far beyond its sources, its right fork, its left fork, every tiny stream that emptied into it, the creek bottoms from rim to rim, the hillsides that drained into them, the hilltops, and tier after tier of bench claims, until there was nothing left for belated arrivals to stake. Yet still they came by the thousands, drawn by the mighty magnet of gold. Many of them wandered over the hills into adjacent valleys far from the creek of the fabulous gravel, still hopeful that they might find gold.

Two of the latecomers drifting about the hills and valleys one day came upon the gulch at Gold Bottom Creek where Henderson was working his claim, all unaware of the commotion his advice to Carmack had started. He asked the strangers where they came from.

"Bonanza Creek," they told him.

"Bonanza Creek," Henderson repeated. "Never heard of it. Where is it?"

His visitors were astonished. They asked him how long he had been working his claim. He told them, and impatiently repeated his question as to the location of Bonanza Creek. They led the way out of the gulch to a hill, pointed the direction of the creek, and bade him look. In whatever direction he looked, he saw tents dotting the land, fires burning everywhere to thaw out the ground, men at work on the creeks piling up the rich gravel. The district was the nucleus of what developed into the Klondike placer gold mine area of about eight hundred square miles in the basins of the Klondike, Indian, and McQuesten rivers.

When Henderson learned that it was Carmack who had discovered all this, he was bitter. He had missed riches by only a few miles. With all the wealth and fluency of vituperation and invectives acquired through years in the Yukon, he cursed Carmack, his squaw, and her brothers for clumsy, blundering fools whose stupidity had led them into wealth and whose selfishness and greed held them back from making him a sharer in fortune that never would have been theirs save for him.

Carmack's luck stayed with him. With his half-breed brothers-in-law he acquired claims on El Dorado Creek which proved very rich in gold. They took huge fortunes out of the ground and proceeded to enjoy life after their fashion. They gave ripsnorting parties at which liquor was abundant, arrayed themselves in fine garments, adorned themselves with huge diamond-set nuggets, and, in general, behaved in the traditional manner of beggars set on horseback. When life in Dawson seemed too tame, they made many trips outside to coast towns. On the occasion of a trip to San Francisco they amused themselves by tossing nuggets from the windows of their hotel to the streets. In less than a minute the streets about the hotel were jammed with a frantic, fighting mob, scrambling for the gold. Street cars were blocked, traffic was stalled, heads were broken, and riot and civil commotion threatened. When the police had dispersed the mob, they persuaded Carmack and his brothers to scatter their gold in a more conventional manner.

They found other ways to get rid of it, for they were easy marks for swindlers, get-rich-quick promoters, race-horse touts, and crooked gamblers. Soon their huge wealth had been spent, and they returned to the obscurity out of which they had come.

Henderson was hardly less fortunate, although surely more deserving. Gold Bottom never panned out and he finally abandoned the claim. The Canadian Government, a few years after Carmack's find, officially recognized Henderson as the discoverer of the Klondike gold fields and gave him a substantial life pension.

I saw Henderson on several occasions when he came into Dawson for supplies. I do not recall that his experience embittered him, but he was an object of sympathy as a man who by all rights should have been rich. "The dice of God are always loaded." They are indeed. Henderson had lost on a throw. He was not the first or the last in the Yukon to miss riches by so narrow a margin. Nor was Carmack the only one I knew of who had blundered into wealth.

CHAPTER IV

WHEREVER MEN FORGATHERED in Dawson's bars, dance halls, gambling joints, and eating places, there were yarns told of the luck, good and ill, of prospectors in the Yukon. Some of them were tragic, others packed with comedy, and among the latter was the story of how "Big Swede" Charlie Anderson was hornswoggled into fortune.

Anderson drifted from Circle City into Dawson after all the choice locations on Bonanza Creek had been staked. About all that was left in that general vicinity was El Dorado Creek, one of the last districts to be claimed, and the old-timers and practical prospectors did not think much of it. They did not fancy the lay of the land in the small valley the creek traversed. Neither the willows nor the birches—none of the timber, in fact— leaned in the right direction. Veteran sourdoughs were agreed that all the signs for a proper gold field were lacking. Only the latecomers, who had no other choice, staked claims on it, and among these were two tinhorn gamblers from Circle City. They soon abandoned all efforts to wrest gold from their claim and concentrated their attack on Lady Luck in Dawson.

When Anderson hit town the gamblers greeted him as an old and esteemed acquaintance. Guessing that he had a full poke, they proceeded to celebrate his arrival with

wassail, trimmed him expertly at faro, and at the appropriate moment when the Swede was dead to the world they
exchanged the rest of the contents of his poke for a transfer
deed to their unwanted claim on El Dorado Creek, all
duly made out in Anderson's name and properly signed,
sealed, and delivered. When Anderson awoke some hours
later and examined his poke he found the deed, but his
five hundred dollars had disappeared. He put up a mighty
squawk and posthaste sought out Major Walsh, in command of the Mounties, clamoring for justice. Major Walsh
sent for the two gamblers, confronted them with Anderson
and heard both sides of the story. The gamblers denied
nothing, except that they had stolen the five hundred
dollars, asserting it was given them in payment for the
deed to the claim. Anderson denied this. The major
directed the gamblers to take back the deed and return the
five hundred dollars to the Swede.

"But we can't do that, major. After the sale we got into
a game of faro and were cleaned out."

Major Walsh investigated their story and found it was
true. He turned the gamblers loose, with a warning, then
advised the complainant.

"I'm sorry, Anderson, but there's nothing I can do about
it. You have no witness to show it was a robbery. The
money's gone, but you have the deed, and that's genuine.
The only advice I can give you is to work the claim for
what you can get out of it."

Sorrowfully Anderson concluded that that was about
all he could do. The gamblers had picked him bare, but on
credit he got a sack of flour, a slab of bacon, a few pounds
of coffee and sugar, and some tinned milk. With his provisions, a pick, shovel, saw, and gold pan, he hit the trail,
heading for his El Dorado claim. He had no fear of hard

work, and he had powerful legs and arms and a strong back. Also, he had a terrible headache and a heavy heart.

He worked like a mule on the claim, sweetening his labor by imagining that every stroke of his pick in the soil was a blow through the vitals of his swindlers. Bedrock was only twenty feet below the surface of the creek and Anderson soon realized he was nearing it. He had let a "lay" to two fellow Swedes on a fifty-fifty basis. A "lay" is an agreement between a claim owner and another, or others, whereby the parties bind themselves to share on the agreed basis whatever gold they dig out.

Anderson was the first to strike bedrock. The first pan he tested contained more than $1,200 in dust. He said nothing about it to the other Swedes, but suggested that they sign a contract by which, in exchange for the lay, he agreed to pay them $25,000 within ten days. They were easily persuaded, satisfied they had the best of the bargain. He paid them well within the stipulated time, and they soon made themselves scarce. Then Anderson prepared to work his claim in a big way.

He hired labor, constructed a roomy cabin, and installed steam heat in it. He built an electric-light plant and a large steam thawing plant to facilitate mining in the frozen ground. Between his task of superintending the mining operations of his laborers and weighing his dust, he relieved the tedium of amassing gold with gay parties almost nightly in his cabin, to which the dance-hall girls and their followers flocked. After working his claim several months, tales of its golden yields interested Captain Healy, then resident manager at Dawson of the North American Trading Company. Healy investigated and asked Anderson his price for the claim. He laughed scornfully when Anderson offered to sell for $500,000, but six months later he offered the Swede $750,000 for the claim. It was Anderson's turn to laugh. He told Healy the claim was not for sale at any price.

Anderson worked the claim for nearly three years, and in that time it was reported he took about $2,000,000 out of the ground. Although he was a glutton for work, he was just as keen for play. While his claim was piling up wealth for him, he made a voyage to Paris, engaging de luxe train, steamship, and hotel accommodations for himself, three or four of Dawson's dance-hall favorites, and the several boon male companions who accompanied him. Anderson scattered money right and left, with the sky the limit for expenditures on the hilarious parties that marked the progress of his travels. When he had exhausted, as he believed, the possibilities of his claim, he sold it for $100,000 to a large dredging company.

Several years later, I met him in a saloon in Ballard, Washington, a sawmill town, now a part of Seattle. He was broke and working in a mill as a laborer at four dollars a day. But he had no regrets, and what a hell of a good time he had had while the pay streak lasted.

But the pay streak had lasted long after Anderson sold his claim and the dredging company that bought it recovered far more gold than Anderson had taken out. In contrast to the primitive methods which he had employed to skim the cream of the gold from his claim, they introduced the most scientific means of operation. Their enormous dredges, costing millions of dollars to set up and operate, ran the gravel contents of the entire El Dorado Valley without losing a color, handling 6,000 yards of gravel in twenty-four hours—a greater quantity of material than a thousand men could work in a like period under the old method of hoisting and sluicing.

CHAPTER V

THREE DAYS AFTER MY arrival at Dawson I was alone,
Lindsay and Moran having left to work for wages on a
claim on Bonanza Creek, attracted by the $2.50 an hour
paid for labor. Their intention was to hire out for about
a month and return with a stake. Then we would venture
out prospecting on our own. I had decided to remain in
Dawson until mail from the outside should arrive, for although I had written home daily up to the time I left
Victoria, and also aboard the *Amur* and at Skagway, Bennett, and Whitehorse, I had not heard from anyone since
leaving New York.

Mail was expected in Dawson any day as it was reported
that a new detachment of Mounties were on their way
from Lake Bennett with a large amount of it from the
outside. While waiting, I got a job at $15 a day for a
twelve-hour shift, stacking lumber at Joe Boyle's sawmill
in Dawson. It was good pay for work calling only for
brawn, but since the mill was selling at three hundred
dollars a thousand feet all the rough lumber it could cut,
working night and day, it could well afford to offer fancy
wages. Boyle had come to the Klondike when everything
was staked, so he set up a sawmill at the mouth of Bonanza Creek and prospered from the beginning. Later he
took up a huge hydraulic concession on the Klondike ex-

Courtesy Department of Mines and Resources, Ottawa, Canada

El Dorado Creek of the Golden Gravel

tending several miles in length and made money in bales. Although I missed my lively companions, I had little chance to become lonesome. I easily made many acquaintances in a community where the formalities were few and the friendships more or less spontaneous. Before I had been in Dawson a month I was numbered among the old residents, for every day new arrivals were pouring into the little settlement from all parts of the globe.

The steamer had landed at Dawson and the supplies it brought certainly relieved the shortages and reduced prices —a little, that is, but not much. Eggs were firm at $2.00 each, raw fresh potatoes at $1.00 apiece, tallow candles at $2.50 each. Later, before the fall freeze, prices for all commodities, and for labor as well, dropped a bit, but just now the high prices demanded were paid without too much complaint. Workmen especially were in clover, for common labor was paid $15 for a day of twelve hours. Carpenters, including any kind of wood butcher, got $2.50 an hour, and that too, without intervention of a union business agent. It was at the restaurant, however, that fanciful prices ran riot. Menus were not elaborate—although one could get an oyster (canned) stew at $15 a bowl—and they exhibited neither a range of viands, nor a flight of imagination in their preparation. Beans, bacon, and bread were the stand-bys in all the eating places of Dawson as well as in prospectors' cabins where a cuisine was part of the domestic menage. But no matter how staunchly one believed in plain living, a triune symbol of simple fare in time became monotonous. It was not until more than a year later, when Jack Dalton had succeeded in herding a drove of steers seven hundred miles over the trail and across the frozen Yukon to Dawson, that the Klondike renewed acquaintance with fresh meat.

In this connection I recall a yarn that was a favorite in Dawson at that time. It concerned a prospector, Boston born, who after fifteen years in the Arctic had struck it rich in the Klondike and sold out to a large outfit for a big sum. During all these years his meals had been as modest and lacking in variety as those of other prospectors. Beans, beans, beans in plenty, but everlastingly. Aboard the whaler on which he took passage, bound for San Francisco, there were more beans and little else. In San Francisco he outfitted himself sumptuously in store clothes, was barbered within an inch of his life, and then deposited his drafts in the bank, drawing generously against them in currency. Then he registered at the Palace Hotel, engaging the bridal suite, and went down to the main dining saloon. He looked like the ready money he was, and the head waiter escorted him to a table on the station of the best man in the establishment. The bean-fed prospector explained to the servitor that he had been so long absent from civilization that he did not trust his own ability to order the dinner he wanted. He handed the waiter ten dollars.

"Bring me the best dinner in the house, without counting the cost, and if I like it, there's another ten-spot for you."

The waiter was on his mettle and ordered for the miner a meal that would be a masterpiece in any man's land. When he had obtained the guest's approval of the items and was about to start for the kitchen, the miner detained him.

"Before you bring on any of that fancy grub, fetch a big platter of beans, any style, and put it right here in the center of the table," he ordered.

And that was done in due time. As each course was dispatched by the hungry guest the platter of baked beans remained untouched. When the last course had been served and the table was being cleared the waiter started to remove the beans, but the guest restrained him. Presently the entire meal had been disposed of and the waiter placed the bill before the guest.

"I hope, sir, your dinner was satisfactory?"

"Best I ever ate," the miner assured him, handing over the promised ten-dollar bill.

"May I ask you a question, sir," the waiter ventured, as he thanked him.

"Shoot."

"The beans, sir? You never touched them."

"No, and I never intended to, and never will as long as I live. I only had them before me so that I could enjoy real food all the more."

In the early days of Dawson there was very little currency or coin in circulation, and practically all trading was transacted with gold dust, which was carried in pokes. These were buckskin bags, the average-sized one having a capacity of fifty ounces, and the largest sized one holding three hundred ounces. Nuggets, that is, pieces of gold weighing in excess of an eighth of an ounce, usually were kept in a separate poke. Dust from the richer claims was sold direct to the banks, or expressed to mints. The ordinary prospector working his claim *solus* usually carried his dust about with him in his poke, paying out of it for his provisions, drinks, tobacco, and other purchases. At all the stores, bars, and other places where trading was done, and of course at the banks, scales were kept to weigh the dust tendered in payment.

The buyer would hand his poke to the seller who would

spill a quantity of dust into a small V-shaped pan with inch-high sides, open at one of the points of the V. Then, in turn, the dust was shaken from the pan into one of the scales in sufficient quantity to strike a balance at a certain specified weight. Any particles of dust remaining in the pan were returned to the poke, which was then handed back to the purchaser. Necessarily, under so primitive a method of payment, both buyer and seller had to beware. For many tradesmen were clumsy and careless in their weighing, as a result of which some of the dust was spilled on the floor or counter. On the other hand, the seller had to look sharp to see that the dust tendered in payment was free of the black sand and brass filings sometimes added by dishonest tricksters.

Whatever had been the fall in prices in Dawson, those at the bars had not been affected. Champagne still sold $30 the pint, beer at $1.00 a glass, case liquor at $2.50 the jolt, with a slug from the "Man with the Cocked Hat," Alaska hooch, lowest in the price scale, sticking at $1.00 a drink—and dear at that.

The name hooch is native to the Northwest, being derived from the Indian word "hoochinoo." Although prospectors drank it when under the compulsion of necessity, they considered it a terrible beverage unfit for white men. It was distilled in several grades, some of the brands being known as "Aurora Borealis," "Koprecof Dynamite," "The Juice of the Snake," and no man could say which brand was the worst.

It was over my first (and last) glass of hooch one night in the Klondike Hotel bar that I heard from a veteran sourdough, whose name I have long since forgotten, a couple of amusing yarns about the Northwest Indians. The first concerned an experience of John G. Brady, one of Alaska's early governors, who, before he entered politics, did missionary work among the natives. Since "coming outside" I have heard the same yarn with Theodore Roosevelt as its central figure, but since I first listened to it in Dawson in 1897, long before Roosevelt was a national figure, I am inclined to believe it never happened to him.

Brady, so the story went, was invited to address the natives on the occasion of one of their annual potlatches, or tribal reunions, at Hoonah, near Sitka, his home. His remarks in English were interpreted for the Indians by a native. As the missionary worker warmed up to his subject, his periods as translated by the interpreter were enthusiastically applauded by his auditors, who punctuated the address with loud cries, *"Bushwa, bushwa."* As the speaker finished, he was gratified at a veritable frenzy of this applause, and beamingly asked the interpreter the meaning in English of the cry *"Bushwa."*

The interpreter, a dignified old Indian, hesitated, but when Brady persisted he answered:

"Oh, *Bushwa*—it's Chinook for 'bull manure.' "

The other yarn concerned another potlatch held at Killisnoo. It is the custom of Alaskan Indians to buy their own tombstones during their lives, and it is the ambition of every native to possess as handsome a stone as his means will allow, with laudatory inscriptions carved on it and everything about it proclaiming it a work of art. In fact, many of them bought monuments beyond their means. Juneau's foremost headstone maker was a shrewd Irishman, one Hogan. A day or so before the potlatch, Hogan went to Killisnoo and sought out the interpreter who was to translate the address of a missionary, principal speaker at the meeting. After plying him with Scotch, Hogan gave him a ten-dollar bill and proceeded to talk business.

He was so persuasive that at the end of the conference the interpreter had agreed to translate the missionary's talk as an eloquent description of the splendid tombstones Hogan made, the bargain prices at which they were sold, and the place of business at which these lapidary masterpieces could be purchased. For each order thus obtained Hogan promised the interpreter a cash payment of two dollars. So well did the interpreter fulfill his part of the bargain that Hogan's marble yard was working overtime for months after the potlatch.

Dawson was booming. I could literally hear, as well as see it grow, and I began to regret that I had not closed on Ladue's deal to sell me a townsite lot for five hundred dollars. Still more, I regretted my refusal of "Curly Pete's" offer, made a few days after Ladue's, to get me a lot for $250 at a forced sale. Pete was a gambler who had been cleaned out at faro and he needed the money. I regretted it more than ever when, two months after my arrival, the Canadian Government bought, for $15,000, that same lot as the site for a post office. I began to think I would steadily go on muffing chances at wealth.

A new and larger gambling establishment and dance hall had been erected on the river front. It was touted to outshine Dawson's pioneer place of entertainment with its new and shining roulette and chuck-a-luck wheels, its keno, faro, poker, and craps, and its many newfangled gambling devices. The bar was an imposing feature, glittering with fancy glassware and stocked with a wide variety of bottled goods. On the great mirror back of it a soap artist had depicted an alluring tropical landscape whose palms and floral luxuriance, and nude beauties basking in the sunshine, served to comfort its beholders in this

Arctic setting. The large dance floor in the rear was such as to do credit to Dawson, the fastest growing community in the Yukon. Most important of all, many new outside girls had been brought in, and they were of quite a different sort from those the mining camp had known heretofore. They were of the "chippy" variety, the *fin de siècle* designation for women on the border line between veteran prostitutes and what some years later were known as "flappers." They were young, pretty, and beautifully dressed. Even at that early date they had all the hallmarks of their profession, which later were to become "respectabilized" by adoption by their virtuous sisters. They were rouged within an inch of their lives, and many of them wore their hair short. Their skirts were abbreviated, their forms uncorseted, and their frocks close-fitting. They wore silk stockings which, although black, was enough in itself in that era to mark them as at least trifling with the occasions of sin. Furthermore, they smoked cigarettes unashamedly and tossed off whisky neat with all the ease and *sang-froid* of a he-man sourdough with a copper-lined stomach. Their badinage and persiflage, the wit and the wisecracks they exchanged with their male companions, were all below-the-girdle stuff. All in all, the atmosphere was as modern as if there had been a projection into the future, to the year, say, 1935, and the place a night club.

The opening night of the new show place was a gala occasion, and whatever of beauty and chivalry Dawson could boast was there. The receipts over the bar for the first night were more than fifteen thousand dollars, and those at the gaming tables probably were many times that amount. Men from points up the river came in droves for the occasion. Others from the placer creeks arrived with full pokes, and left a goodly part of their gold behind them.

CHAPTER VI

LINDSAY CAME BACK FROM Bonanza Creek with a little
more than five hundred dollars to show for his twenty
days' work. Moran turned up several days later and that
was the last we were to see of him. For one day while
Lindsay and I were absent, Moran helped himself to some
of my provisions and disappeared. Later we heard that he
had joined a party that poled a small boat to the mouth
of the Yukon, two thousand miles distant, and from there
had made Nome. He was one of the first arrivals in the
rush that started upon the news of the new gold strike
there. He staked an original claim and turned out rich,
but died soon after from the effects of dissipation and exposure. His little ball of yarn was wound up, and I for-
gave him his treatment of us.

Now that Lindsay had returned, I was eager to be
about the business on which I had journeyed thousands
of miles from civilization. The tales I heard every day in
Dawson about fabulous riches being taken out of the
ground by men no more remarkable than myself were
making me impatient to have a try at it. Besides, our location on the outskirts of the town was getting crowded,
for the thousands of arrivals were overflowing the little
city into the near-by districts, and firewood was becoming
scarce. So I quit my job at the sawmill and we selected a

location a few miles up the Klondike on a small flat opposite the mouth of Bonanza Creek. Lindsay and I had pooled
our earnings and we began construction of a small log
cabin for our future home, using for the flooring the
timbers of our boat, which we took apart. It required
about ten days to complete the cabin, and when we had
moved our tent and its contents to the new location we
were well pleased with it.

We would have been even better pleased with it had we
known anything about gold mining. Years later, after
we had abandoned the site, the small flat was mined and
an immense fortune recovered from dredging operations.

But hills are greener far away. Although we failed to
see the possibilities of the ground on which we were located,
our imaginations were fired by those of another spot far
distant, and nothing would do but we must go there.
Lindsay had heard of ground open for location on a small
stream emptying into Dominion Creek, near its mouth,
about ninety miles distant, and we decided to investigate.
So, at the end of July, we packed our blankets and a week's
grub and set out afoot for the new property.

The trail led up the left fork of Bonanza to its source,
thence over the divide known as the Dome, with its highest point about two thousand feet, then down into the
Indian River placer district to a point near the junction
of Dominion Creek and Indian River. It was a stiff mush,
for the trail was deep in mud and the myriads of mosquitoes
gave us no rest day or night. In fact, they made life a
torture. It was my first experience on an Arctic trail in
summer; beside it the winter trail seemed no more than
a picnic hike. Any strong healthy person can travel an
Arctic trail in winter, no matter how low the temperature,
without too much discomfort. Even in a temperature of

seventy degrees below Zero he can stop, build roaring
log fires, park himself in his blanket between them, and
rest out the blizzard. But in summer there is no escaping
the mud and the mosquitoes. As you struggle and sweat
through the mire, billions of these buzzing pests, thirsting
for your gore as they thirst in no other clime, blind you as
they swarm about your head, bore through your stout
canvas clothing as though it were netting, and madden you
with their hum. We had been bothered by them in our
cabin, but it was possible there to get some sleep by building a smudge fire of bark in a gold pan, letting it burn for
an hour or so in the cabin, and then retiring into the air
tight room. One got some rest that way, even though it
was at the cost of a splitting headache and a heavily coated
tongue in the morning.

This was not possible on the trail. We tried draping our
blankets over our heads and shoulders, but when we found
that this was ineffective—after nearly smothering ourselves and becoming limp and weak from sweating—we
gave it up. With all the fluency of the Yukon we cursed
our tormentors, but they continued to hum defiance. We
flailed our arms about to ward off their attacks, but this
served only to augment their ferocity.

Of a sudden Lindsay stopped and drew his sharp hunting knife. I thought he had gone berserk in his misery,
but he was only trying an experiment.

"Watch this, Ed," he said, as he swung the knife through
the air, thrusting, jabbing, and crosscutting through the
swarms like a cavalryman.

When he had tired he showed me the knife. It was
blood-stained and the forms of some of our tormentors
stuck to the blade.

"I'll bet I killed hundreds of 'em," he announced exult-

CHAPTER VII

WE NEVER WENT BACK TO the Dominion Creek claim, for before we heard the bad news about it, we were off on a new scent we were sure would lead us to wealth.

Several days after our return from the creek we observed smoke rising from the top of Steamboat Hill, opposite our cabin, on the other side of the Klondike. We had not noticed it before, and it could only mean that prospectors were at work in a district theretofore unexplored. We decided to investigate, so we crossed the river and climbed the hill and there found four men sinking a shaft. They evidently had staked there while we were on the trail, for they had built a cabin and sunk a shaft, they told us. They were friendly chaps and showed us gravel, all white quartz. Their tests so far had shown only colors, they asserted, and they were confident they would strike pay dirt at bedrock. It looked good to us.

Later that day we went to Dawson for supplies and there Lindsay met Jack Dobins, a practical miner from the Fraser River country whose acquaintance he had made at El Dorado. Lindsay told him about the new diggings on the hilltop and Dobins immediately was interested. We agreed to pilot him the next day to the location and have him size it up. He appeared to be favorably impressed by his observations at the shaft and examined the gravel closely.

"They're probably over gold," he said when we had left the hilltop, "but I'm afraid they'll have to dig to China before they hit a pay streak. They'll have to sink their shaft five hundred feet to reach bedrock. There ought to be an easier way than that."

On our way down the hill he made several stops to examine the terrain. He carried a small prospecting pick with which he loosened the thick moss and vegetation in an effort to find the original rimrock, which at length he located near the bottom of the hill, some two hundred feet above the level of the Klondike River. Here he built a fire and thawed out some gravel. Excitedly he declared that the gravel had the same character as that being hoisted from the shaft on the hilltop.

Using our bandanas, we made several bundles of the gravel and brought it to our cabin, where tests in the gold pan showed plenty of colors and a few grains about the size of mustard seeds. On Dobins' recommendation the three of us prospected the place for about a week. We made many tests, and finding no blank pans we decided to stake claims. We defined the rimrock location for about a thousand feet, and we each staked a hillside claim two hundred and fifty feet wide by one thousand feet up the hill. This procedure was simple. We merely noted on the markers we used to define the location the numbers of our mining licenses, and our names and the date of staking. Then we hurried back to Dawson where we waited in line twelve hours at the Gold Commissioner's office to record our claims.

Dobins told a few friends, in strict confidence, of the new location. Lindsay did the same. So did I. Before our claims had been filed the stampede to the rimrock was on. Each friend to whom we had spoken in strict confidence had promptly passed the news on to other friends, under a similar injunction of secrecy, and they in turn to their friends, until all Dawson had heard—in strict confidence —of the new gold field. By the time our claims were on record and we had returned to the location, the whole hillside, from the mouth of the Bonanza up to Bear Creek, a distance of about five miles, had been staked out, and, in addition, many bench claims had been taken up.

Dobins assured us the location was well worth working, but, as he needed money for a winter's outfit, he left for El Dorado to work for wages. Before he went we threw the three claims into a partnership, Lindsay and I agreeing to prepare the ground for prospecting on his return. We stripped the hillside at a point where Dobins had indicated that it would be advisable to start tunneling into the hill, then cleared and graded a space about twenty feet above rimrock for a cabin that we built of the spruce and birch with which the hill was abundantly timbered. Next we cut and piled huge quantitites of logs for use in thawing the ground, and after six weeks of this constant labor we were ready to start tunneling operations whenever Dobins returned.

As a diversion we made a trip into Dawson and there met Dr. Burke and his party, with whom I had parted in Victoria. They had landed in Dawson only about a week prior, but the energetic doctor and his son John, the doctor's brother Tom, and Julius Ullman, the artist, had erected a building on the river side of the main street fronting the water and had taken up their residence. The doctor's office was in a large room facing the street, and their living quarters overlooked the river. Already he had established a thriving practice at an ounce a call. Sixteen dollars an office visit served to make amends for the hardships of their trek over White Pass and the subsequent trail.

Never have I seen, outside the circus or a burlesque theater, any human being rigged up as the doctor was. He wore fawn-colored English riding breeches, very tight at the knees and flaring widely at the sides, with drab-colored puttees wound about his calves. A tight-fitting jacket came just to his waist, and about his rotund stomach was wound a vivid red scarf, the ends of which dangled at his knees. Surmounting this bizarre outfit was a little pillbox cap, set at an angle of forty-five degrees atop long white hair which fell to his shoulders. His headgear was kept in place by a chin strap, beneath which his beard straggled to his waist. To complete the effect, he carried a staff, about seven feet long, tipped with an iron ferrule. I think he had found the staff useful on the trail and was unwilling to abandon it.

If Dawson's sourdoughs were amazed at this sartorial splendor they gave no sign of it. Perhaps it was well that none of them did, for the old fellow was a peppery campaigner who walked with a smart military stride and carried himself with a certain arrogant dignity. Apparently they liked the show, for we had evidence during dinner at his home, to which he insisted on bidding us, that his practice was as flourishing as he said it was. Twice while we were at table he was called to attend patients in his office, each call netting him an ounce. It seemed to me almost as lucrative as an El Dorado claim. And the returns were quicker, if not as heavy.

We dined bountifully, if not well, on a six-pound steak (three dollars a pound, I mentally noted) and boiled fresh potatoes (at not less a pound). The cooking was not such as to do justice to costly viands, for Johnnie performed the honors in the kitchen, and he was as poor a cook as any at whose hands I have ever suffered, and in the Yukon I had experience with many who deserved no less than death for their culinary crimes.

The doctor was interested in hearing of my experiences since we had last met, but he was not enthusiastic over our plans for working our claim. He strongly advised that we give over the idea until others had proved that there really was gold in "them thar hills." As a counterproposition, he urged that we go into the freighting business, citing the demand for transportation in the gold fields and the money that was to be made that way. His arguments won us over, especially as he agreed to finance the undertaking to the extent of $3,500 cash, with which we were to buy thirty dogs at $100 each, and three good sleds, two for hauling freight and one (a basket sled with a capacity of two) for passengers. Lindsay and I were to do the mushing, or driving, and handle the freight. Johnnie was to do the cooking. It speaks volumes for the doctor's powers of persuasion that, with this dinner before us as a sample of Johnnie's culinary art, we allowed ourselves to be talked into a venture where he would be in charge of the commissary.

Definitely we put over until the next year all thought of developing our hillside claim and sent word to Dobins of the change in our plans. During the weeks until the snow came, we put in much of the time in Dawson selecting our dogs and sleds and getting ready to launch the freighting business.

CHAPTER VIII

Jack London, who was to give the Yukon a place in literature, was not one of Dawson's celebrities. I first met him, a newcomer, in the fall of 1897. He did not leave California for the Klondike until a little more than a month after I had arrived in Dawson. He made no great stir in society of the place, for he was only a youth who had not yet made a name for himself in the world. It was not until five years after he ended his short stay—he left the Yukon in 1898—that the publication of *The Call of the Wild* made him famous overnight. After he became a star in the firmament of letters, I talked to many men who must have met him frequently during barroom sessions in Dawson but they were honest enough to say that they had no clear-cut recollection of him, and certainly did not suspect him of latent genius. London in all truth had had few enough acquaintances in Dawson who credited him with any extraordinary gift. Both before and after his stay there he met with many discouragements in his attempts to sell his stuff. Yet when his book became an immediate success, there arose many who proudly claimed his friendship and who admitted that they had always known he had it in him.

I first met London in a Dawson bar in the late fall of 1897. I never knew him well, for I was a few years his senior, and he probably considered me too near his own age, too little seasoned, to be worth his while as far as an acquaintance was concerned. For London was surely prospecting, but it was at bars that he sought his material. I believe that he had staked a claim, and it is probable that his hatred of capitalism did not extend to acquiring wealth for himself, but I never saw him working one, never met him on the trail, and do not remember ever having seen him except in some Dawson bar. I think he preferred to delve in the rich mine of Dawson life and to examine the characters of the sourdoughs who made the life there unique and interesting. Although I was not in his confidence (I doubt if any person in Dawson was), I have always believed that London did not go into the Arctic to "rape the Yukon" of its gold, but heeded the urge, which in him always was irresistible, for adventure and a life lived in the open.

I remember him as a muscular youth of little more than average stature, with a weather-beaten countenance in which a healthy color showed, and a shock of yellow hair, customarily unkempt and in keeping with his usual slovenly appearance. It seemed to me that whenever I saw him at the bar he was always in conversation with some veteran sourdough or noted character in the life of Dawson. And how he did talk. Men of derring-do, his seniors by several years, whose lives had been spent amid dangers of as many kinds as St. Paul enumerates in his Epistle, listened to him with respect. For although he was but a youth—only a few months past twenty-one—they recognized in him a blood brother. Since early boyhood he had drifted to far places, living haphazardly by what work he might. Like the men he met in the Yukon, he had known

life in the raw. He had known the insides of more than one
jail—for offenses no more serious than infractions of police
rules—and in experience he was a man of years. Although
a great reader, he had a wealth of knowledge "not strained
through books." As rancher, salmon fisher, oyster pirate,
longshoreman and able seaman (at seventeen he had
shipped before the mast on a voyage to Japan), he could
talk the language of men whose souls were as restless and
questing as his own. His final claim to a place in the
brotherhood of the Yukon was the fact that he had made
the trail through Chilkoot Pass, afoot and carrying his
pack.

It has always been a matter of wonder to me where the
money came from to finance London's trek to the Klondike
and his stay in Dawson. His people were desperately poor
(he was one of a family of ten children), and to go to
Dawson he had quit a job in a cannery which could not
have paid him well. He had no job while there, for two
San Francisco newspapers had refused his application to
represent them as their correspondent in the Klondike.
Nor do I remember him as a gambler, and hence winnings
as a source of his income are eliminated in my mind. Yet
he was a pretty steady patron of the bar, and liquor in that
day in Dawson was steep in price. Undoubtedly, while he
drank, thus accumulating some of the material for his
John Barleycorn, he was at the same time saturating himself with the spirit and lore of the Arctic as he caught it
from his sourdough drinking companions.

One of these in whose company he was often seen was
George William Gates, "Swift Waters" Bill. Gates was an
owner and operator of rich claims in the Klondike. His
soubriquet had been conferred on him a few years before
when, on the trail, he had insisted upon walking around a

point in a river where the current was swift and the rocks plentiful, while his companions went through safely. Which was more evidence of good sense than I had ever seen him exhibit during the time I knew him in Dawson. "Swift Waters" was a high roller and lavish spender, a constant patron of the bars, gambling joints, and dance halls. He had fallen hard for the charms of a dance-hall girl, and he lavished attentions and money upon her. For all his wealth and his willingness to spend it upon this light-o'-love, "Swift Waters" was soon to experience the truth that "the course of true love never did run smooth." His girl tired of him and transferred her affection to another and handsomer suitor. And this, to be sure, was not difficult, for Bill was no Adonis.

"Swift Waters" was inconsolable. Repeated overtures to be restored in her favor found the lady stonyhearted. He moped, drank heavily, and, as his love turned to hatred, plotted revenge.

Among the whims of fancy in which he had indulged her was an inordinate fondness for fried eggs. She was noted in Dawson and throughout the Klondike for the neatness and dispatch with which she could dispose of a platter of a dozen fried eggs, washed down with a pint of champagne, at a single sitting. Three times a day, week after week, no amount of them was sufficient to diminish her enthusiasm for the deilcacy. It became a belief in the Klondike that chickens squawked in terror at the mention of her name.

In his sad recollections of the happy days passed in the favor of his lost love, Bill recalled her appetite for eggs. And in his resentful being a fell vengeance formed. Keeping his own counsel, he began, both in person and through agents, to buy, at two dollars apiece, every available egg in

Dawson, and when he had cornered the supply, his agents went through the outlying regions of the Klondike seeking, by offers of a premium, to entice eggs from the outfits of prospectors.

When at length he was convinced that he had become the owner of every egg in Dawson and points near by, "Swift Waters" prepared to dramatize the vengeance he had planned. He chose an hour when he knew his faithless love would be awake and stirring, and a place where she must witness his performance. Then the eggs he had garnered were brought up to a spot on the banks of the Yukon. In crates, boxes, hampers, and baskets they were delivered to where Bill stood guard over them. Delving into the receptacles while most of Dawson looked on, he removed the eggs, one by one at first, then in handfuls, and cast them far out into the muddy waters of the Yukon. When the last egg had found its grave in the river, he turned to the awe-struck spectators with a grim smile of triumph.

"Now, we'll see if that damned tart will have any more fried eggs."

"Swift Waters" was permanently cured of his infatuation for the faithless one. Not long after this coup he married a dance-hall girl of Dawson. He liked the family so well that he married two of her sisters in succession, but whether it was death or divorce that cleared the way for his matrimonial encores, I do not now recall.

As I scan the pages of my notes covering this period of my Yukon days, I observe the name of one who stands out from among the hundreds of others, prospectors, miners, mushers, gamblers, and soldiers of fortune. He is so dissimilar in character and background from the run of Yukon humanity that I cannot forbear mentioning him briefly in order to show that men of lofty purpose and high ideals labored side by side with the gold grubbers, gamblers, and wasters who infested the region in those days.

Father William Henry Judge, a member of the Jesuit order, was then building a log hospital in the lower end of Dawson, the only provision for the care of the sick in the town. Almost before it was completed it was to prove a veritable godsend, for that fall an epidemic of scurvy raged in Dawson and its vicinity, and thousands were affected. Although he had planned the hospital in advance of what were then considered Dawson's immediate needs, it was taxed far beyond its normal capacity for months, and many patients were accommodated in the corridors.

Father Judge was a veteran of the territory, having worked among the natives and the few white people in the Northwest as a missionary for seven years. When news of the gold strike in the Klondike reached him at his station at Fortymile, a mining camp forty miles distant from Dawson, he immediately set out to heed the call. But the call he heard was not for gold, but for service among the thousands who were seeking the precious metal in the Klondike. He had already purchased several lots in Dawson for a church and hospital site when, about the middle of March, 1897, he packed a sled and, with only one dog, started for Dawson, where he arrived after a two-day journey. He immediately set about building first a hospital and next a church, that of St. Mary.

The priest was a virile, active man whom the hardships and dangers of the Arctic left wholly undaunted. For years he had traversed many hundreds of miles of Arctic territory, visiting the widely separated huts of his parishioners, traveling alone over the trail with a sled drawn by only one dog, for he could not afford more than that. With a rope over his shoulder he helped the dog pull the load. He was tireless in his activity, but never too occupied to befriend the friendless, no matter what their creed (or whether they had any at all), or to assist with his counsel, his ministrations, or the work of his hands, those who needed help. I once overheard a waiter in a tent restaurant explain to a stranger who the man was who had just gone out.

"He's a preacher," he said. "But nobody that knows him holds that agin' him. Everybody can't be a miner, or a dog-musher, or a gambler, and somebody has to do the preaching. And, stranger, I don't know no sky pilot that's a better scout than Father Judge."

That seemed to be the unanimous opinion of Dawson, where he was well loved. When he died, about two years after his arrival, there was a day of mourning, and Dawson's entire population, swelled by hundreds from the vicinity, turned out to attend his funeral. A tall, thin figure, with drawn and wrinkled visage, I had met him often on the trail and had supposed him to be an old man. He was, in fact, but forty-nine years of age when he died. The rigors and hardships of his years in the Arctic had worn him down.

It was not until the first frenzy of the gold rush had subsided and not until life in Klondike settlements had become less raw that very many women, other than dance-hall girls and the like, ventured there. But there were a few of the other kind—in the Yukon women were of but two classes—who were no less stouthearted than men in braving the perils and discomforts of pioneering in the Arctic. Two of those whom I remember particularly were Nellie Cashman and Kate McMulrooney.

Nellie sticks in my mind because she was the first woman

I had seen since leaving Skagway with Hamilton on the long trail to Dawson. We met her, as I related earlier in this narrative, a lone, undaunted figure in the wilderness, who had surmounted all the obstacles with which nature had beset her path, and had talked out of existence all those put in her way by men. I was glad to meet up with her again in Dawson in a locale less forbidding than the one in which I had last seen her. She was a unique and arresting figure in the early life of Dawson. She had known life in many mining camps in the western states and she could talk the language of prospectors. After leaving Dawson she went to Nome and later to Fairbanks, and when I last heard of her she was "somewhere in Alaska." The polar breezes of the Arctic were the very breath of life to her, and I am sure she will not be content to end her days anywhere else.

Kate was one of the early entrepreneurs in the Klondike, to which she had come in the first stampede. She was a stewardess on the *City of Topeka*, operating on the Alaskan run, and when the first news of the gold strike reached the outside world she promptly chucked her job. In the Klondike, she opened a tent restaurant at the Forks, where she dispensed meals consisting of bacon, beans, bread, and coffee—most often without the incidentals of butter or milk—at a uniform price of $2.50 a meal. Eggs, when she had them, were extras at a dollar an egg, at the diner's risk. That is, if the first egg chanced to be too ancient to be edible, he had the privilege of ordering another—if he paid for it—and so on, ad infinitum, until a good egg appeared or the supply was exhausted. Of course she made money in her restaurant business, and she was never reckless with it. She had staked a bench claim on Cheechaka Hill just above the original Carmack claim on Bonanza

Creek. She worked this claim and it proved fairly rich.

Between her catering and mining activities—she was interested in several claims in the district—Kate prospered and her rise in the social scale was climaxed by her marriage to a man reputed, in Dawson, at least, to be a count. Whether or not the lucky bridegroom was a titled man, I do not know. I suspect the legend was born of the circumstance that he was a foreigner and a notorious ne'er-do-well. In any event, he has always had my heartfelt sympathy for I am certain that if, indeed, he was a drone, Kate took it out of his hide. I base this surmise on my own experience with his bride. For while she was having her Cheechaka claim worked, I was employed on it shoveling gravel at a dollar an hour to tide over a temporary financial embarrassment. On one of her daily tours of inspection Kate took immediate and violent exception to the size of the long-handled shovel I was using and fired me on the spot. The offending shovel was one belonging to her which had been furnished to me by her foreman. Through much use it had been worn down to a tithe of its original size. Until that moment I had never questioned that Miss Mc-Mulrooney belonged to the Irish, not the Scotch, division of the Gaelic race.

CHAPTER IX

BY THE APPROACH OF WINTER Dawson had grown so that four large gambling resorts were not more than adequate for the needs of its population, fixed and floating. These Arctic casinos included bars and dance halls in their attractions and were the centers of Dawson's social life. Unlike the clubs of the Victorian era, they were not exclusively for men. Women were welcome; indeed, they were important to the success of a place, but of course the frequenters were exclusively of the demimonde. There were practically no other women in Dawson at that time.

Nearly everyone in the town sought one or other of the gambling houses for diversion, if not to participate at the gaming tables, then at the bar or on the dance floor. Many of them sampled all three forms of pleasure impartially. For in a land where life is a hazard and wealth and ease may come on a single turn of Fortune's wheel, it was natural for men to seek the gaming table and its adjuncts, women and booze, for their relaxation. In the Yukon the stakes were their lives against gold, and in time hazarding fortune became a fixed habit with most of them. Those who had wrested the coveted treasure from the earth gambled it with others who had struck pay dirt. And they played always for high stakes for, as fortune had been lavish with them, they could not be pikers. Besides, effort

—whether work or play—for small returns was not their dish.

Gambling in Dawson was open and, as open gambling goes, it was fairly honest—the Mounties saw to that. The commandant had served notice on the resort owners that no person under the influence of liquor should be permitted to play. The resorts were regularly policed and the orders were strictly obeyed. Similarly, players were watched and any crooked gambler, or any loiterer not known to have a job, received a "blue ticket" from the police. That is, he was warned either to get a job or take a walk, or a boat, down the river. The order usually was obeyed without question. Failure to comply with it brought on the recalcitrant a term in the "skookum house" (jail) or on the municipal woodpile.

The Yukon never was a gunman's paradise, nor was the knife customarily used in a quarrel. Men reserved those weapons for use only against wild beasts. The rugged men of the trail, whose mettle had been tried by the hardships and dangers of the Arctic, considered them the tools of assassins, weaklings, and cowards. I saw many battles in the gambling houses in Dawson, and in its streets and on the trail, but I never witnessed one where anything more deadly than fists and feet were employed. Men were quick to resent insults, and trail and mining claim disputes often led to hostilities, but they rarely ended in death, or even maiming. They were rough-and-tumble affairs in which fists flew and men wrestled. If a combatant was lucky enough to fell his opponent with his fist or a club, or throw him at grapples, it was always fair and within the rules to finish him off by applying "the boots" to the prone adversary. The theory was if you let him up he would renew the combat, and if he threw you he would give you "the boots." So a fallen enemy was booted until he cried "quits" or became unconscious.

In the gambling halls men lost fortunes on the turn of a card without batting an eye. The loser either had plenty more dust where what they had lost came from, or else they were confident of making a lucky strike, either at cards or prospecting, to recoup their fortunes. I saw Jack London's friend, "Swift Waters" Bill, playing pool one night in a Dawson saloon for one hundred dollars a game of one frame, the first one to get eight balls to be the winner. Bill didn't have a Chinaman's chance, for his opponent was an expert known up and down the Yukon as one who could charm a pool ball to do his will. He lost game after game in short order, almost before he could pocket a ball, and he was soon out several thousand dollars. But his losses bothered him not at all, for the game had a large gallery and Bill strutted importantly, satisfied because he was in the limelight.

Another gambling plunger of quite a different stripe was Humboldt Gates, no relation to "Swift Waters," of the same surname. Humboldt was a Californian who, at its very start, had joined the Klondike rush from Circle City. He owned and operated one of the richest claims on El Dorado Creek and had become immensely wealthy in almost no time. He was one of the most colorful figures in the Yukon, greatly different from most of the rough-and-ready prospectors who peopled it. Tall, broad-shouldered and athletic in appearance, his manners were those of the cultured gentleman he was. The conventional Yukon canvas attire which he customarily wore in the gambling houses of Dawson, or at the Forks, was always immaculate, and when he put on miners' rig, it was with the air of one more accustomed to the black and white of

evening dress. Although the sourdoughs sensed a difference
between him and them, they did not hold it against him,
and he was much liked everywhere in the territory.

Gates was not an inveterate player, but whenever he
made a bet it was always for high stakes. He rarely placed
a bet until he was almost ready to leave the gambling hall,
but he liked to stand around with the gang, watching the
seated players. Then, when the last case-card bets were
about to be made, he would haul out a bulging poke and
coolly stake a thousand dollars on the high card. Win or
lose, he rarely made a second bet that same night. If he
won, he invited everybody in the house up to the bar to
drink on him. If he lost—and he did frequently—it was
all right with him. He laughed lightheartedly, remarking,
"Better luck next time," and with a pleasant good night
to the gang, he would jump into his sled for the drive
to his cabin.

Gates's team was the wonder and envy of all beholders.
He had assembled twelve of the finest dogs in the Yukon,
paying ten thousand dollars for them. The harness, silver-
mounted and of fine leather, had cost another two thousand dollars. The Huskies were matched in size, color, and
markings, were slim and swift, and never in their lives
had they drawn a loaded sled. They passed everything on
the trail, even the fleet sixteen-dog team driven by "Big
Mike" Sullivan, Klondike's mail carrier, and their swift
coming was always announced far in advance by the
jingle of the many silver bells on their harness.

Gates was a bachelor, and when he struck it rich on El
Dorado Creek, he sent for his sister, in California, to join
him. She was a tall, slim, pretty girl of about nineteen
years, with olive skin, dimpled and rosy, and golden-
bronze hair. She was a thoroughbred like her brother and

the day-after-tomorrow personified. She could handle
Gates's dog team with all the dash and expertness that he
did, and she was a familiar and always-welcome figure on
the trail. It had been many weary months since the men
in Dawson had seen a woman not of the dance-hall or
brothel sisterhood, and this girl captivated all of them.
To see her flashing by on her sled, to hear the cheery "hello"
she had for all wayfarers, and, best of all, to see her
friendly smile parting lips that showed even teeth of a
whiteness to rival the snow, put gladness into the hearts
of the dourest sourdough or the orneriest dog-musher in
the Arctic.

Three men, who many years later became famous, or at
least notorious, stick in my memory as being among the
hundreds I met in Dawson's resorts. "Tex" Rickard, who
was to get gold as a prize-fight promoter, was among the
early arrivals in Dawson. He was prominent in the sporting fraternity in the mining city, and a familiar figure in
the places where its members congregated. I do not recall
that he ever actually prospected while in Dawson. At
any rate, before I finally had "come outside," he moved
on down the river to Fairbanks and Nome.

John Considine, who later went to New York and became the owner of the Metropole Hotel was another
prominent member of Dawson's gambling set. Considine
was a claim owner and operator in the Klondike, having
brought his claim with him into the territory. Whether
he won it at cards or acquired it by purchase, I do not
know. In the intervals between working his claim he
operated "off the arm" in Dawson saloons and dance halls.
When not in his waiter's uniform he took a fling at the
gaming table, and it is my belief that he amassed more

gold that way than he ever took out of the ground. Like
Alexander Pantages, a contemporary of his in Dawson,
who also both worked a claim and wore the white apron,
he was thrifty. They belonged in the category of those
who "stacked" their coin, in contrast with the happy-go-
lucky brotherhood who "rolled" it. For it was a saying
in the Yukon in those days that coin was minted flat so
that it could be stacked, and round so that it could be
rolled. They were wiser in their generation than the
wasters who liked to see the ducats roll, for they both
prospered. On his Klondike winnings Considine reared a
fortune as mine host in New York. Pantages became a
theatrical magnate of sorts on the Pacific coast, but the
pleasure of his affluence was marred somewhat when he fell
afoul of the law. Even before that he had had a taste of
litigation, and found it bitter in his mouth. There was
"Klondike Kate," a dance-hall habitué of Dawson, with
whom he was enamored. After he became wealthy, she
alleged an early partnership agreement and sued him successfully for a share in the fortune he had amassed from
his claim.

CHAPTER X

THE VISCOUS MASS THAT overlay Dawson's street and paths was beginning to freeze up a little, and on the hills and trails the snow was sticking. The long Arctic winter was setting in and we were all ready to inaugurate our freighting service out of Dawson to points north, south, east and west—wherever the business lay. We had our dogs and our sleds. We awaited only the Arctic's good-roads maker, snow, and within a few weeks there was plenty of it.

Our first haul was to the Forks, twelve miles distant, where a settlement had sprung up at the junction of El Dorado and Bonanza creeks. We left Dawson with two full loads of one thousand pounds each, twelve dogs to the load, making the round trip inside ten hours. It was good time, for we had extended ourselves and the dogs to make an auspicious beginning of the service. We were fortunate in having for the inaugural trip a trail that was in good condition and not too difficult at any point. There were no steep grades, only a gradual rise of less than 1 per cent a mile. The only difficult places were where the trail crossed the creek. Malamutes do not shine at pulling loads uphill, and we learned to adopt the principle of a Coney Island switchback, going downgrade at a speed sufficient for the momentum to carry the load up the next rise.

Our dogs, all Malamutes, behaved splendidly. They were well fed, well trained, and well rested after the summer's idleness. Prior to launching our freighting venture Lindsay and I had had no actual experience with Arctic dogs, but we studied the brutes, their habits and dispositions, in the time we had before hitting the trail. We thought we knew a bit about them but we realized on this first trip that our knowledge was elemental. For the Arctic dog is in a class by himself. Any ordinary dog expert who has never known the Malamute or Husky must begin all over when he undertakes to handle the Arctic dog. Even the Master of the Buckhounds himself would be put to shame by the least of Yukon dog-mushers.

Arctic dogs are of two varieties, the Malamute and the Husky. The first-named is bred from the wild dogs that from time immemorial have roamed the Arctic in packs; the other, from the timber wolf of the North. Of the two, the Husky is the larger, grey in color, with a long coat under which, in winter, is grown a fine, soft fur. Neither breed ever barks, and hence they are useless as watchdogs. But they become vocal at the sound of music of any kind. Lindsay had a puckish humor, and it was his delight at a stop on the trail to sing at the top of his voice. Whereat the brutes would squat on their haunches and send forth a chorus of discordant wails. Also, they are the world's most accomplished snarlers, and in their incessant fights their terrific growling brings to the spot every dog within hearing distance.

I can't give them a character for either honesty or sweetness of disposition, for they are inveterate thieves to whom stealing is second nature, and they will fight with or without provocation, and in a melee their fangs know no brother. On the trail the food must be securely tied

and covered with canvas to guard against their stealing it
at night, and great care must be exercised so as not to
stop near another team, or even to drive too close in
passing one, for they love nothing better than tearing into
each other. They are cowardly fighters, though, for all
will turn upon a dog that is down and rend him to bits.

But how they can work! A team of twelve good dogs,
either breed, on a fairly level, hard trail will move a
thousand-pound load at an average speed of four miles
an hour, and they can do it daily on a rest of not more
than six hours a day. Traveling light, the same team can
average fifty miles for the six hours. On a steep upgrade
they are not adequate, for they tire very quickly, but
with all the will in the world they will pull until they
drop in their tracks.

The secret of getting the best out of a dog team is to
feed them well and to treat them with a sternness unre-
lieved by the slightest show of affection. For the Arctic
dog will work his head off if he is given plenty to eat. But,
being incapable of affection, he will take a mean advantage
of any musher weak enough to indulge in it. Just let a
misguided musher pet a dog, and the beast will maneuver
to capitalize on this partiality by faking weakness or lame-
ness, or by fudging on the hauling even to the extent of
managing to ride the sled with the load. For all their surli-
ness and lack of responsiveness, they are clever in dog ways.

On the trail they are fed only once a day. As feeding
time is always at night, they are eager to be harnessed in
the morning so that they may get under way and moving
toward the next meal. There is no fear of their straying on
the trail. The sled carries their food and they know it.
When the food supply fails, they will unhesitatingly eat
dog, and for this they should not be judged harshly. Many

prospectors in like straits have done the same thing, and, perforce, liked it.

However much a dog-musher may admire the few good traits in his Huskies, it is next to impossible for him to have for them the affection one has for dogs in milder climates. Hence it is not surprising that Arctic dogs rarely are named. "Rex," "Rover," "Prince," or "Towser," would mean nothing to a Husky or Malamute. The only form of address they recognize is "mush" (a corruption of the French *marchons*), and to them that means both "go ahead" and "get out of the way."

I remember a yarn about an English tourist in Seward who observed the idle dogs roaming the streets or sleeping in the sunny spots on the sidewalks. Hearing the word constantly addressed to them by those passing in the street, he was greatly puzzled.

"St'rordinr'y," he remarked to a friend. "There are hundreds of these brutes in this town, and every bally one to the last is named 'Mush.' "

It appeared that the freighting business would be a go, and we were greatly encouraged. Our rates seemed to be right, twelve cents the pound being average, with differentials according to the distance. The maximum was forty cents on some long hauls over difficult trails, and the minimum was eight cents. We made trips out of Dawson before the winter was well on, and we began to envision ourselves as the future magnates of a Yukon transportation system reared on our pioneering enterprise. "Gold is where you find it." So far, we had found none in Klondike soil; perhaps we were to find it in the freighting venture.

Best of all, we were in superb health, and we were a congenial crew of three young men with a glorious life ahead. Gloom or heaviness of mood could not long abide in the

Morgan Driving Sleigh

Courtesy Canadian National Railways

A Husky Poses for the Camera

same atmosphere with Lindsay. His irrepressible spirits constantly found expression in songs roared out on the frosty air, in droll imitations of Dawson characters, and in an inexhaustible flow of fun and witticisms that lightened the arduous labors of the trail, tasks in which he took his full share. Johnnie Burke's cooking had improved under threats of dire consequences, and after we had had our supper Lindsay would roar out songs, the three of us harmonizing more or less successfully in the choruses. It delighted Lindsay when the Malamutes responded to his obbligato with their dismal wailing—which seemed all the more pronounced when he sang one of his favorites, "Tim Toolin, the Stout Man from Tipperary." Probably for the reason that he always sang it fortissimo, and *con amore* and *con espressione* as well.

"Shut up, you don't know good music when you hear it," he would shout, belaboring them vigorously with the butt of his whip handle.

We experienced no great distress from the cold on the trail, for we had learned how to dress for it and we came to know much of the lore of the Arctic, which enabled us to defy its rigors. We wore heavy underwear, woolens of fine texture, and heavy woolen socks. Our shoes were of heavy felt, high above the instep. Hard leather is of no use in the Arctic. Stout canvas breeches, wool-lined, were stuffed in our shoe tops. A canvas coat, of the same texture as the trousers, a cap and a parka completed the costume. The cap was of canvas-covered fur—rabbit or gray squirrel is the best—with the fur worn next to the skin. The cap extended to cover the back and sides of our necks, and fastened around the throat so as to cover the chin to the mouth. In extremely low temperatures we customarily wore a silk handkerchief tied around the cap and over the nose and mouth, just below the eyes. We resorted to this only on rare occasions because the breath, freezing on the handkerchief, necessitated removing it frequently, and that was a nuisance.

Save by those who ride, fur (except in the cap) is never worn when traveling in the Arctic, for it causes one going afoot to sweat. When that happens it is necessary to stop, build a fire, and dry out. Otherwise, one would freeze to death. We wore no gloves, but heavy woolen mittens, over which we put another pair of canvas ones, worn separately to permit easy drying. Our parkas, which we pulled on over our other clothing, were sleeved, and hooded, loose-fitting canvas garments, in shapelessness somewhat like the old-fashioned nightshirt. They hung from the neck to the shoe tops, and had openings only large enough to put the head through. The neckpiece was fur-trimmed and closed with a drawstring.

Accoutered thus, we suffered little from the cold. In severe blizzards we stopped in our tracks, put our backs to the snow and wind and sought what windbreaks were handy, and rested out the storm. In extremely low temperatures there is rarely any wind, and then we pursued our way warily.

On one of our hauls, while on the return trip to Dawson, we stopped at a roadhouse on the trail for a snack and a smoke. It was very cold and there was a group around the red-hot drum stove. In the manner of all having acquaintance with the etiquette of the Yukon, several of those hugging the stove gave place to the new arrivals. After the icicles on my eyebrows and lashes had melted and I had thawed out sufficiently, I rolled a cigarette and asked the chap standing at my side for a match, which he politely furnished, looking at me closely as he did so. Now

that my eyes had become accustomed to the cabin's twilight I saw that he was a colored youth of about my own
age.

"Mistuh," he said, "You sho remind me pow'fully of a
gen'man ah knew back yondah in N'Yawk."

"Well," I told him, "I'm from that neck of the woods."

"Sho 'nuff," he said delightedly, showing two rows of
brilliant white teeth. "Now ain't dat wondaful? But this
gen'man ain't you, ah knows, 'cause he done got too much
sense to come to this heah country what de good Lawd
done forgot."

"What was your friend's name?"

"His name's Mistuh Ed Morgan," he answered.

He had me. I didn't remember him from Adam's off
ox.

"I'm Ed Morgan, but darned if I know you."

He was delighted. He laughed, slapped his sides, did a
buck-and-wing step or two, and shook my hand heartily.

"Why, Mistuh Morgan, doan you 'membah me? Ah
knowed you back in 1896, 'fo' ah come out heah to freeze
in this God-awful lan'."

I was getting every moment more curious.

"Well, where was it you knew me?" I demanded impatiently.

"Why, doan' you 'membah Henry, de hat-check boy,
at de Ice Palace, up at One Hundred and Seventh Street
and Lexington Avenue, and ah sho wish ah wuz theah
right now."

With that, I remembered him. No wonder the Ice
Palace, in his longing, seemed to him like the tropics. It was
sixty degrees below zero outside on the trail at that
moment.

Henry told me he had staked a claim on Hunker Creek

and worked it for eight months without success. Then he had obtained a job at the roadhouse as a roustabout at ten dollars a day. He was saving up his fare, and in the spring, when navigation on the Yukon opened up, he was going back to New York.

"And dey ain't nothin' evah goin' to get me out o' dat town no mo'," he declared.

I never saw Henry again, but I hope he got back safely to New York and the Ice Palace.

On the trail a few weeks later, I met another old acquaintance. He was the only one of my fellow passengers aboard the *Amur* that I had met since coming into the Yukon, and I did not recognize him when he hailed me. It was the Fat Boy, but now so sadly changed as no longer to merit the nickname. He had lost one hundred and fifty of his three hundred pounds, and his clothes hung on his gaunt frame like a tent. But he was a good sport and a brave spirit, and although he had not yet struck a pay streak, he regretted not an ounce of the excess flesh with which he had larded the Yukon trail. I was glad to have met up with him, for he was a link with the life aboard the *Amur,* an experience which now seemed impossibly long ago and not nearly so unhappy as I had thought it at the time. Also, he was the only man that I met in all the Yukon who had known Hamilton, and I wanted to ask him if in his travels he had ever chanced upon him.

But he had not. Although I had no sense of guilt for the circumstances of our parting, it saddened me to think what fate Hamilton might have met with in that awesome wilderness of snow and ice after we had gone our separate ways.

CHAPTER XI

BY THE MIDDLE OF NOVEMBER our freight-hauling service
was fairly established. We were reasonably busy handling
freight to and from the locations, with time in between
for odd jobs. We were known as the pioneer freight line
out of Dawson. Now we were to add to our hauling
activities that of Arctic ambulance service. This came
about through no ambitious reaching out on our part, but
through an emergency call we could not refuse.

Tom Sullivan, a miner working a claim on a lay with
Jim Stringer (that wasn't his name, but I'll use it) in
Diamond Creek, at its junction with Twelvemile River,
near the headwaters of the latter, lay helpless in camp there.
Both his legs were frozen from about six inches above the
knees to his toes. His partner had come to Dawson and
engaged us to bring Sullivan back by sled to Father Judge's
hospital. The location was eighty-five miles distant by trail
following the Yukon twelve miles downstream from
Dawson, thence up Twelvemile River to Diamond Creek.
Overland it was about thirty-five miles, with two ranges
to cross. Stringer agreed to pay us five hundred dollars for
getting Sullivan to the hospital.

Because of the urgent nature of the job we decided to
go in two parties to the camp, Lindsay taking the river
trail with the basket sled and our ten best dogs. I took the

overland trail, accompanied by Stringer, and carried provisions sufficient for only one meal, Stringer assuring us there was plenty of food at his camp. Lindsay, who expected to reach the camp in quicker time than I, took only blankets and dog food.

Except for his knowledge of the trail, Stringer proved a liability rather than an asset on the journey. He was rather a sniveling weakling who insisted on frequent stops for rest, making the excuse that his journey to Dawson had used him up. So many were our stops that we made no speed, and I would have gone on ahead except that I was unfamiliar with that part of the country and feared to miss the gulch where the suffering man lay. Nevertheless, we arrived there at nine o'clock that night. We had lost two hours because the chuckleheaded fool, Stringer, had guided me into the wrong gulch and we had gone five miles before he discovered his mistake. By the time we had backtracked and found the right gulch, Lindsay had arrived at the camp two hours ahead of us.

Although Sullivan was suffering agony, we decided that it would be most unwise to start back on the return trip without some rest. Our dogs were tired after their splendid run and we ourselves were ready to drop in our tracks for want of sleep, and were numb from the intense cold and fatigue. So, after some six or seven hours' rest, we loaded Sullivan in the basket sled and started on the return journey. We had left Stringer behind, rolled up in his blankets, for he had not volunteered to accompany us and his helpless partner to Dawson. The dogs were in fine fettle, for they had had a good feed the night before, and a dog team always shows much pep on a return journey, knowing that more food and rest await them at its end.

One of my legs was a bit stiff from a bad fall on a down-grade the evening before, but I soon worked the stiffness off. We chose the river trail for the return trip, anticipating not too much difficulty, for it had proven the quicker route of the two. Lindsay, coming up to the gulch, had had some trouble with the many windfalls on the trail, but they were as nothing compared to what they proved to be when we had a sled laden with a sick man. Every time we had to tilt the sled over a big log the poor devil cried out in agony, and we had gone no more than half a mile when we realized that we would need Stringer's assistance if we were to insure his partner as much ease as possible on the rough journey.

I returned to the camp to explain our need, but the callous brute refused my entreaties to return with us. Weakly, I abided by his answer. I was not hankering for his company on another voyage anyhow, for I had had my fill of him on the trail the day before. But when I returned without him and explained why, Lindsay was enraged.

"Won't come, won't he, the yellow bastard!" he roared. "Well, we'll see if he won't."

He grabbed the sled axe and started off toward the camp. In half an hour he was back, with Stringer in tow, and we resumed our journey.

Even today, nearly forty years later, I shudder at the recollection of the horror of that trip. It was bitter cold, the trail down Diamond Creek to Twelvemile River was beset every few steps with windfalls, around which we must pass or ease the sled over. When we had to do the latter, Sullivan suffered the most excruciating torture, for every jolt caused him agony in his frozen members. Unable to stand it without outcry, he would now curse us horribly, now plead with us, at first together, then separately, "for the love of Christ and his Mother," to knock him on the head with the axe and put him out of his misery.

Sometimes he was in a delirium, and then he would sing at the top of his voice the words from some Catholic hymn remembered from his boyhood, strangely alternating this with the refrain from a popular song of the day.

> The Bow'ry, the Bow'ry!
> They say such things, and they do
> strange things
> On the Bow'ry, the Bow'ry!
> I'll never go there any more!

Again he would pray—and from what I later heard of Tom Sullivan, I know that only a delirium, no less, could have moved him to that. Or he would plead in the most heartbreaking tones: "Oh, Doctor, dear, don't you be cutting off me legs. Sure, what use would I be, at all, at all, without me two legs?" Then, in terror as he in his ravings saw the doctors approach him, he would try to rise, shrieking out, "Stand back, you —— sawbones, I'll not have you cutting off me legs."

It was horrible, and in the face of his suffering we were silent, helpless to alleviate his pain. At length we came to Twelvemile River, and here we halted. Lindsay, with a black scowl on his countenance, turned to Stringer.

"Now you can go back to your blankets and your tent, you white-livered quitter."

Stringer, shamed, hesitated to move.

"Get out," Lindsay roared, fingering the axe, "or by God, I'll fix you so you can't."

Stringer left without debating the point.

We drove ahead all day, delayed by the many windfalls

and the care we had to exercise to spare our maimed passenger whatever added pain we could. Despite our efforts
Sullivan suffered terribly and his cries, his delirious cursing
and pleading for us to put him out of his misery, harrowed
our nerves and increased the travail of the trail in the
bitter cold. For the first time in our mushing together
over Yukon trails I did not hear Lindsay's cheery voice
roaring out in song. To make it worse, the stiffness from
my injured leg had come back, and I was not able to relieve it by riding the sled runners. A basket sled, such
as the one we were using, has handle bars extending back
about a foot on each side, and by these the driver of the
team guides the sled. Also extending back about a foot
are the sled runners, on which the driver can stand and
ride for a considerable distance when the going is good.
On a long journey this affords him frequent rests, but he
cannot ride continuously, for he soon becomes too cold
in this standing position and is obliged to run with the
team to warm himself.

I could not avail myself of this opportunity for an
occasional rest because, early on the voyage, I had split my
breeches at the crotch and my parka was insufficient to
protect that part of me from the intense cold. As night
came on, my strength was diminishing momentarily and
I felt my endurance near the breaking point, but I considered it was out of the question, in view of Sullivan's
desperate situation, to suggest a rest. Try as I would I
could not maintain a pace that would keep me abreast of
the dogs. Lindsay would forge ahead with them, and
when perhaps half a mile away, he would halt until I came
up. Each time I would urge him to go on without me in
order to get Sullivan to the hospital, and each time he
would answer:

"To hell with Sullivan. You and I get to Dawson together, or not at all."

After a seemingly endless succession of hours, I no longer
tried to keep the pace. I felt a languor that was almost
pleasant stealing over me. Time and place were ceasing to
exist. I did not seem to care what happened, or how soon it
happened, to Sullivan, to Lindsay, or to me. All I wanted
was to rest. I had never before felt as I did just then. I
halted and Lindsay came up to me. He eyed me closely,
with a seriousness in his expression I had never before
seen there.

"Are you coming, Ed?" he asked.

"No," I told him. "You go on with Sullivan, I've got to
rest. I'll follow you to Dawson tomorrow."

Wearily I took the hand axe from the sled and started
toward the riverbank.

"Where are you going?" he asked.

"I'm going to build a fire here, get warm and rested,
and follow you later."

I went on a few steps, but he was at my side, his hand
on my arm.

"Come on, Ed, we're just a few hours away."

"No, by God, not another step until I get some rest,"
I answered doggedly. Then with a flare-up of energy I
cursed him soundly, ending with a foolish laugh as the
languor and indifference returned.

Quietly Lindsay took the axe from me, and the fight
was on. Ordinarily, I believe, I would have been a match
for him, even though I knew him to be a parcel of wild-
cats when he engaged in a scrap—which was not often.
It required an unusual amount of provocation to arouse
him to that point. He was just an inch short of six feet in
height, with powerful shoulders, a forty-four-inch chest

and thirty-inch waist. His one hundred and fifty pounds of flesh were well distributed over his frame and every ounce was firm. His fists packed wallops like a mule's kick. Almost before I had time to get in a lick he had me groggy, and as soon as I was prone on the snow Lindsay gave me "the boot," everywhere except on my face, until weakly I cried "quits." Even then he would not let me up until I had promised faithfully that I would go along with him to Dawson.

I think the anger he aroused in me was the thing needful to dispel the torpor that was enveloping my mind and will, just as the fancy shellacking he gave me was, I know now, what saved my spent physical powers from quitting utterly. Although sore in body from the trouncing I had received, and indignant at his treatment of me, I was no longer indifferent to what might happen to me, and I determined to make good on my promise to stay with him until we reached Dawson together.

We delivered Sullivan at the hospital at four o'clock the next morning. It was sixty degrees below zero in Dawson, lower than the temperature was on the Yukon. From the hospital we drove the half mile to our camp, fed and put up the dogs, and made for our shack to get some food for ourselves. We had not eaten since the day before. All our larder contained was about five pounds of stewed prunes, but we cleaned them up and longed for more. But, even more, we longed for sleep. And so, our hunger unsatiated, we curled up in our bunks and slept the clock around.

When I awoke I was unable to rise and experienced excruciating pain in my abdomen, the flesh of which felt as though it were clutched by red-hot pincers. I knew the symptoms of frostbite but I wanted conformation, so I called to Lindsay.

He took one look at my burning region.

"I thought so," he said. "A touch of frost."

Then I understood fully what fear had actuated him when he fought me so tigerishly the night before on the trail.

"Lindsay," I said contritely, "you saved my life."

"Yes," he admitted readily, "but I had to nearly kill you to do it."

For the next week he nursed me with all the delicate care and solicitude of a mother, cheering my convalescence with his repertoire of song, mimicry, and spontaneous humor of the sort now known as wisecracks. Brave, loyal, truehearted Lindsay, what a pal you were. Truly "the bravest are the tenderest."

We never collected a single yellow grain of the five hundred dollars promised for getting Sullivan to the hospital. But we were not too disappointed, for Sullivan's legs were saved. A conclave of doctors at the hospital were for cutting them off pronto, but Doctor Burke avowed he could save them, and he did, although it took a long time.

Lindsay discounted nonpayment of the five hundred dollars, promising himself, and me, that he would take twice that amount out of Stringer's hide at the very first opportunity.

In this, too, we were to suffer disappointment, for never again did he cross our path.

CHAPTER XII

OUR FREIGHTING ENTERPRISE continued active and as we got deeper into winter we had few idle days. The cash receipts, it is true, were not large, for most of the business was done on credit extended to working mines that would not make or sluice their gravel until the spring thaw provided water sufficient to wash out the "pay," or gold. Until that time, we could not collect, but we felt that the risks were good. Although we frequently passed within three miles of Steamboat Hill on hauls, we had no opportunity to visit our claim. We heard occasionally about the progress of work on other claims near by, and what we heard was not very reassuring. The outfit working the hilltop had abandoned operations, after having sunk their shaft to a depth of 240 feet. Three hillside claims near ours were being worked, but we heard no reports of sensational results. Dobins, the experienced prospector upon whom the success or failure of our claim must largely depend, was still working for wages on El Dorado Creek, and we did not anticipate resuming operations on the location until the freighting season should end with the coming of spring.

In the meantime Dawson had heard of our ambulance service for Tom Sullivan and a few days before Christmas we were engaged to haul a claim owner, John King, from the hospital in Dawson, where he had been under treatment for heart trouble, to his camp on Quartz Creek, in the Indian River district. It was a forty-five-mile trip with one divide to cross, and we agreed, for $250, to deliver King to his camp within a day, starting on the morning of Christmas Eve. Normally the journey could be accomplished easily in twelve hours, and although King weighed two hundred pounds, we decided that one man was sufficient for the trip.

I called at the hospital for King at four o'clock in the morning. He was ready and waiting for me, and so was his baggage. Nothing had been said to us about luggage when the contract was made. When I saw a hospital attendant following the patient with a huge grip weighing more than a hundred pounds, I was aghast. I protested to King that no team could haul him and his trunk over the mountain trail within the time stipulated. He was insistent, finally offering to raise the hauling fee to three hundred dollars, and I weakly yielded. The trail was up the Klondike River to Hunker Creek, thence up Gold Bottom, over the summit of the Dome, an altitude of two thousand feet, and thereafter down a steep miner's trail to King's camp on Quartz Creek.

My passenger was one of the most cantankerous and all-around disagreeable persons I have ever met. He was in haste to be home for Christmas, but his holiday spirit did not include me. He had been querulous and complaining from the beginning, but no crisis arose until we had proceeded about five miles up the Klondike to a point where there had been an overflow just prior to our arrival. These overflows, caused by the swift current forcing an outlet through the ice, are serious hindrances to anyone mushing on the trail. For if the musher's feet get wet, he must stop, build a fire, and dry his footgear. Otherwise, frozen feet would be the result. They are no less serious for the dogs, because the water, freezing between their toes, forms ice which cuts the balls of their feet and causes them to go lame. Both the dogs and I got our feet wet, so I told King we would have to halt until we had dried them.

Although, as an old miner, he was familiar with the problems involved in mushing Arctic trails, the old coot immediately set up a profane protest against the delay. When I insisted, he conceded, but declared half an hour should be sufficient. I paid no attention to him, but halted until the dogs and I had thoroughly dried out, which took three hours. With the dogs rested, we made good time to the foot of the hill in Gold Bottom Gulch, where the ascent to the Dome begins. Here we stopped to give the team a rest of two hours and to have our lunch. The morning's wetting had taken plenty of pep out of the dogs and I feared for their ability to make the steep grade in anything like good time. I suggested to King that he cache his big grip, but he refused, saying that it was full of Christmas gifts and must go with him.

We made the summit by eight o'clock in the evening, but it was a hard grind, accomplished only after giving the dogs repeated rests. Here I decided that the team must have a two-hour respite before setting out on the dangerous drop downgrade, and my passenger again protested, this time surpassing himself in his profanity, which sweepingly included the dogs and their paternity as well as myself and my forebears. He was getting frightfully on my nerves, and I was in a smoldering rage. I wanted to turn on him and give him an overdue licking, but he was sixty years old and an invalid, so I gritted my teeth and held onto my fists and my temper.

Going down a steep trail is perilous in daylight; going down it at night is doubly, triply, dangerous. King was for making the descent with a minimum of delay; I was equally determined to proceed with all caution. I rough-locked the sled runners, winding some dog chains about them and making them fast. Just before we reached a bad turn near the bottom of a hill I stopped.

"I think you'd better get off the sled and walk around the turn," I suggested. "It would be safer."

"To hell with the idea, and you too," he roared. "I'm paying to ride and I'm going to ride." And shouting out a tirade of abuse and curses, he refused to leave the sled.

I drove on, King cursing me, the dogs, and the sled without pausing for breath. He was still at it as we carefully negotiated the dangerous turn. Just as we reached it, he ripped out a particularly offensive epithet and this was the breaking point for me. Without a word in reply, I lifted on the inside handle bar of the sled.

Over went sled, passenger, and dogs, pell-mell, a drop of twenty feet. I was alone on the trail, sobered on the instant, my sudden rage just as suddenly cooled, and beset with dreadful imaginings. I feared I was a murderer and I loathed myself. For while the drop probably could not kill, or even maim the old man, the shock might easily prove fatal to a heart patient. Fearsomely I descended to where the dogs and the passenger had plunged into three feet of soft snow. Divine Providence was with me—and King—for he was unhurt and sputtering lurid oaths. The blankets in which he was swathed and the snowbank had cushioned his fall. Now I had a revulsion of feeling and regretted that the spill had left him unscathed, or at least still able to curse so fluently. But I was thankful that none of the dogs was hurt.

Courtesy Canadian National Railways

Husky Mother and Family

Courtesy Department of Mines and Resources, Ottawa, Canada

Rest Period for the Dog-Sled Team

It took me an hour to get the dogs, the sled, and King back on the trail, and we pulled up at the old man's cabin just before midnight. King tendered payment of the three hundred dollar hauling charge in dust very dirty with black sand. To have accepted it would have meant a loss of at least fifty dollars to me, and I refused. His wife, a pleasant old lady, pleaded with him to pay me in currency, but he would not do it, and with a string of oaths he declared I would take the dust or nothing. While the hubbub was going strong, Mrs. King slipped out of the room and presently returned with her son-in-law. At a look from him, I left the room and went to his cabin on the same claim. There he paid me in full in currency.

"Why didn't you leave the old coot in the hospital, or on the trail?" he asked me.

I didn't tell him how near I had come to doing the latter, but I believe that he would have understood the provocation.

After a four-hour rest at the King claim, we took the trail and were back in Dawson at noon on Christmas Day. It was much the same as any other day in the little town, except that the saloons, dance halls, and gambling joints had slightly better than their usual attendance and the eggnogs, Tom and Jerrys, and punches, the special tipple appropriate to the holiday season, were more in evidence. The new dance hall that Charles Meadows, "Arizona Charlie," had opened up earlier in the year, was the center of attraction in Dawson that day. For it was known throughout the Klondike that the proprietor's Christmas gift to his ladylove would be on exhibition in a conspicuous place in his establishment.

The gift was a full-length portrait in oil of the lady, and Arizona Charlie, his inamorata, and all Dawson agreed that it was the finest work of art in all the Klondike. Charlie had commissioned Julius Ullman, who had come to Dawson in Dr. Burke's party, to paint the portrait from life, agreeing to pay him $1,500 for the work. Charlie's girl was a stunning blonde, perhaps the most striking in his collection of dance-hall girls, all of whom were remarkable for their good looks. For a month she sat for Ullman, costumed in a frilly, lacy, beribboned gown of the late nineties. When Arizona Charlie, his girl, and their friends saw the finished work, they were unsparing in their praise of it. Charlie had it gorgeously framed, and he declared that the most fitting place for it to be exhibited was in the front room of his Palace Dance Hall, where all Dawson could see and admire it. And a goodly part of Dawson was doing just that this Christmas Day.

When Arizona Charlie commissioned Ullman to do the portrait, the agreement had been that the fifteen-hundred-dollar price should be paid, cash on the nail, on delivery. However, when the portrait was finished, the dance-hall proprietor, like many gamblers, was temporarily short of funds. Ullman, with none too good grace, allowed Charlie to stand him off, though the artist himself was experiencing financial stress. He had prospered ever since his arrival in Dawson, but after the manner of artists, he was a poor manager. Furthermore, he lived like a fighting cock, eating and drinking without regard to expense, smoking cigars that cost a dollar apiece in Dawson (five cents in the States), and on every possible occasion tried his luck at roulette, or at calling the high card. He had made some excellent sketches in oil of Dawson scenes which he sold at good prices, and at El Dorado and at the Forks he had done many crayon sketches and oil studies for wealthy claim owners, for which he had also received high prices. But now his poke contained only colors. He needed money badly and he had counted heavily on the fifteen hundred dollars Arizona Charlie had agreed to pay him.

The portrait was Dawson's sensation during the holidays, but Ullman was still without his fee. He had called on Charlie several times during the week, but on each occasion this patron of the arts had put him off with excuses. About then, Lindsay and I went to Dawson, where we came across Ullman. The artist was stone broke, he said, and sunk forty fathoms deep in despond. He told us about the portrait, and at his invitation we accompanied him to the Palace to view the masterpiece. Charlie was there, and so, too, was the girl. Both of them beamed as we admired the portrait, Charlie suggesting the various angles from which to view it, the better to appreciate its fine points. All the while Ullman stood by, silent and unhappy.

When we had exhausted our adjectives and a lull came in the flow of admiring comment, Ullman broached the subject of payment to Charlie. Charlie tendered him five hundred dollars on account, promising to pay the balance within a reasonable time. Ullman refused to accept anything on account, declaring angrily that he wanted all or nothing. Charlie shrugged his shoulders and walked away. We drew Ullman aside and urged him to accept a part payment, assuring him he would undoubtedly be able to collect the balance very soon. He was stubborn and declared that it must be a full payment or none.

Almost before we realized what he was about, he had approached the portrait on its easel, before which Charlie was expatiating on its perfections to a newcomer. Without a word, Ullman brushed by him, whipped out his jackknife, and opened it. With a series of ripping thrusts he slashed the portrait to ribbons.

Then he strode haughtily away. Arizona Charlie was too dazed for speech. His girl had fainted, and was on the floor in a heap.

Courtesy Canadian National Railways

A Reposeful Moment for Prospector and Dogs

CHAPTER XIII

WHEN SPRING COMES IN the Yukon the season for mushing with dog teams closes. For the thaw makes the trails too soft during the daytime, and at night the freeze leaves many bare spots. About the middle of April our first freighting season ended. By all the signs we knew that it would be our last. Horse-drawn wagons were supplanting sleds and dog teams. Dawson already had many horses and they were proving that one good horse could pull a load that forty dogs could not keep moving. We realized this, and without indulging any sentimental regrets, we sold our dogs for what they would bring. Before the first of May we disposed of the lot, giving away the last two, who were crippled.

When we reviewed our venture we found that we had realized more enjoyment than money from it. We had lived well, worked hard, and reveled in the free life in the open, but we had not much in the way of money to show for it. True, we had made considerable on our hauling jobs, but our expenses were large. On the trail the plainest meal—bacon, beans, bread, and coffee—cost a minimum of $3.50, with a top of $5.00 in remote places. While there was a trifle of $16,000 in credits on the books at the season's end, there was little actual cash in the outfit's general poke. Less than a fourth of what was owing the business was ever collected. Our dogs had been sold for less than a third of the total we had paid for them. Dr. Burke lost heavily on the venture and so did we, for the only dividend declared at the end was a bill of provisions for six months, for which the doctor paid.

Dr. Burke was a good sport and pocketed his loss without complaining. His practice was growing daily, for he had definitely established himself as Dawson's leading physician, with a creditable record of success with most of his cases. But Dawson was growing too, and needed wharfage and docks and space on the river front occupied by many of the buildings erected by early arrivals. Accordingly, the police notified all occupants and owners that their buildings must be removed from the area by May 1. This meant, among others, the Burke domicile. While we were mushing we had our dog kennels under the street level of his living residence, our living quarters in the rear along with his own. We cached our provisions in our cabin on the Steamboat Hill claim, and in obedience to the police order vacated the house well in advance of the dead line.

But not Dr. Burke. He went on the warpath, served public notice on the police that he intended defying their order, wrote long and indignant letters of protest to the Parliament at Ottawa and to the Privy Council in London. He organized and held indignation meetings at which, in fiery language, he denounced the police ruling and declared that he would never yield to it. Toward the end of March some of the occupants of stores, restaurants, and other buildings on the water front began to vacate, but Dr. Burke held out. The police be damned, he shouted. They could not force him off his own premises, and he never would leave voluntarily. He was an Irish gentleman who had served the Empire in thirty years of foreign service in the British Army. He had been retired with the rank of surgeon major, and he'd like to see the day when any policeman, anywhere, could put him off British soil. While others abandoned their riverside buildings, he stuck it out, until he was alone.

All the while that Dr. Burke shouted defiance at the police, no retort came from them save only the cold, official notice that any building remaining on the river front subsequent to May 1 would be dismantled by the police after they had removed from it the occupant, or occupants, if any. Both parties to the dispute stood by their guns. When May 1 arrived, Dr. Burke held the fort in his office, while a squad of Mounties bearing picks, axes, and crowbars, and leading a gang of prisoners told off as a wrecking crew, deployed on the Burke dwelling. Dr. Burke was escorted from his office to the street by a Mountie. While the crew fell upon his residence, demolishing it steadily, the doctor mounted a barrel and harangued the crowd that watched the work of destruction. He was a ludicrous spectacle in his bizarre outfit, his long hair and beard floating in the wind as he flailed his arms and swayed his body in impassioned protest. He hadn't progressed very far in his incendiary oration when a police sergeant kicked the barrel out from under him. A Mountie caught the orator as he pitched from his rostrum, and the Dawson Civil War was ended.

With his usual ebulliency of spirit the doctor accepted the situation. Without loss of time he was established on another site where he immediately began the erection of a one hundred thousand dollar hospital.

So much has been written in praise of the Mounties that anything I could add would be supererogatory. Yet from my close observations I have conceived an admiration for them as the last word in police organization. Although they were but a handful of men in a community to which many untamed characters had swarmed, and where others, unruly to the point of lawlessness, were moving in, they governed Dawson and the surrounding districts with an iron hand, administering impartially a rough justice that was always arbitrary, yet it created but a minimum of friction. In their smart uniforms, bright red coats and blue-black trousers, with a broad yellow stripe on the outside of each trouser leg, they were a picturesque symbol of the might of British Law. At every station along the trail to the Yukon, from the summit of White Pass to Dawson, each person entering the territory had to pass inspection by them. At Dawson the inspection was repeated, and it was close. It was due to the Mounties that this mushroom mining town never achieved the notoriety which lawlessness ordinarily brings to such communities. Punishment for infractions of the law was swift and certain and the woodpile, where offenders worked out their sentences, no matter what the weather, was a terror to the gunfighters, cheats, and other lawless immigrants from Skagway, Juneau, and the coast towns. Many of them needed only one look at it to heed the advice of the Mounties to "keep moving down the river."

The police had a sense of humor which customarily kept them from a tyranical exercise of their authority. I recall an occasion when a husky miner with a full poke lurched out of a saloon on the Dawson water front, and stepping to the middle of the street, uttered a maudlin sound intended as an imitation of a bear's growl.

"I'm a Kodiak bear!" he roared. "And can I fight! Step up, some one, and try me."

A good crowd had collected, but no one accepted the invitation.

The miner, evidently believing his overpraise of himself had intimidated his audience and ruined his chances of a fight, shifted to a different impersonation. He flapped his huge arms up and down several times in crude imitation of a bird.

"I'm an American eagle," he bellowed. "And how I can scrap! Won't some one please step up and try me?"

Still there was no response from the crowd. Instead, a trig Mountie sidled up to the challenger and regarded him quietly for a moment, thumbs stuck in his belt.

"Trying to make the woodpile, Eagle?" he asked. "Better hunt your nest."

The Eagle subsided on the instant, all thought of combat gone from him.

On another occasion I saw a frowzy drunk propelled out of a Dawson saloon by a husky bartender and projected into the mud of the street by a final well-directed kick. A Mountie also witnessed the exemplification of the "bum's rush." He walked quietly to the saloon, stood in the doorway, and curtly ordered the barkeeper to come out.

When the barkeeper obeyed, the policeman commanded, "Pick up this chap, put him in a back room, and let him stay there until he sleeps it off."

When his order had been complied with, the Mountie, following him to see that it was done, told him, "I'll check up on you to see that this fellow stays here until he sobers up. If you throw him out again, it's the woodpile for you. He got the hooch here and while his money held out he was welcome."

When we closed our freighting venture and vacated the Burke mansion, Lindsay and I were two unattached mushers without occupation. Not having found gold in the ground, we had sought it on the trail. That failing us, we must turn again to mining. We could not work the hillside claim, for that involved technical operations wholly beyond us, and for help we would have to await the return of Dobins, who was still working for a stake at El Dorado. So we took a fifty-fifty lay on a fractional rimrock bench claim on Cheechaka Hill, owned by Fred Striker. We had to earn a stake with which to buy a small steam boiler and sufficient provisions to enable us to prove up on our claim on Steamboat Hill. The gravel on our lay was not very rich, but at the end of four months our share of it was two thousand dollars, and at the end of September we quit Cheechaka and moved into our cabin on the Steamboat Hill claim.

CHAPTER XIV

FOR A MONTH OR MORE ALL Dawson had been agog. Gold strikes and rumors of gold strikes in the Klondike had become of secondary interest compared to another rumor that had reached the mining town about mid-September, brought by the mysterious Arctic grapevine telegraph. It was reported that Jack Dalton, an Oregon cowman, was on his way over the frozen Yukon with a drove of 150 head of steers. He had landed in Pyramid Harbor, twelve miles south of Skagway, with his beeves, and early in September had begun driving the cattle over the trail to Fort Selkirk on the Yukon, 500 miles distant from Pyramid. From Fort Selkirk to Dawson, 150 miles, the cattle were being driven over the frozen Yukon, and as the daring journey drew to its end and reports of its progress were received daily in Dawson, the interest became more intense. For the Klondike was hungering for beefsteaks and prime rib roasts as well as for gold.

When Dalton and his aides at length ended their journey, with the loss of a negligible number of head, they were lionized. Had Dawson rejoiced in the possession of a brass band, assuredly it would have been on hand to welcome them. In fact, Dalton deserved the honor accorded him, not alone for his service to the appetites of sourdoughs, but for the really notable feat he had accomplished. From

Pyramid to Fort Selkirk, he had blazed and made his own trail, which later was to become known by his name. This trail proved to be an easier one than that from Skagway, being very nearly a water-level route to the interior, or upper Yukon, country. Had the engineers who surveyed the route for the White Pass and Yukon Railroad known of the Dalton Trail, many millions of dollars could have been saved in its construction, and other millions in its operation and maintenance, for the snowslides encountered in the narrow clifflike channels cut through White Pass became a problem. It also would have obviated the long river-steamboat trip through the swift current of the Yukon above Fort Selkirk to Whitehorse.

Just then it was the part that the cowman had played in relieving the fresh-meat shortage that weighed uppermost in the minds of his Dawson admirers. Dwellers in metropolitan centers, where supplies of beef and milk are at all times plentiful, can hardly realize the yearning for them that possesses those who have been denied these staples. In the Klondike at the time there were so few cows that the very sight of one was almost as much a novelty to a veteran sourdough as it would be to a city urchin on his first excursion into the country.

While George Dare and I were working on the Steamboat Hill claim in the summer of the next year a cow strayed onto our property. Dare, who had been a farmer in Scotland, acted, at sight of her, as though he had never before seen one. His eyes bulged and for a moment he was speechless. Then he dropped his shovel and in one bound reached the cow and tethered her, calling to me to fetch a pail from the cabin. Then he milked her. He had not tasted fresh milk in two years, and he declared he would keep the cow until the owner claimed her.

Courtesy Commissioner, Royal Canadian Mounted Police

Canadian Troopers Before a Northwest Station

Courtesy Commissioner, Royal Canadian Mounted Police

They "Always Get Their Men"

For two days he held the cow incommunicado in the tunnel, which he blocked, milking her regularly and feeding her on rolled oats and the sparse grass on our location. At the end of that time I urged him to turn her loose, assuring him that she would find her owner or that he would find her. Dare wanted the man to come looking for her, and it was only when I reminded him that he could hardly find her while she was hidden in the tunnel that he resolved to set her free. We might better have kept her, for she met a sad fate two weeks later when she wandered to a small gulch on Bear Creek, about two miles up the river. There a startled Swede prospector saw her in the distance and shot her for big game. When the owner discovered the slaughter, he demanded an explanation from the guilty man.

"Ay tank him moose," the miner told him.

Dalton's epic cattle drive of 1898 was succeeded by many others over this trail in the open, or summer, seasons. There was enough rich grass to feed the cattle as far as Fort Selkirk. There they were loaded on scows and freighted down the Yukon to Dawson, where they were landed in marketable shape.

Dalton was a diminutive figure with broad and powerful shoulders somewhat out of proportion to his stature. He was always pre-eminently fit and in condition, as he would need to be to perform on the trail as he did. He was an agreeable and square-shooting person to meet or do business with, but a bad *hombre* to cross or run up against. He was proficient with his fists and, once he engaged in combat, he stayed with the fight to the finish. He was reputed to know no fear, but he was not foolhardy, as one incident I heard of him proved.

On one of his many cattle drives to Dawson a few steers

strayed from the herd and he and Henry White, one of his assistants, went back on the trail to round them up. White was mounted on a cow pony and Dalton was afoot. They had located the strays and were driving them back to the herd when they encountered a brown she-bear with her two cubs. The mother immediately charged the two cowmen. Both men were unarmed and White shouted to Dalton to jump up on the pony behind him.

"To hell with the pony," Dalton yelled, as he started legging to safety. He outran both the pony and the mother bear.

When things began to get slack in Dawson and cattle driving ceased to be profitable, Dalton struck up with Ed Hanley, another cowman from Oregon who had been operating a claim in Bonanza Creek, and together they purchased a big hydraulic mining property in the Porcupine Mining District some twenty miles distant from Pyramid Harbor, north from Haines, Alaska. Dalton was not a teetotaler himself, but he had set ideas about the evils of drink, especially as impairing the efficiency of his workmen. Accordingly he served notice upon Tim Vogel, a saloonkeeper and trader of Haines, to keep himself and his wet goods away from his property, for Vogel had been making trips to the district with a pack train and had been dispensing hooch by the keg to Dalton's men.

Vogel was sufficiently impressed by Dalton's earnestness, and by his knowledge of Dalton's prowess in battle, to heed the warning. He remained away from the property a long time, but at length he yearned for the profits to be had from slaking the thirst of Dalton's men, and he became incautious.

Dalton had gone into Haines several times on business since warning Vogel, and on each occasion made studied

efforts to avoid a face-to-face meeting with the man, crossing to the opposite side of the street whenever he saw him.
Vogel had always fancied himself to be a scrapper and this
gave him new courage. He got the impression that Dalton
was afraid of him. He knew that Dalton's men, after a
long dry spell, were ripe for a sale, so one day he loaded his
pack train with hooch and set out for the Dalton property.
Dalton met him on arrival.

"Didn't I send word to you, Vogel, to keep away from
here with your hooch?" he demanded.

"Oh, to hell with you. I go where I please," the publican
answered.

Then the battle was on. Vogel's life was saved only by
Hanley's interposition. When his partner dragged Dalton
away, Vogel had been beaten to a pulp. It was weeks before he was up and about. He never again went within
miles of the Dalton property.

Although their location was rich in gold, hydraulic
operations were unprofitable on account of the heavy
boulders in the gravel, and the partners sold out to the
Porcupine Gold Mining Company. About that time
Michael J. Heney was constructing for Stephen Birch the
Copper River and Northwestern Railway to Kennicott,
Alaska, where Birch's great Bonanza and Jumbo copper
mines were located, and was just finishing the construction
of the railroad's ocean terminal at Controller Bay, a huge
rock bulkhead erected to make a harbor for ships to dock.
Three thousand men had been engaged continuously for
two years on the work. Dalton, who knew Heney very
well, viewed the Controller Bay project as it was nearing
completion, and he told the engineer that, in his opinion,
the bulkhead would never stand up against heavy seas if
the wind should last any considerable length of time.

Heney, a most capable engineer, was confident the bulk-head had been built for keeps. A few months later the costly work was battered to extinction in a single night.

Dalton had been making trips to the western side of the delta at the mouth of Copper River and he knew the region well. He offered to show Heney an all water-level route up the river and a natural deep-sea harbor in Cordova Bay. Heney inspected the route and the bay and was convinced. The original route was changed and a large terminal dock was constructed on Cordova Bay. A few years after the railroad had been in operation, hauling copper ore from the mines to the dock for shipment to the smelter in Tacoma, it came to light that Dalton had staked a copper mine on the site of the terminal dock. The startling news broke when Dalton notified Birch to take his railroad and dock off his property. Of course, litigation ensued, but the dispute never got to court. Birch settled the case out of court, paying Dalton more than a hundred thousand dollars for his claim—on which, it developed, no copper existed. Dalton returned to his native Oregon where he bought himself a show ranch, married, and settled down.

CHAPTER XV

JACK DOBINS HAD EARNED his stake at El Dorado and joined us on the Steamboat Hill claim. By pooling our resources we were able to outfit with a winter's supply of food and necessary tools, and install a small steam boiler. George Dare, who owned a bench claim above us, threw in his lot with ours and Julius Ullman, the artist, joined the outfit as cook. After his homeric revenge on Arizona Charlie, Ullman's fortunes had gone from bad to worse. In his first few months in the Klondike he had made a great deal of money by painting sketches in miners' gold pans at twenty-five dollars apiece. As it took him no more than two hours for each job (and he sold many), it was a lucrative sideline while it lasted. But after the first year the quotations for art in the Klondike dropped and the best price he could get for a gold-pan sketch was ten dollars. Haughtily he refused to prostitute his art at this figure, declaring he would starve first. He was likely to do just that when I induced him to sign on with our outfit. He was a delightful addition to it, for he was prime company —even if not too good a cook. He could tell good stories well, discourse on art to the comprehension of sourdoughs, and keep our camp happy with the music of his voice and his guitar.

At last we were all set for our try, in a big way, for the

Klondike's gold. It was Dobins' theory that, somewhere in the hill, there was an original main channel of the river bed from which the gravel in the present formation had been deposited. A fortune awaited the discoverer, for the ground certainly should contain rich pay dirt. Dobins was skeptical regarding the success of the men who were sinking the shaft on the top of the hill, for, like most placer miners, he believed that gold was only to be found near the creek bottoms. Yet there were striking exceptions to this generality. One of the most notable was the rich claim that had been developed on top of Gold Hill. Pete Scouse and Charlie Block, coal miners from Nanaimo, British Columbia, had staked bench claims above hillside claims on the left limit of El Dorado Creek. As their claims were about one thousand feet above the creek-bottom claims, most of the placer miners thereabouts thought them crazy. No one had ever heard of staking claims on a hilltop and, until then, placer gold had never been found at an elevation.

"But what else could you expect of a couple of tarnation coal miners?" the sourdoughs asked of one another.

Almost without digging, the two coal miners had recovered gold from their hilltop claims, for the gravel was very shallow and very rich. Also, it was dry, and could be worked without thawing, for the sun had drawn out the moisture. Scouse and Block took the gold out hand over fist and continued to do so for a long time. When they had amassed their pile and abandoned operations, they left enough gold on the claims to make it very profitable for hydraulic working. When the orthodox placer miners saw the yield of the hilltop claims, they were astounded, and some of them reversed their opinion of the coal miners.

"I'd stake a claim on the moon if them two did," one sourdough declared.

Digging for our tunnel was hard work, but we welcomed it in the expectation of a rich reward. Lindsay's job was firing the boiler, keeping up steam for the ground-thawing, which had to be done at night. Dobins' and Dare's assignment was to run the tunnel, or drift, into the hill. Mine was to furnish the motive power for the wheelbarrow from the face of the drift to the dump outside the tunnel mouth. Later, as we got deeper into the tunnel, we laid wooden rails on which we operated a makeshift car to replace the barrow. Between times, the three of us gathered and stacked snow to be melted for Lindsay's boiler. We worked every day, including Sundays, and eventually mined 870 feet into the hillside in search of the wavy formation of the bedrock, and timbered the tunnel for the entire distance. Every shovelful of gravel carried some gold, our daily tests showing some as high as $1.10 to the pan, with gravel taken out four feet above the bedrock testing only four cents to the pan. But never any blanks.

For weeks on end the pay indications were fine, and we were happy. Fatigued as we were after our hours of delving, we would loll about the stove after supper, enjoying Ullman's songs and yarns, indulging our pipe dreams and discussing plans made against the day we struck it rich. Trips around the world aboard de luxe steamers, with the accompaniment of wine, women, and song, were the least of our programs once we had acquired the Midas touch. But there were intervals when the tests showed poor ground, and immediately the atmosphere became charged with gloom, and amid the sound of bursting bubbles each man would seek his bunk, silent and morose.

When I joined the Klondike gold rush I had only the haziest notions as to how and where the gold I sought was to be found. I probably believed that it could be dislodged from rocks in great chunks with a pickaxe, or shoveled from the ground in great quantities, like sand on a beach. I did not know the difference between "hard-rock" and "placer" mining. Certainly I had had no sort of understanding of placer mining—the kind we were doing, and which was the only kind in the Klondike—or of the ardors and disappointments involved. Nor could I then have known that only a very few of those who stampeded to the Klondike for gold were destined to be successful in finding it in paying quantities. Years later it was estimated that only 2 per cent had been that fortunate. Even had I known, it would have made no difference, for why should not I be among the very few? Nor could I know of another disheartening calculation of statisticians—that each ounce of Klondike gold, valued at $16, cost $246 to produce. All I certainly knew about placer mining, once I was on the ground in the Klondike, was that in prospecting a claim the first thing necessary was to find out if the sand or gravel contained any gold. It was only later that I learned how to make this test.

Under the primitive methods employed by the first arrivals in the Klondike, an ordinary shovelful of gravel was put in the testing, or gold, pan. This implement, without which no prospector ever traveled, was a flat, round, iron vessel about eighteen inches in diameter and four inches deep. The pan, with its gravel contents, was submerged in a creek, or in a container filled with water, and it was twisted about vigorously with a rotary movement, the motion causing the top gravel to wash off. If the pan contained gold, the particles of the precious metal sank to

Courtesy Canadian National Railways

Placer Miner Panning Gold

the bottom, being heavier than the gravel. The agitation of the pan in the water, at first violent, gradually decreased to a gentle motion. When all the gravel had been washed away, any remaining gold residue was visible on the bottom of the pan. This "dust" was then dried out, either in the sun or by the heat from a stove, weighed, and pouched.

Where large quantities of pay gravel were mined, it was shoveled into sluice boxes a foot to six feet wide, the height of the sides varying according to the amount of water available and the quantity of gravel to be tested. Sluice boxes were laid at certain grades to each ten feet of their length, the coarseness or fineness of the gold, as shown by the tests, determining the pitch at which the boxes should be placed. On the bottoms of the boxes, at right angles to its sides, there were iron obstacles, or riffles, to catch the particles of gold as they sank to the bottom. Water directed through the sluices carried the gravel away. On small, individually operated claims the box was cleared every day, the water being diverted from the sluices, the riffles lifted, and the gold removed. On claims where labor was employed, and where the sluicing was continuous, the boxes were cleaned every two weeks, the gold shoveled out into heavy iron boxes or buckets. Our dream was to reach the point in our operations where we would be shoveling out the gold dust.

More than once I had seen sluice boxes containing dust in sufficient quantities for it to be removed in shovelfuls. One day, as I was on the trail passing by a claim on the El Dorado owned by Alexander MacDonald, the "Klondike King," a gang of men had just shut off the water from the big sluicing boxes bearing the washings of ten days past. For a distance of one hundred feet the bottoms of the boxes were covered with masses of golden grains. Mac-

Donald was an original staker on Bonanza Creek, and he
added to his holdings by purchases on El Dorado Creek and
by grubstake agreements on nearly all the rivers and creeks
throughout the entire Klondike region. No wonder he was
able to shovel gold dust! And no wonder he transported the
yield of his claims by pack train!

About a month after my arrival in Dawson I was on
the trail, toting a seventy-five-pound pack on my
shoulders, and I had sat down on a log to rest. Presently
a big Swede, carrying a pack even larger than mine, joined
me on the log. While we mopped our perspiring features
and fought off the mosquitoes, a train of twelve mules
went by. They were on their way to Dawson from one
of MacDonald's El Dorado mines, and each mule was laden
with two hundred pounds of gold dust.

My chance companion looked curiously at the mules,
then at the packs at our feet.

"Partner," he remarked, "Ay tank you and me ban the
mools, not dem fallers."

All placer gold, when first mined, contains some black
sand, the quantity depending on the district. There were
places in the Klondike where the gold was so fine and the
black sand so prevalent that it did not pay to mine it.
Where the dust was not too dirty, the sand was removed
by blowing. Where it occurred in large quantities magnets
were used.

There was one worry we did not have to experience in
working our claim. This was the danger of having our
gold dust "high graded," a problem with which the owners
of rich claims had to contend. "High grading" was a
euphemism of those days for stealing gold dust, a feat
which was not too difficult of accomplishment under the
crude mining methods then employed. In some of the

very rich claims on El Dorado and Bonanza creeks the ground was so rich that the coarse gold was plainly visible. It was an easy matter for a miner working on wages to slip a few handfuls of rich earth into his pockets as he shoveled pay dirt into a barrow at the bottom of a shaft. I remember an occasion when the owner of a claim of this kind took me down into a tunnel and showed me the bedrock at the face of the drift. Covering it an inch thick was a layer of coarse gold, and hours thereafter, its yellow splendor dazzled my vision.

For more than two months we had been working steadily on the drift, now elated at the gravel tests and dreaming golden dreams, now sunk fathoms deep in despondence at the poor showing of the pay. Of late, the occasions for gloom had been steadily increasing. The pan tests showed no blanks, but they certainly produced no results to justify us in believing that the claim was being operated at a profit. Our gloom was accentuated by the fact that Christmas was approaching and the general poke would soon be showing nothing better than colors. The chances were that, whether or not we had any great cause for rejoicing, we would be lacking the wherewithal for celebrating the holiday.

It was then that Lindsay rose to the occasion. He declared that Santa Claus would not be permitted to pass up our claim if he could do anything about it. So he built a small rocker and rigged it up over the panning box behind the cookstove. We had at the face of the drift plenty of bedrock that we had regarded as too poor to bother with. Now, in our poverty-stricken plight, we ran the despised gravel through the rocker, and by dint of any amount of work in our spare time over a period of several weeks we recovered about $150 in dust for our Christmas fund. Part of it went for necessities, but the major share was spent for such delicacies as Dawson's one store afforded.

Two weeks before Christmas a flock of ptarmigan, a bird similar to the pigeon, had flown in near our claim. They are foolish creatures, and without much trouble I knocked off about three dozen of them. They were promptly put in cold storage to pinch-hit for the turkey in furnishing the Christmas board.

Christmas Eve we knocked off work on the tunnel and prepared for the holiday. It was decided that the day would be incomplete without wassail, and Dobins and I were told off to hike to Dawson for four quarts of the dew of Scotland. We set out early in the morning and shopped around for various items of Christmas cheer—and the Scotch. The four quarts of liquor took $120 out of the poke, but we did not begrudge it. It was evening when we returned to the claim. The ascent on the last fifty feet up the hillside to the cabin was very steep and we had cut steps in the ice and snow to ease the climb. With Dobins leading, we mounted until, when near the top, I stumbled, slipped, tried to recover my balance, and rolled headlong down the steps, landing in a heap on my back.

There was a mighty crash of glass, for the four quarts were in the pack I carried. Dobins hurried to me, and in an awe-struck voice inquired, "The whisky, Morgan?"

I nodded weakly. I knew too well its fate, for I could feel the broken glass prodding me and the warm moisture of the liquor soaking through my clothes. Lindsay, who had been watching for us at the cabin door, saw me fall and heard, to his horror, the sound of breaking glass. Now he was at my side, making frantic efforts with a shovel and a couple of gold pans to salvage some of the Christmas cheer. He might as well have tried Mrs. Partington's stunt. The Scotch that had not soaked into my clothes had seeped away into the Arctic snow.

Slowly we entered the cabin. The gloom that descended over us was real, not mock. I was in despair and in disgrace. No one had helped me to my feet after my fall. No one cared whether or not I was hurt. In fact, no one talked to me at all, or even looked at me. It was a tragic moment in my life. I could not have felt more culpable and deserving of punishment if I had been caught redhanded robbing a poor box. I am sure that my abjectness must have been such as to melt a heart of ice, but no sign of forgiveness came from anyone, until at length Lindsay relented.

"Pardner," he said, with a depth of feeling in his tones as he laid his hand on my shoulder, "you're the last man in the world I ever thought would be guilty of such carelessness."

Then he rigged himself for the trail, and at the door sang out, "Some one watch the boiler. I'm off for Dawson."

He was back at midnight, having made the round trip, fourteen miles there and back, in a temperature of sixty-five degrees below zero. He unstrapped his pack and held aloft for our inspection six quarts of Scotch.

For a moment we were speechless, then we fell on his neck, hugged him, and cried out our joy in admiration of such a man.

"But how the hell did you do it?" we asked when our first transports of joy were over. "There wasn't an ounce left in the poke."

"On tick, of course. I put up such a spiel to Arizona Charlie about home and mother and the sadness of four poor mushers away from all this at Christmas time that I had him almost cryin' before I got through."

He paused a moment, then added with a note of regret in his voice, "I think if I'd gone on just a minute longer he would've given me the stuff."

CHAPTER XVI

IT HAD BEEN A GRAND Christmas, but with the holidays, especially New Year's Day, came the inevitable retrospection and introspection—that spiritual stock-taking that is seasonal. It was nearly two years, on January 10, since I had left home. I had been in the Klondike, in the very heart of fabulously rich diggings, for a year and a half. And what had I to show for it? Nothing, I reflected gloomily, except an empty poke, a share in a few holes in the ground, my original five-thousand-dollar stake gone to the last penny, and not even a golden dream left to me. For by this time I was beginning to lose confidence in our claim as a future Golconda. So were the others, but we all kept doggedly at work.

We continued driving the tunnel into the hillside until the end of April. Then we quit. Like most prospectors working claims in that district in those days, we had extravagant ideas. We were willing to suffer any hardships and work to the limit of our endurance in the quest for gold, but we wanted to find it in thousand-dollar pans on the bedrock. We would not be satisfied with anything less than pay dirt such as the rich claims on Bonanza, El Dorado, Gold Hill, and other sensational diggings were yielding. But after months of toil we had not found the center of the original channel where Dobins was confident rich pay was. We despaired of ever finding it, and doubted that it existed. We were wrong. Had we crosscut our tunnel where the bedrock waved in small humps a foot high and followed these mounds in whatever direction the pay dirt or gravel led, we would have found it. Some five years later it was found, but not by us, and the immense fortune that had lain within our grasp went to others.

I had sprained my back a few weeks before. Tunneling operations were stopped and for the next twelve days I was laid up in my bunk with two temporarily paralyzed legs. By the time I was up and about Lindsay and Dobins had taken a lay on a Gold Hill bench claim and were working it from an open cut. Dare and I remained on the Steamboat Hill claim and dug a series of ditches to catch the water when the thaw came, intending to wash the gravel that had accumulated on the dump at the tunnel's mouth. Our ditches did not give sufficient volume for the whole recovery of all the gold, and never at any time was the supply of water adequate to wash out the gravel in any quantity from the sluice box, but we hung on until about the middle of May. By that time all the snow had melted off the hill, and the water quit. There was nothing for us to do then but to quit also. We had recovered about ten thousand dollars for our half-month's work, but most of it went to pay for supplies.

Ullman, his occupation gone, abandoned cooking for good in favor of a job as an illustrator on a new newspaper just started in Dawson. Telegraph communication had been established with the outside world and Dawson was emerging from its awkward, ungainly adolescence into something like a city. Dare went on to work for wages at one dollar an hour on an El Dorado claim. I went to Gold Hill where Lindsay and Dobins were operating their lay

on an ambitious scale, having engaged six men at one
dollar an hour, payment to be made on the wash-up. They
invited me to join them, but the layout did not look attrac-
tive to me. For one thing, the fuel supply was scarce, since
the El Dorado operators had used up every stick of wood
within a mile, and the long haul for timber would prove
costly. Besides, I had another plan in mind.

While I lay disabled in my bunk late in March, I had been
doing some tall thinking and had come to a conclusion. It
was that if we were ever to realize on our Steamboat Hill
claim it would have to be through hydraulic operation.
Not the puny sluice-box process we had engaged in, which
was nothing more than a slightly glorified pan test, but the
large-scale scientific methods that already had been introduced in this district and were now washing out millions in
gold from claims from which the cream had been skimmed.
But that required capital, and we had none. It was up to us
to get it.

During the time I stopped with Lindsay and Dobins in
their Gold Hill camp we reviewed our situation ex-
haustively and they agreed with my conclusions. We
figured that, on the basis of the cubic-yard volume of
gravel on the Steamboat Hill claim, estimated at an average
value of $1.50 the yard, the value of the whole deposit was
more than two million dollars. We had the record of all
our pannings to back up our claims of gravel values. Anyone on the spot could verify for himself the volume of
gold-bearing gravel. He could see also that large-scale
sluicing alone would do the trick, and we had the data to
show that in California big money had been made by
ground sluicing.

Lindsay and Dobins financed a survey of the claim made
by C. R. Hawkins, a mining engineer, whose tests of gravel

from different points in the tunnel, as well as from the surface of the rimrock to the limits of the claim, showed values far in excess of our estimates for the entire contents. On this showing, I obtained options for six months on the two hillsides adjoining our claim on the east, the two claims to the west of it, and on eight of the bench claims above and adjoining it. Only a small down payment was required to bind the options. The money for this, as well as for the engineer's maps and reports, was furnished by Lindsay and Dobins. They also advanced a thousand dollars for my trip to San Francisco and Seattle in an effort to interest capital in the proposed hydraulic operations.

The work preliminary to presenting our proposition for the consideration of capitalists had used up the better part of a year, during which time I was kept pretty busy. Fortified with maps, reports, engineering data, and samples of pay gravel, I left Dawson by steamer on July 2, 1900, and fourteen days later I landed in Seattle. I had left Dawson in high hopes, confident that I would be back within a few months with money in my poke (or pledged) that would enable us to install hydraulic equipment with which to wash vast quantities of gold out of the gravel of Steamboat Hill.

I have never seen Dawson since the day I left it. My mission was fruitless. For weeks after "coming outside" I oscillated between Seattle, Victoria, San Francisco, and Portland, haunting mining-company officials, bankers, and financiers in my efforts to interest them in our proposition. I spent hours every day for weary weeks on end, talking, explaining, and pleading, trying to interest someone with money, but I had no success. I had many promises, but they were all like piecrust, made to be broken. My bank roll was sadly shrunken. I decided that I would abandon my role of prospector and, somehow, return to Dawson.

Fate decreed otherwise. Lindsay and Dobins worked their Gold Hill lay until the freeze-up. Then they went haywire. For when the wash-up was finished they had cleared just enough, no more, to pay the men they had hired. So they quit, and went to work for wages at one dollar an hour on El Dorado Creek. They worked steadily the entire winter. I had given Lindsay a power of attorney for my interest in the Steamboat Hill property, and in the spring of 1901 he sold the claim for $9,000.

Six months later the purchaser, William Foster, sold it to the Yukon Gold Company for $125,000. This outfit bought up the entire hill, from the two claims east of our location to the point, or end, of the hill, west to the mouth of Bonanza Creek. Some few years later, through hydraulic operations, they began to take enormous quantities of gold out of the property.

Of course, without capital, we never could have done this. But even using our primitive methods, if we had hung on, we would have made a handsome profit out of our claims. Others did. George Parks, who owned the fourth claim a thousand feet east of ours, stuck it out for ten years after we quit, operating with lay men on a basis of 40 per cent to the owner and 60 per cent to the lay men. His income from this claim was $20,000 a year. When he decided to retire to a California ranch he sold his claim for a handsome figure to a hydraulic outfit and they took more wealth from the ground.

Well, Fortune is a fickle jade, full of whimsies, and she bestows her favors where she listeth.

Book 3

THE UNSINKABLE MARINER

CHAPTER I

IT WAS A HUMBLING REFLECTION that after a month I had been no more successful in obtaining capital for the development of our mining property than my partners and I had been in extracting dust from it in paying quantities. It was maddening, too, for I knew the gold was there to make the fortunes of those who went after it the right way. But we were just not equipped to do that. I hated to confess defeat and return empty-handed to Dawson, but that was what I would have to do because my poke was about empty. The trips between Dawson, San Francisco, Portland, and Vancouver, and my sojourns at hotels, while waiting upon the pleasure of men with money, had all been expensive. Then, too, I had had to outfit completely. So, as the end of August approached, my financial rating every day sank lower, until at length I was "more broke than the Ten Commandments" and had not even the price of my passage back to Skagway.

Nevertheless, I was going to return and work the claim, in a primitive way at least, since I could not do otherwise. On August 29, at Seattle, I shipped aboard the *Dirigo*, of the Alaska Steamship Company, as pantryman at thirty-five dollars a month. It was my intention to jump ship at Skagway and from there make my way over the trail to Dawson. The fluctuations in my career of late had been so diverse as to amuse me even in my disappointment. From mine owner to promoter, to dishwasher! For pantry-man was only a nice-sounding name for my work, which consisted principally of "diving for pearls." Although simple, it was also monotonous. The grub was good, the *Dirigo* was a staunch craft, a floating palace compared to the *Amur*; and the skipper, Captain J. C. Hunter, and the chief steward, Henry Sims, were agreeable superiors to work under.

The *Dirigo* had a list of fifty passengers and my work was not too arduous. Our crew was composed mostly of wild, seafaring men whose most absorbing thoughts were of where the next drink was coming from and of the benders they would go on when we reached Skagway. Most of them, like myself, intended to jump ship. The passengers were, in the main, serious-minded, sedate folk. They were quite unlike my fellow passengers aboard the steamer on which I had left Skagway a little less than two months before. Then, every mother's son of them had had a poke full of dust which he was intent on spending, and not one of them could wait until he had reached land before beginning to dispose of it, knowing that he had plenty more to his credit. They were long-haired, wild-eyed, and dirty as pigs. Their clothes were often tattered; they were delirious with joy and liquor and full of bawdy talk. Once the vessel was under way, all hell had broken loose, and pandemonium reigned until the ship docked. There had been continuous heavy drinking and gambling, only slightly interrupted by many fierce brawls, sometimes with knives and guns, in which the crew had not dared to inter-vene. Everything went but murder, and even that would have resulted had not the North made these returning Argonauts too tough to kill.

Aboard the *Dirigo* we had none of that wild roistering for the passengers were going to the gold fields either to make their pile for the first time, or to rebuild their dissipated fortunes, and they were a sober and grave-minded lot. There were a few sporting women aboard, on their way to Alaskan dance halls, and of course there was some drinking, principally by the women. One of the women, an Alaskan madame known as "Jew May," had a huge bank roll with which she was not niggardly. She liked to play hostess to her ship acquaintances and she entertained them lavishly in her suite, keeping the room steward busy bringing drinks to her quarters night and day.

The chief steward and second steward, heedless of the reprimands and warnings of the ship's commander, were frequent guests of the madame, and they were not at all backward in accepting her liquid hospitality. The revelry in "Jew May's" suite lasted throughout the passage to Skagway, culminating in a noisy jamboree the night before we were due to land. At Skagway the chief and second stewards accompanied the woman ashore. They were gloriously drunk, but she was perfectly sober. The skipper, scowling but silent, watched the three go down the gangplank. I tried to collect the few dollars coming to me, this to serve as a meagre fund for the trail to Dawson after I had jumped ship. But the purser told me I would have to wait until the chief steward, my immediate superior, approved the voucher for my wages. So I hung around the ship until he showed up.

About six hours later the chief and second stewards returned arm in arm. They had improved the hours ashore by visiting all the bars in Skagway, and had added considerably to the cargo with which they had left the ship.

As they lurched up the gangway they were met at the side by the skipper.

"You can't come aboard. You're fired," he told them sternly. Then turning to me, he demanded, "Here you, Mister, do you want the chief steward's job? I think you can hold it down."

The suddenness of the question nearly bowled me over. I did some rapid thinking. Most decidedly I did not want the chief steward's job, or any other job aboard the ship. The only job I wanted was that of working our claim on Steamboat Hill. Yes, but how to get there? Uneasily I had been calculating that the few dollars coming to me as pantryman's wages would hardly be sufficient to outfit me for the trail to Dawson. Perhaps it would be wiser for me to accept this providential chance, to make a few trips in order to add to my slim money resources, and then to go to Dawson over the ice. It would mean a delay of only a few months. Besides, it would give me the opportunity I had craved to see more of Alaska—a craving incited eight years before when I met John Muir, the great naturalist, who had fired my imagination with the glowing descriptions of the grandeur and beauty of Alaskan scenery.

"Yes," I told the skipper. "I'll take the job."

"Very well. Get the keys from those two swine, have their gear and clothes put on the dock, and then the purser will pay them off."

Thus I became chief steward of the *Dirigo*. The few trips I had it in my mind to make were to multiply, and the period during which I was to remain with the Alaska Steamship Company was to lengthen out to twenty-eight years. I was to experience in my long service perils of the sea in greater number than falls to the lot of most seafaring men, to suffer shipwreck, to escape death many times, to meet many individuals—trail breakers, empire builders, soldiers of fortune—with whom acquaintance was a privilege, to know the Inside Passage almost as one knows the way to his office, and to become so enamored of the beauty and grandeur of Alaska's terrain and waters that even now to remember that great country is to cause a nostalgia that is almost pain. I was to serve the steamship line in various positions, as chief steward, second steward, freight clerk, ticket agent, auditor's clerk, purser, then general agent in Alaska, and again as purser. I was to serve, in all, on a dozen or more ships and to be aboard on some twelve occasions when accident or shipwreck occurred.

I had not made many trips in my new calling before Lindsay and Dobins went to Fairbanks upon news of the gold strike there. They staked on the Dome, and their claim was to ground about 125 feet above bedrock which was rich in the precious metal. They sank their shaft and wealth beyond their dreams was theirs for the taking. At long last they had reached the end of the rainbow. Then Dobins was killed by a fall to the bottom of the shaft. Lindsay had become greatly attached to his partner, and his death broke him up. Regardless of the prize within his grasp, he would not work the claim any longer. Even remaining near the property was abhorrent to him, and he was eager to be away from the scene of his partner's terrible death. He sold out for thirty thousand dollars—a sacrifice figure—to Dobins' heirs and set up a saloon in Fairbanks. Here he married and raised a family, content to forego prospecting, mining, and mushing for the comfort and content of domesticity. But Fairbanks, like the Klondike, had its day, and when it was "dug out" Lindsay went to San Francisco where he fitted up an elaborate saloon on Market Street. Fourteen months later, prohibition came along and Lindsay's place made its exit before he had realized enough to pay for his investment. The simple-minded sourdough had not the stomach for bootlegging. He returned to Alaska and in Anchorage opened a pool and billiard hall.

Dr. Burke conducted his hospital in Dawson for years, competent, confident, and now only mildly truculent, a strange figure at whose eccentricities nobody dared laugh and for whose solid worth everybody had respect. He hung on in Dawson long after the camp had been dug out. Then about fifteen years ago, aging but indomitable, he removed to Vancouver where he established an office and died after a few years' practice. His son, Johnnie, remained in the Yukon, working a claim in the Fortymile district. Although not taking out gold by the handful, he was untroubled by its seeming scarcity, for he had the gold of a sunny nature and that sufficed for his lack of the coarser metal. Julius Ullman left Dawson about 1905, went to Seattle, and established himself in a studio where he has been successful.

CHAPTER II

LIKE THE SHELL PICKED UP on ocean sands, which ever after holds within it the roar of the surf, all unconsciously I had retained my affinity for salt water, a heritage of my birth within sound of the waves. For now that I was following the sea for my livelihood, my love for it was reawakened, not reborn, for it had never died. It held me, as the crisp delights of the Arctic trails, the Yukon creeks with their alluring promise of golden treasure troves, and the untrammeled life in virgin wilds could not. Yet I had not abandoned all thought of returning eventually to the Klondike and there wresting from its gravel the gold that so far had eluded me. For a long time I told myself each sea voyage would be my last until I returned with a poke full of dust and more gold in banks and mints. The more often I put off my return to the Klondike, the better I realized in my secret soul that I would never go back, that I did not want to go back, that I cared more for the sea than for gold, and that I had made the better choice. The claustrophobia, which had had me in its grip as a boy, when even the meaning of the word was unknown to me, by now had become incurable. Even matrimony had not cured me. I had married about a year and a half after leaving Dawson, but I continued my service at sea.

Other factors than my love of the ocean had contributed

perhaps to my waning gold fever. In the Yukon I had
known countless instances where wealth, gained suddenly,
it is true, but at an antecedent cost of effort, hardship, and
disappointments, had brought no luck or happiness with
it; and indeed, in most cases, no constancy of possession.
The wealth so gotten, it seemed to me, was nearly always
"fool's gold," no matter what its mineralogical genuine-
ness, for too often it seemed to induce in its possessor a
maniacal quality. "Hard come, easy go." To that refrain
too many of those who struck it rich had feverishly dissipated the fortunes which they had spent their best efforts
to gain, and in the end, when their gold had taken wings,
their last state was worse than their first.

During my twenty-eight years at sea in Alaskan waters
I saw many other instances that proved, to my satisfaction
at least, that too often a miner's luck ceased when he
reached the pay streak. One of the most striking examples
of this was the case of Antone Stander, an Americanized
Greek whom I had known in the Klondike. He was an
original staker on El Dorado Creek and had taken nearly
two million dollars out of his claim. Stander was a man of
sybaritic tastes to whom wealth meant the opportunity
for unlimited indulgence. He married in Dawson, then removed to Seattle where he acquired much property and
built a hotel which he operated on a lavish scale. But he
was a high liver and his convivial habits and extravagance
exhausted his fortune. When I last saw him he was flat
broke, on his way back to the Klondike to try his luck
again. He was working his way to Skagway, peeling spuds
aboard a vessel of the Alaska Steamship Company.

An even more notable example of the transitory nature
of the wealth amassed by gold finders was that of Joseph
Juneau. The sole reminder of the discoverer of the great

gold field of this district is the fine town, now Alaska's capital, which bears his name. In 1880 Juneau and Richard Harris, hard-rock prospectors, staked claims on the site of the present city. The ground was rich in gold-bearing ore and the partners became wealthy, eventually selling their claims, which then passed through a succession of ownerships. Juneau's wealth dribbled between his fingers, and at length he drifted to the Klondike. When I last met him he was conducting a restaurant in Dawson. It was a typical mining-camp eating house, not an opulent dining salon *à la Pierre*.

Japhet Lindeberg, who discovered the Nome fields, was another instance of the short-lived possession of good fortune that seemed to attend upon gold strikes. Lindeberg, a Laplander in charge of a herd of reindeer sent into Alaska by the government in September, 1898, came upon gold on Anvil Creek, in the hills back of what is now Nome. He and two companions staked three claims, which under the liberal regulations of the American registration laws gave them practically the whole creek. The claims proved very rich ground and the three partners took a huge fortune out of them. A few months after they had staked, word of the strike reached the outside world and another historic gold stampede was on. The creek monopoly of the original stakers had not cornered the gold field, for rich placer gold was found on the shores of Bering Sea, and almost overnight the town of Nome sprang up, with an initial population of twenty thousand. It was no trick to get there, for there were no forbidding passes to make, no ranges to climb, and no trails to mush over. Stampeders had only to board a steamer at Seattle and within fifteen days they were landed at Nome, ready to prospect on the beach right at hand.

Its ease of access brought to Nome by the thousands a class of people whom the hardships and dangers of a long, hazardous trail would have discouraged. Soon Nome was by way of being what it ultimately became, the toughest, most lawless mining camp in the world, the paradise of thieves, thugs, cheats, outlaws, and the most degraded types of sporting women and their parasites. Although the season was short, three months, many of the prospectors made fortune in a brief time, for some of them recovered as much as a thousand dollars a day from the gold-bearing sands.

The man whose discovery was responsible for all this did not long enjoy prosperity. Some ten years after the gold strike Lindeberg financed and opened a large bank in Seattle, with a branch in Nome. Neither he nor his associates in the venture were bankers, and eventually the institution crashed as the result of poor loans and bad investments. Some of its officers were tried, convicted, and sentenced to short jail terms. Lindeberg was stripped of his possessions to the last penny, and never again attained affluence.

Perhaps Pierre Erussard, who sold for a pittance the location of one of the world's great gold mines, was wiser in his generation than other discoverers whose wealth brought them only troubles. Erussard, known throughout the territory as "French Pete," in the early eighties discovered low-grade gold quartz on Douglas Island, Alaska, opposite Juneau, at the head of Gastineau Channel. "French Pete" sold the location to John Treadwell for four hundred dollars. In the thirty years of its operation the Treadwell Mine paid, in dividends, more than a hundred million dollars, besides huge sums in wages to the three thousand men on its payrolls.

The case of Edward DeGroff, enriched by the Chichagof Mine, one of the greatest gold quartz mines in the world, seemed to me a particularly poignant example of what was becoming a fixed belief with me. I knew DeGroff, and knew him as the salt of the earth, honest, steady, generous, and lovable, a compact of such merits as surely were deserving of good fortune. He was an American who had for years owned and operated a general merchandise store in Sitka, then the capital of Alaska. He was a genial, friendly man who conducted his business on lines rather too liberal to make him prosperous. For years he had been extending credit to everyone who asked for it or needed it, and, indeed, to many who did not deserve it. He was also forever grubstaking prospectors, too often on nebulous partnership agreements to make him sharer in their profits, if there were any. He had followed this course so consistently that he was about at the end of his rope, and his own credit with the San Francisco and Seattle wholesale supply houses was saved only because their regard for his lovable qualities made them stretch a point or two in his favor.

When DeGroff's fortunes were at their lowest ebb two Indians walked into his store one day and displayed the contents of a small sack they carried. The rock they showed him glittered with gold. They told him they had located the ore in surface outcroppings on Chichagof Island, west of Admiralty Island in southeastern Alaska, and that the location was about fifty miles distant from Sitka on the east coast of Chichagof. They wanted from him a four-months' grubsteak, tools, and powder to blast the outcropping. DeGroff knew Alaskan Indians. He knew by bitter experience that credit to any of them on anything was bad business, for while their intentions were

the best in the world, the only way the creditor could collect from them was to stay with them on the job and to
take out of their fishing, trapping, or mining proceeds the
amount of credit extended to them. But he was too kindly
and generous to refuse their pleading.

He gave them a four-months' grubstake, the necessary
mining tools, some powder, and a quantity of sacking
sufficient for ten tons of rock. In return he drew up an
agreement whereby he became a partner with a one-third
interest, and promised to continue to furnish supplies
necessary to prove the mine. Then he loaded the outfit into
the Indians' small sloop, but firmly refused their request
for cash with which to buy medicine. He knew that
"medicine" meant hooch. But the Indians got their hooch
anyhow. For fifty dollars they sold to one Kelly, con-
nected with the mission house in Sitka, a one-eighth share
in their remaining two-thirds interest in the enterprise.
With the fifty dollars they bought six quarts of liquor.
Then with two other Indians aboard, they pushed off for
the Chichagof claim.

At the end of four months DeGroff, as he had promised
his partners, sent a scow to Chichagof to take off the rock
they had mined. Ten tons of it were sent to Tacoma to be
smelted, for which DeGroff received more than twenty-
seven thousand dollars. He reinvested all of it in the
property, erecting a stamp mill of five tons capacity, and
arranged with his Indian partners to conduct the actual
mining operations while he attended to the necessary
financing and provisioning in Sitka. Big gangs of native
workers were employed, but they were inefficiently directed and in six months they had produced only about
half of the mill's capacity, and the mine showed no profit.
DeGroff then went to Tacoma where he induced William

R. Rust, a smelter operator, to organize a company to take over the mine. Besides Rust and DeGroff, the incorporators were Hugh Wallace, of Tacoma, a banker and, later, American Ambassador to France; and Captain Jarvis, United States Collector of Customs in Alaska.

The newly organized company bought the interest of the two Indians for one hundred thousand dollars each, and Kelly's one-eighth share for eighty thousand dollars, put first-class engineers in charge of operations, and erected a fifteen-ton stamp mill on the location.

The mine soon proved far more valuable than the expert employed by Rust had estimated. It made the fortunes of its owners, but DeGroff's enjoyment of his new wealth was short. I met him aboard the steamer which brought him to Sitka upon his return from Chichagof. The new management was well launched and the mine was proving itself. He was elated and told a group of us of his plans for the employment of his wealth. His intentions were all worthy ones in which he took keen pleasure. He would expand his business, build a new store, warehouse, and dock, and erect the finest residence in all Alaska, a place where he could entertain his friends more comfortably than in his store. There, everyone had had to sit about the big stove. He was happy, in the manner of folk with generous natures, that his money would enable him to be useful and to give pleasure to others. That night in Sitka, a few hours after I had parted with him, he was seized with acute appendicitis and died following an operation.

Although DeGroff did not live to enjoy the fruits of his many years of honest effort, his wife and daughter were made very wealthy by his mine holdings, for the Chichagof

property, in the comparatively short time it was operated,
produced more than twenty million dollars in profits.

Another of the original incorporators to whom the
Chichagof gold seemed to have brought little good luck
was Captain Jarvis. While the mine was making him
richer every day he was mentioned as being involved in the
Alaska coal scandal. Jarvis was a proud and sensitive nature,
and brooded over the fact that his character was under a
cloud. Then one day, unable to endure it longer, he blew
out his brains. He had been too hasty, for some time later
Rust, who was himself the soul of honor, assured me that
the investigation of the scandal had not revealed anything
that reflected upon Jarvis' honesty.

Hugh Wallace, who owed to Rust's friendship his
opportunity to be a sharer in the Chichagof gold yield, had
become ambassador to France in 1919, and during his two
years in Paris he was very popular. He could afford to
maintain his ambassadorial state in a manner calculated
to make him a favorite in both the official and the social life
of the French capital, for he was a wealthy man even before he acquired his interest in Chichagof. From this
alone, his income was never less than four hundred thousand dollars a year. Whether it was the atmosphere of the
diplomatic world, the formality of Old World manners
and society, or his sense of the overwhelming distinction
of the Grand Cross of the Legion of Honor, conferred on
him by the French Government, that was responsible, I do
not know, but in Paris he had acquired a manner more
highly starched than that of his Tacoma days.

Wallace had been urging Rust to visit him in Paris, for
he really had a sincere regard for the man. Rust, a college
man and an outstanding mining engineer, had added to his
training by wide reading; he was a culitvated gentleman

of charming manners and he exhibited a genuiness of character that endeared him to all who knew him. When Rust sold his Tacoma smelting property for several million dollars, he and his family went to Europe. In Paris, meeting Wallace in the lobby of the Hotel Crillon, Rust approached him with outstretched hand and the hearty greeting, "Hello, Hugh."

Wallace's response was so restrained and formal as to chill his old friend. And the Ambassador's next words were hardly calculated to do away with his discomfiture.

"In future, Rust," he said coldly, "please do not address me in public except as 'Excellency.'"

Rust bowed, talked briefly with his old friend, then left him. Deeply hurt by Wallace's cold manner and his rebuke, he left Paris almost immediately, returning to Tacoma after only a brief time on the Continent and in England.

A few months later the waters of the Pacific flooded the Chichagof Mine and caused it to cave in. And Hugh Wallace's huge income from this source ceased.

AN INTERLUDE IN MY ALASKAN sea duty came late in 1903 when I was detailed to accompany Captain John Johnson to Chicago, where the Alaskan Steamship Company had bought the *Indianapolis*, a lake vessel, for the run between Seattle and Tacoma. With him also were other members of his staff, First Mate William Jansen, Chief Engineer William Bishop, and First Assistant Engineer Allen Hunt. I went along as purser. We made the trip to Chicago by rail, but were to return to Seattle aboard the *Indianapolis*, by way of Cape Horn, in all, a voyage of some sixteen thousand miles. Any one of us, I believe, might have been hesitant about making this long voyage aboard a Great Lakes boat under any other skipper save one possessed of the extraordinary ability of Captain Johnson. Had we known what lay ahead of us, our confidence in the captain might, even then, not have been enough to allay our uneasiness.

For the *Indianapolis* was only a ferryboat which, up to time of her purchase, had been making two round trips daily between Chicago and Fair Haven, Michigan. She was only 185 feet in length with a 32-foot beam, a 17-foot draught, and a displacement of about 900 tons. She had a steel hull and a superstructure of wood, and was comparatively new—built in Toledo in 1900—and for all her diminutive proportions and her single-screw propeller she was staunch and speedy, capable of an average of sixteen knots with her 2,700-horsepower engine.

From Chicago the first leg of the little vessel's long voyage was through the Great Lakes and the Welland Canal to the St. Lawrence River, thence to the Atlantic and to New York, where the *Indianapolis* was to be over-hauled at Hoboken and transformed into a deep-sea vessel. When Johnson attempted to clear the vessel for the voyage, the custom house at Chicago ruled that neither he nor Chief Engineer Bishop could qualify to take her through the Great Lakes to the sea. This, despite the fact that both had unlimited papers qualifying them for any ton-nage, any waters. A Captain Dougherty, a Great Lakes skipper, was put in charge of the *Indianapolis,* with a chief engineer of his own choosing, for the voyage as far as Montreal. Johnson and his staff went along as passengers.

Captain Dougherty was a competent skipper, but per-haps a bit overcautious. In a spot of heavy weather, during which the little ferryboat's rolling and pitching gave one somewhat the sensation of being on the hurricane deck of a bucking bronco, he ran the vessel into a small bay on the New York side of Lake Erie and anchored there. When I asked him why he had tied up, he answered that the lake was too rough to proceed.

"Well, the ocean is a sight rougher than this and there are no anchorages at sea," I told him. "How the hell do you expect us to get her to Seattle?"

"I don't," he said. "And, if you ask me, I think you're a parcel of nuts even to think of attempting it."

At Montreal Captain Johnson took over the command of the *Indianapolis,* and Dougherty and his chief engineer remained aboard as passengers as far as New York. Off the coast of Newfoundland we struck a bit of weather, a New York gale, with a heavy swell which the little craft rode gallantly, never a drop of water boarding her. True, she rolled terribly, and no one aboard her could stand, or even lie down, without hanging onto a heavy stanchion. I think Dougherty and his chief had qualms about her sea-worthiness—I know they were seasick—and looked forward to the time when their voyage would end at New York.

When we docked at Hoboken they were the first to land. They told us ruefully they feared we and the entire crew of the *Indianapolis*, assuming we could get one, would be lost at sea. A few years later, Dougherty, commanding a heavily laden freighter, was lost with all hands aboard when his vessel foundered in Lake Erie.

The *Indianapolis* lay up in the Tietjen and Lang ship-yards at Hoboken for six weeks while the work of over-hauling her and converting her into an ocean-going ship was being done. At length, with condensers and donkey boiler installed, and her hull strengthened, we were ready to begin the second leg of our voyage. All we needed was the crew. Getting one was no easy task, and we were ten days at it. Invariably, after one glance at the diminu-tive steamer, the hard-boiled sailorman would shoulder his duffel bag and go away without signing on.

"What, go 'round the Horn in that punt," more than one of them exclaimed. "None of her for mine, Mister."

That was the general sentiment of the veteran seamen. But at length we shipped a crew, all but cooks. The men were a Falstaff's army, the rag, tag and bobtail of flop-houses and Bowery dumps, barflies, saloon hangers-on, hopheads, sodden bums, graduates of jails, the human flotsam and jetsam of many nationalities and races. I doubt if in the lot there was one real seaman.

With this motley crew Captain Johnson took his ship down the bay to Staten Island and anchored off Tompkinsville at midnight. He chose the dark to bring aboard two Japanese cooks we had succeeded in signing on, for coming aboard at midnight they had less chance of accurately gauging the ship's size and, most likely, reneging. Those cooks were the only two men worth hell-room among a crew of thirty-two scuts as worthless as ever cumbered the earth. They knew how to cook and their proficiency bolstered up the morale of the ship's officers, at times appalled by the difficulties of the long voyage, and, I do not doubt, did much to avert mutiny among the unruly spirits of the crew.

Our first port of call was Saint Lucia, in the Windward group of the British West Indies, where we stopped for fuel. The *Indianapolis* could carry only five hundred tons of coal, and at that every inch of available space was used to stow it. I think it was loaded everywhere on board except in our berths and in the lone bathtub the vessel boasted. Captain Johnson, who had made shift with his worthless crew only because of his masterful handling of them, thoughtlessly gave them shore leave at Saint Lucia and a small advance on their wages. When the *Indianapolis* had coaled at the end of twenty-four hours and was ready to resume her voyage, her crew was missing. To a man they had deserted.

The purser was sent ashore to appeal to the police to round up the missing men. I was unable to kindle in the commandant any faint spark of concern about our plight until I laid a twenty-dollar bill on his desk. The effect was instantaneous. The official was galvanized into activity

which, in the tropics, can be induced only in one way.
On the moment a squad of Negro military police were
summoned, black faces and brass buttons gleaming, and the
commandant gave them instructions to visit all the hook
shops, saloons, dance halls, gambling hells, and underworld
joints of the town and not to rest until they had routed
out the truant crew of the *Indianapolis*. Within a few
hours every man jack of the crew was aboard, some of the
tardy or more reluctant ones marching up the gangplank
with their rears menaced by a bayonet in the hands of a
grinning cop.

The men were not very amiable about their enforced
return, but they made no actual trouble over it. There
was something about the appearance of our cool, self-
reliant skipper, quiet, fair spoken, but hard as nails, that
made even the sea lawyers of the fo'c's'le hesitate to start
anything.

At Montevideo, Uruguay, our next port of call, we
profited by our experience at Saint Lucia. There were no
docks there and the ship coaled while at anchor in the
roadstead off the city. No shore leaves were given the crew,
but dozens of small boats came out to the ship, offering
to take passengers ashore at twenty-five cents a trip. There
was danger that most of the crew, at the first opportunity,
would slip over the side and use the small boats to get away.
I again invoked the magic of a gold note judiciously invested. A twenty-dollar bill to the captain of the harbor
police boat not only insured that none of the crew would
be permitted on the small boats, but it removed temptation
from them, for the pests were ordered away from the
steamer, and they obeyed.

Within thirty-six hours the ship took on six hundred
tons of coal, one hundred tons in excess of her normal

capacity. Under that weight she stood so low that at times the water washed over our main deck alarmingly. It was a risky thing for any vessel, large or small, but the skipper declared that by the time we reached the Horn most of it would have been consumed and she would be in good trim in case we encountered bad weather. He was right. Rounding the Horn, we ran in a gale with a long, heavy swell on which the tiny ship rolled and pitched to her heart's content, but without shipping so much as a spoonful of water. She rode the waves like a sealed bottle. At no time, in fact, during the entire voyage did she ever ship a sea, although we met or passed vessels of far greater tonnage whose docks were awash in bad weather. The *Indianapolis* unquestionably was a staunch little craft whose behavior was especially admirable in heavy seas, but, of course, much of the credit for her performance was due to her masterful handling by her skipper.

After coaling at Coronel, Chile, our next port upon rounding the Horn, six thousand miles of sea lay between us and San Francisco, which the skipper hoped to make without stopping to coal. The most remarkable stretch . of fine weather I have ever known at sea enabled him to do it. Over the entire distance, the ocean was as calm as the ponds in Central Park. The weather held until we arrived at our destination, Seattle, but the skipper, of course, could not know this, so, as a precaution, he stopped at San Francisco to take on 250 tons of coal.

The stop meant trouble for us. The crew demanded shore leave, and Captain Johnson, kind and considerate, for all his rugged insistence on discipline, thought they rated it after the long drill aboard from Saint Lucia. But they got no advance on their wages. Despite this, more than half of them managed somehow to get a skinful ashore, and when they came aboard there was hell to pay. Fortified by San Francisco redeye and tarantula juice, they somewhat lost their awe of the skipper and the ship's officers. They demanded their wages in full and their cash fare back to New York. It was the agreement when signing them on in New York that the return fare of every man who completed the voyage to Seattle would be paid at that port. Johnson stood on this, steadfastly refusing their demands, and ordered the men to their stations preparatory to sailing.

When we left San Francisco it was with all hands aboard, but they were drunk and nasty, on the very brink of mutiny. The officers feared some sort of outbreak, but did not dream it would come as soon as it did. Hardly had the *Indianapolis* pulled away from the bunkers when the smoldering fire burst into flame. The ship was yet in the bay when the ringleaders of the disaffection attempted to take charge of the vessel. There was a heavy fog over the bay and the skipper was at the side of the harbor pilot, aboard to take the vessel out over the bar at the entrance to the bay. While the *Indianapolis* felt her way cautiously, her foghorn sounding mournfully and all her officers looking sharp, three of the crew, led by a great hulking brute known only as Big Sam, attempted to rush the skipper and the pilot. They were unarmed, but the forty-rod rotgut they had been imbibing ashore had made them reckless.

The skipper was caught by surprise, but went into action promptly and with all the cold, battle fury of his Viking ancestors. With a crashing blow of his fist, planted squarely in Big Sam's pan, he laid his cheek open almost to the bone and sent him reeling. He followed up his attack with a rain of blows under which the mutineer went down. Then over his body Johnson engaged the two other seamen whom he had shaken off, but who now had returned to the fray and were pressing him hard. The skipper was giving a good account of himself, but he was outnumbered and might have fared badly, had not the mate hurried up to his assistance.

While the two officers were subduing the mutineers, some dozen of the crew were milling about and showing signs of a disposition to go to the aid of their shipmates who were now getting a first-rate mauling at the hands of the skipper and mate. When the melee had threatened to become general, I had hurried to the purser's office and was returning to the deck with a brace of navy barkers, fully loaded, when I ran into Allen Hunt, who had been sent up from the boiler room by the chief to learn the cause of the racket on deck. I turned over one of the revolvers to him and with these we stood off the group of seamen. They were drunk and surly and needed only a little encouragement to make them rush us and go to the help of their leaders.

"Get back, you bastards," Hunt ordered them waving his gun barrel in the direction of the fo'c'sle.

None of the men moved.

"Get back, I tell you, or so help me, I'll drill the first one that tries to start anything."

This time several in the group wavered and one or two slowly gave ground. Hunt advanced step by step as they retreated. One of the men sidled around the fringe of the group with intent to attack the young officer on the flank. Hunt saw him out of the tail of his eye, wheeled on him, and fired a shot into the deck planks almost at his feet. The fellow stopped short, turned and ran towards the fo'c'sle with the others following.

While I stood over them with my revolver, the assistant engineer went to where the skipper and the mate had now thoroughly subdued the three mutineers and assisted in putting them in irons. In all, twelve of the most unruly of the crew were shackled. Ten of them were chained to a heavy stanchion on deck. Big Sam and a companion were shackled apart, but, unfortunately, in a place within reaching distance of a rack containing fire axes and a heavy sledge hammer.

With these axes they succeeded in liberating themselves. While Big Sam swung the murderous sledge about him, the two rushed to the group of mutineers chained to the stanchion and attempted to free them. The fight was on again. Hunt and I, with our revolvers, held off others in the crew, while Johnson and the mate engaged the two escaped men, and after a brief struggle, took from them the sledge and the axes.

Then they were again put in irons and this time chained to the stanchion along with their fellows. The two men who had freed themselves had hacked their arms and legs in their efforts and were in bad shape from their wounds and the beatings they had received. The blood from their wounds had made the deck slippery. The cries and curses, the thud of hard fists upon flesh, the murmurs of the crew, the shuffling of feet as the struggle raged, and always the hoarse undertone of the foghorn—all contributed to the pandemonium.

When the abortive mutiny had been put down, and the *Indianapolis* approached the Marine Hospital near the Golden Gate, Captain Johnson signalled, and a tug from the hospital put out and came alongside with two doctors. They stitched the wounds of the two emancipators and patched up some of the other mutineers whose bruises and contusions from the fists of the skipper and officers made them fit subjects for attention. Then the ship resumed her voyage. Until she reached Seattle it was necessary to keep six of the crew, the most vicious of the lot, in irons.

At Seattle they were lodged in jail, charged with mutiny on the high seas. Despite the testimony of the skipper and his officers, no indictments were found, and they were turned loose. Then, through a shyster, they brought suit for heavy damages against the steamship line, and a weak-kneed jury found for them in a small amount.

The *Indianapolis* had made the wide arc of her swing down toward the nether side of the world and back to within striking distance of the Arctic Circle in forty-nine days, less stops—a record at that time—at an average speed of a little better than fourteen knots. She was a grand little ship. When I last heard of her she was in service on the run from Seattle to Tacoma making her five round trips daily, rarely missing one and never getting into trouble of any kind. It seemed a prosaic career for this converted Great Lakes ferryboat that took so naturally to the sea, and to which a maiden trip of sixteen thousand miles, with a maladroit and mutinous crew aboard, was but an incident.

CHAPTER IV

EARLY IN MY SEAFARING career I experienced my first (among many) accidents at sea. They were then more common than now because of the almost total absence of any aids to navigation in the Inside Passage. It was on my first voyage with the *Dirigo,* that which marked the blasting of my hopes of success as a gold-mine promoter, that I had my baptism as a sea casualty. The *Dirigo* was a converted steam schooner of about fifteen hundred tons, used to carry freight and passengers in the run between Seattle and Skagway.

On the homeward-bound trip, after leaving Skagway, we had stopped at McHenry to load copper ore, and in McHenry Inlet the *Dirigo* fetched up on a rock off Prince of Wales Island.

We had thirty passengers aboard, and there was no panic among them when the ship struck. Yet even today I can recall with startling clearness the grinding, rending sound —new to me then, but later to become all too familiar—as the *Dirigo's* wooden hull slid along the rock. I did not know what had happened except that, whatever it was, it was serious. There was something about the hushed atmosphere aboard, immediately after the crash, that was almost as terrifying as the impact itself. One could sense that some fate impended by the tenseness of officers and crew as they stood by for orders, while on the bridge the skipper, calm but serious, quietly telegraphed the engine room, gave unhurried directions to the quartermaster at the wheel and to the mate, and by his entire demeanor in the face of danger allayed the fears of passengers and crew. In a crisis, there is that about the appearance and conduct of the Old Man—all skippers, no matter what their years, are that to the crew—that inspires confidence even in the timid.

The *Dirigo* was not badly damaged, but she was fast on the rock and it was evident to her skipper that, despite his efforts, she would remain there until the tide floated her off. Captain Hunter ordered the lifeboats launched, and all the passengers were taken safely ashore without so much as getting their feet wet, at least from the sea. It was raining hard and the weather was chill, and the only warmth was from fires built ashore while the passengers waited for the next high tide to release the vessel. In due time, the *Dirigo* proceeded on her way to Seattle.

Once again, a year later, the *Dirigo*, this time with Captain McGregor in command and a British pilot navigating her, came to grief when she struck a buoyed reef in Nanaimo Harbor, Vancouver Island. She was floated off by the incoming tide without her passengers leaving her, and docked at Victoria. I began to think an evil fate pursued this vessel and I was glad when I was transferred from her to the *Dolphin*, under Captain Hunter, with whom I had made my first voyage on the *Dirigo*. The *Dolphin*, formerly operated as a fishing vessel in Atlantic waters, was purchased by the Alaska Steamship Company and brought around to the Pacific by Captain John A. O'Brien, known throughout the shipping world as "Dynamite Johnnie" O'Brien.

Sandwiched in between the various assignments during
my first few years of service, I went as freight clerk to the
steamer *Clallan*, and had not been serving aboard her very
long before I experienced my first marine disaster of any
magnitude. The *Clallan* was a brand-new ship of two
thousand tons, wood construction, which made daily trips
between Seattle and Victoria, ninety miles through Puget
Sound and the Strait of Juan de Fuca. She had been in
this trade only five months when, one morning in November, 1905, shortly after leaving Seattle with 150 passengers, water was reported coming into the hold through
a broken deadlight. The heavy seas had smashed the two-
inch glass of a porthole, behind which was an iron plate
that locked tightly. This plate, however, had not been
fastened in place, and when the mischief was discovered
it was too late.

With water pouring into the hold through the deadlight the *Clallan's* engines were soon out of commission
and the vessel lay helpless in the trough of the seas. Immediately panic ensued among the passengers, who demanded that the skipper, Captain George Roberts, launch
the lifeboats. Roberts very properly refused to order them
launched, for no lifeboat could have lived in the seas running at that time. The plight of the *Clallan* was observed
by a deep-sea tug which came up to her assistance.

Lines were made fast to the distressed vessel and the
tug began to tow her. Instead of trying to take her to the
lee of Smith Island, which was nearer, and where the
Clallan would have been afforded some respite from the
heavy seas, the tugboat captain attempted to bring the
vessel to Port Townsend, Washington, near the entrance
of the strait. With the *Clallan* momentarily settling deeper
in the water because of the weight of the incoming seas,

her progress was slow and becoming increasingly uncertain. At length she became thoroughly waterlogged, and, with little warning, she foundered.

There was not time then to take to the lifeboats, even if they could have lasted in the rough water. As I felt the vessel going under, I jumped from her. Many others of the passengers and crew did likewise, but most were trapped and went down with the ship. Since I had not time to obtain a life belt, when I came up after my plunge I struck out to escape being engulfed by the suction of the foundered ship.

I had not been in the water more than four or five minutes before I saw a spar, or piece of driftwood, floating a few yards from me. I clung to that providential flotsam for the next two hours, watching the tug pick up others from the water, wondering all the time when I would be observed. They came just when, chilled and numb, I could not have held on very much longer.

I was safe aboard the tug, and on my way back to Seattle, but ninety passengers and fifteen of the crew had gone to their death in the water. Captain Roberts lost his command, and the chief engineer and his assistant their papers.

CHAPTER V

WHEN THE *Clallan* FOUNDERED and I discovered myself
among the survivors, I began to consider myself "a fool
for luck." It was my first serious experience with shipwreck, although prior to that I had been aboard vessels
which had been in difficulties that might have had a serious
outcome. Looking back on my experiences, it seems a
marvel that I was not in danger oftener, for the vessels in
Alaskan waters at that time were, in truth, not the best of
craft, the Inside Passage was beset by hazards, the aids to
navigation were few, and the weather for much of the year
was such as to demand the utmost in seamanship of the
masters navigating vessels in these waters. Seamanship,
that was the answer! The average ability of the ships'
masters was very high, and they possessed courage and
skill of a high order.

Notable instances of these qualities came under my
observation in the years 1907 and 1908 while I was purser
on the *Dolphin* under Captain Johnson, the same who had
taken the *Indianapolis* around the Horn. The *Dolphin*
was a vessel of fifteen hundred tons, with an iron hull and
a superstructure of wood. She was used to carry passengers
and freight between Seattle and Skagway. On a voyage
in 1907, when outward bound from Seattle with 150 passengers and a heavy cargo, she encountered a heavy sea

in Queen Charlotte Sound between Vancouver Island and the mainland. Lumbering through the water in the early dawn, a tremendous sea struck her abeam and split her port side. Immediately the water poured in and it seemed that the ship was doomed.

Captain Johnson, cool and competent always in the face of danger, and in control of his ship and her crew every minute he was aboard, got busy without delay. He impressed into service every hand who could be spared and after an hour of feverish activity he had stopped the hole with bales of hay from the cargo, with mattresses and tarpaulins. Then, his engines saved from the threatening waters, he worked his ship around to the lee of Egg Island, where he anchored her. For thirty-six hours he rode out the storm, while temporary repairs were made. When the seas subsided, he resumed the voyage and brought the *Dolphin* safe to harbor at Skagway.

A year later the *Dolphin*, while proceeding south from Juneau to Petersburg with two hundred passengers and crew aboard, headed into a heavy southern gale. A tremendous sea boarded her, crushed in the pilothouse and social hall, flooded the dining room and burst the inner partition of the purser's office. It was early in the morning and the skipper had just arisen.

Without pausing to dress, Johnson went out on deck in his underclothes and gum boots and took command of the situation. While the rudely awakened passengers looked on, too impressed by the skipper's calm demeanor to show panic, he directed that the wrecked parts be inclosed in tarpaulins. Then, when the dining room had been baled out, breakfast was served as Johnson brought his ship to anchorage behind Cape Fanshaw. There temporary repairs were made, and after fourteen hours the *Dolphin* proceeded on her way.

Still another example of the courage and capability of this skipper in the face of danger came under my observation while serving as purser on the *Dirigo* under his command. The *Dirigo,* homeward bound from Skagway to Seattle with seventy-five first-class and one hundred steerage passengers, fetched up one morning on Whitestone Rock in a fog in Milbank Sound. There was a falling tide, a moderate sea, and no wind, and all the passengers were safely taken off in lifeboats. Johnson and the crew remained aboard, and I was ordered to proceed with the passengers to Bella Bella, where we were well cared for and fed at the Presbyterian missionary settlement. The *Dirigo* was floated off that evening at high tide, her passengers were picked up at Bella Bella, and the voyage was resumed.

Captain Johnson's enviable record for the safety of those aboard vessels in his command was destined to continue, even when in August, 1910, his ship was lost in a wreck. He was then skipper of the *Ohio,* a six-thousand-ton passenger and freight vessel. Although I was not aboard her, I was on the vessel that came up to rescue her passengers. On the second day out from Seattle to Cordova, at one o'clock in the morning, the *Ohio,* with three hundred passengers aboard, struck a reef at the entrance to Graham Reach after leaving Milbank Sound. There was a smooth sea and the moon was at full. The boats were launched promptly but some of the passengers, in their panic, had jumped overboard, and for hours we cruised about the landlocked waters searching for them. Only one man, a soldier, was lost, and the passengers were taken ashore where fires were built for warmth. When the *Ohio* struck, her wireless summoned assistance, and the next day the *Jefferson*, Captain J. C. Nord commanding, was at the scene. I was aboard the *Jefferson*, having been transferred to her as purser from the *Dolphin*.

Among the *Ohio's* passengers was one who had distinguished himself by his heroic and unselfish conduct in the wreck. This was Michael J. Heney, builder of the White Pass and Yukon and of the Copper River and Northwestern railways. Heney had worked unceasingly, at times in the water, to rescue passengers. When all were ashore and fires built, he had refused to avail himself of the warmth until all the women and children had dried their clothes and been cared for. A man about fifty years old and of sturdy, athletic frame, he was, when I saw him, obviously suffering from exposure.

With the other passengers he proceeded to Cordova. I never saw him again, for early in the following October he died in a San Francisco hospital as a result of his sufferings in the wreck of the *Ohio*.

Although not a college man, Heney was well-read, polished, and all things to all men. An Irish-Canadian of humble parentage, he had been engaged in railroad construction since he was fourteen, had made and lost several fortunes by the age of thirty-five, and at his death was regarded as the foremost construction engineer in the Northwest. He was a man of indefatigable energy, of great resourcefulness, but with a very human liking for the company of congenial companions, with whom he could sit up the better part of a night, turning out for work at five in the morning without showing the least evidence of lack of sleep.

He was especially fond of Captain "Dynamite Johnnie" O'Brien, and in his frequent Alaskan travels he arranged, whenever possible, to book on O'Brien's ship. Once aboard, he and "Dynamite Johnnie" were inseparable, the skipper obliging with his repertoire of songs, among which "Sweet Rosie O'Grady" was his favorite. Heney, although an astute poker player, always managed to lose to the skipper, who was nothing to brag about at cards. I think he had a double purpose in this. It was the only way he could, without offense, give money to O'Brien, who was always broke. Also, he enjoyed hearing the skipper rally him on his losses and his inferiority as a poker player.

When Heney died he left an estate of several millions. One of his bequests was a pension of $250 a month for life to "Dynamite Johnnie."

CHAPTER VI

IF THERE WAS AT THAT TIME in Alaskan waters any more colorful and picturesque seafaring man than "Dynamite Johnnie" O'Brien, I never met him. Not that he was impressive physically, or that he was of the roaring, swashbuckling, buccaneer type of sailor. He was diminutive in stature, about five feet four inches, and pudgy and rotund in frame. Also, except on occasions, he was quiet-voiced, suave, a marine Beau Brummel whose uniform was of the best material and cut, with every button in place and his gold braid glittering. Yet for all his lack of inches, and for all his geniality, he was courage incarnate, uncowed before danger from the sea or any other source, and a raging tempest of action and withering, blistering oaths when aroused.

When I first became acquainted with him he was in his late fifties and going strong, although he had crowded into his lifetime experiences and adventures that would more than suffice for a score of ordinary mortals. Born in Cork, Ireland, he had gone to sea as a boy, serving an apprenticeship on deep-sea, full-rigged sailing ships. He had sailed the South Seas and to the Orient, and had been a famous gunrunner and organizer of Fenian raids into Canada before coming to Alaska. When he died in Seattle in 1931, he had a record of having navigated Alaskan .

waters for many years without a single mishap of any importance.

I remember an instance of his consummate courage on a voyage I made with him as purser aboard the steamer *Northwestern* about 1910. The vessel had a large passenger list bound for Seattle, among them an insane passenger in charge of a keeper. While the midday meal was being served the madman eluded his custodian, made his way to the cook's galley and seized a meat cleaver. He was a miner of powerful physique, weighing more than two hundred pounds, and as he ran out on deck, laying about him with the cleaver, he spread panic among the passengers, who fled for their lives. Officers and crew were unable to get near enough to disarm him, and the maniac had soon cleared the deck, terrorizing all as he chased them, making swings with the murderous cleaver.

A seaman, pale and terror-stricken, ran to the dining room to summon O'Brien who was at a table with several passengers. The skipper calmly excused himself and went out on deck, where only the lunatic was in sight, raging up and down, howling and hacking the air with the cleaver. O'Brien advanced upon him unarmed, and as the madman poised the cleaver for a blow he sprang upon him and gripped his arm, at the same time grasping the man about the body. The suddenness of his attack diverted the cleaver's blow, but the madman continued to fight. Despite the difference in their weight and size, the struggle was not one-sided, for O'Brien's strength was equal to his courage, and the two men were locked, the skipper gripping the maniac's cleaver-arm and trying desperately to throw him, the madman striving to free his arm for a finishing blow upon his antagonist. Twice the maniac struck the skipper on the shoulder; although they

A Kodiak Bear, Biggest of 'Em All

were glancing cuts, they brought the blood. Ignoring the pain, the skipper hung on. For perhaps less than five minutes, which to the frightened spectators seemed hours, the struggle lasted. Then the ugly weapon clattered to the deck, as O'Brien, with a mighty effort, tripped the frenzied man, threw him, and sat upon him until he was put in irons.

This was perhaps the only occasion upon which "Dynamite Johnnie," in a tight place, did not make the welkin ring with profanity, at which he was a past master. He was, normally, urbane and well-spoken, but, let anything go amiss with wind or weather, with the crew, or the officers, and the floodgates of his profanity were unloosed. I have heard the foremost exponents of swearing in action, men like mule skinners, dog-mushers, longshoremen, and truck drivers, who put a world of sincerity and ingenuity into their coinage of strange oaths, but never have I heard anyone who could hold a candle to O'Brien. He combined all the best features of the master swearer's oaths with his own interpellations and refinements, drawing on a wealth of epithets, invectives, and mixed metaphors to round out tirades that were perfect. He swore by the Bones of the Twelve Apostles, by the memory of the Seven Wise and the Seven Foolish Virgins, by the great horn spoon, and embellished his remarks with adjectives unprintable. Oaths such as never were heard on land, and only seldom on sea; deep-sea profanity that grew in intensity until it evolved into blood curdling, awe-inspiring sacrilege; marine curses that left the hearer dazed and wondering; billingsgate that seared and blistered came from his lips in uncontrolled torrents. When aroused he seemed, like Gladstone, to be intoxicated by his own eloquence and loathe to stop.

Yet he was a clean-living man, a sincere believer in his

Maker, genuinely devout, and would not think of missing Mass while in port. And for all his iron courage, he had a streak of superstitious fear of the supernatural, which was amusingly evident on one occasion when his ship was taking on a load of corpses for burial in the States. While the work of loading the coffins was going on, I had occasion to go on the dock, and I stepped over one of the coffins. O'Brien, who was standing near by, saw me, and a look of awe came over his features as he crossed himself. He was too horrified for oaths.

"Morgan," he said solemnly, "would you walk on the faces of the dead? Why, man you'll never have any luck in your life, at all, at all."

Another time, at Cordova, while his ship was loading copper ore, he came aboard at midnight. He had been ashore with some congenial spirits, among whom, I have no doubt, Heney was one, and as he made his way along the main deck he failed to notice an open hatch. He fell through it to the lower hold, a drop of forty-five feet. First Mate Hanson saw the skipper fall and hurried below, expecting to find him dead. O'Brien was in a heap, groaning out oaths.

"Are you hurt, Captain?" Hanson asked.

The inanity of the question infuriated the skipper, who launched out on a stream of oaths that left Hanson dazed, though he himself was no slouch at nautical billingsgate.

"Shall I get a doctor?" the mate next inquired.

"No, to hell with the doctor. Get a priest, you blithering ———— ———— ———— ————."

O'Brien was a skipper who thought of himself as host, as well as protector, of his passengers. He was popular among those who traveled Alaskan waters for his genial manners and his courtesy, and many distinguished men and

women were pleased to number him among their acquaintances. It was then, as it is now, the custom for the officials
of steamship companies to "recommend" to the commander of a vessel for special attention passengers of note
booked on his vessel. O'Brien always took pleasure in complying with such requests and did it so wholeheartedly
that the recipients of his attention were flattered.

On one of his voyages three ladies of rather precise demeanor were "recommended" and the skipper, as usual,
played host to them charmingly. He had invited them to
the bridge, a signal honor, and was explaining to them the
uses of the instruments and the duties of those responsible
for navigating the ship. The ladies were delighted and
interested and enjoying a pleasant time when suddenly, a
fog came up.

O'Brien immediately lost interest in the social side of
his duties. He wanted his guests off the bridge, anywhere
aboard the ship but there, but he was too polite to ask them
to leave. Also he wanted to swear, for the occasion called
for it. But all he could do was to pace the bridge, wring
his hands, and repeat over and over: "Dear me, oh dear
me." His guests, at length sensing that the skipper was
worried about the fog, had the good sense to leave the
bridge.

That night, while the ship lay in dock at Valdez, unloading, the ladies in their berths heard a long-continued
bombardment of oaths so horrible that they covered their
ears and lay cowering in momentary expectation of a rain
of fire and brimstone from heaven to punish the offender.
It was O'Brien swearing at the mate, but of course they did
not identify the swearer with the polished skipper who had
entertained them that afternoon on the bridge. In the
morning they sought out the captain and earnestly com

plained to him about the horrible oaths they had heard in the night. O'Brien was shocked and grieved. Like Admiral Sir Joseph Porter, K.C.B., he would have no profanity aboard ship.

"Ladies, I am indeed sorry to hear this," he told them, and there was sorrow in his tones. "I will have no profanity aboard my ship. I shall investigate this and when I find the guilty man, I assure you I will discharge him."

CHAPTER VII

WHOEVER HAS LIVED IN THE Northwest will back the
Kodiak bear, for size and ferocity, against any other member of the animal kingdom, bar none—this, whether or not
he has ever seen or hunted one of the creatures. The fame
of this most distinguished inhabitant of Kodiak Island is
such that Alaskans resent any intimation that hunting him
is just big-game hunting, no more, no less.

On one of my voyages northbound on the old *Excelsior*,
which, at that time, 1910, was the only ship besides the
Bertha in the Western Alaska-Prince William Sound run,
we had aboard Lord Vivian Drumgoole, a mighty hunter.
You won't find that monicker in Debrett or Burke, for it
isn't really his name. But he was a titled Britisher, all right,
and a good sort at that. He was accompanied by a valet
who, besides looking after his lordship, was in charge of his
master's many guns, rifles, and hunting gear, which had
been brought along for the conquest of Alaskan big game.
Lord Drumgoole was a bland and somewhat childlike
person, but thoroughly likable, democratic in his manner,
and a good sport generally. He had not been aboard long
before he was on good terms with all of the few passengers,
and particularly with George Max Esterley, a mining engineer and veteran sourdough, well-known throughout
Alaska and in New York also.

Esterley, besides being a topnotcher in his profession, was prime company, for he could mix drinks superbly, spin good yarns innumerable without ever once repeating himself, and hold his auditors spellbound by the flow of conversation which tumbled from his lips with all the sparkle of, but with a velocity greater than that of a glacier cataract. He and the English hunter hit it off beautifully at once, but when his lordship proudly displayed his high-powered rifles and elephant guns, and related his exploits in Africa and India, and gloated over his many bags of lions, tigers, rhinos and elephants, Esterly felt that his supremacy as a teller of tall tales was being challenged. To do that was to arouse him.

"H-m-m-m," said George at a pause in the Englishman's recital, while he examined the visitor's armament. "What were you intending to hunt in Alaska?"

"Kodiak bear," the other answered promptly.

Esterley raised his eyebrows. "Kodiak bear? With these?"

"Certainly, why not?"

"Oh, well, I suppose they would do very well for Alaska moose, but for Kodiak bear—well, hardly."

"I say, I think you're pulling my leg," Lord Drumgoole told him good-naturedly.

"Not me, Pardner. I tell you, on the level, these here rifles and elephant guns may be all right for lions, tigers, and rhinos, but when you hunt Kodiak bear, why, they simply ain't there. Unless you strike the heart or some other vital spot on the first shot, I'm tellin' you, you'll sure be up Salt Creek."

He spoke with such gravity and evident sincerity that the Englishman could not believe he was being spoofed. Amazed at the existence of any beast that could not be bagged without too much difficulty with his big game arsenal, he begged Esterley for further details about the Kodiak bear, and that facile and amiable liar only too willingly proceeded to enlighten him. He filled the inquiring sportsman so full of information—none of which the closest student of the animal would have recognized as authentic—that in no time he had his hearer goggle-eyed and speechless.

"You don't have to take my word for it," he assured him. "When we get to Valdez I'll show you a sample of 'em, and when you see for yourself you'll realize that artillery of yours wouldn't be no more than popguns against those critters. Why, man, they have hides six inches thick and tougher than steel. I've seen 'em bigger 'n elephants, and their dispositions are meaner 'n hell."

Lord Drumgoole was mightily impressed, but he was a thoroughbred and his sporting blood was up. When he got his second wind he was keener than ever for a go at Kodiak bear, be the limitations of his armament what they might. In fact, the more Esterley embroidered his narrative about the dimensions, habits, viciousness, and virtual indestructability of the Kodiak bear, the greater became his lordship's yen for a shot or two at one of the monsters.

Valdez was the *Excelsior's* last port of call, and she was to start on the return voyage after twenty-four hours' wait there. Esterley had been in Valdez two months prior and he knew that his friend, Red Ellis, had killed, just before that, a whacking big Kodiak whose pelt measured fourteen feet from tip to tip. The hide had been nailed to the side of Red's house to dry, and Esterley hoped it was still there. When the *Excelsior* docked, Esterley was the first passenger ashore. Ellis, of course, was at the dock, for the whole town always turned out when a ship arrived. He took Ellis aside.

"Red," he asked, "is that bear's hide still nailed on your house?"

"Sure," Ellis answered.

"Fine. Leave it there, won't you, until further notice. I'm bringing a Britisher over in a little while to see it, and I want you to back me up on everything I tell him about it, no matter how strong I make it."

"I'm on," Ellis promised him.

Esterley sought out his English friend and presently they came upon Ellis, to whom his lordship was introduced.

"I've been tellin' the lord here about that Kodiak you killed when I was here last," Esterley remarked after the first greetings were over. "By the way, Red, I hope you still have the hide. I'd like to show it to him."

"Sure." Ellis answered, "it's still nailed up where you saw it, and I'll be glad to have the lord drop around any time and look it over."

But the visiting hunter could not wait. There and then he urged his friends to lead him to a sight of the pelt, and they politely obliged. When they reached the house, Ellis pointed to the skin which covered the better part of the side wall.

"Yonder's the cub's hide," he said casually.

"Cub?" the Englishman gasped, as he stared in amazement at the huge pelt, measuring its dimensions with his eyes.

"Yes," Esterley interposed, quite as casually as Ellis, "that's the one I was telling you about. Tell him how you bagged him, Red."

But Ellis was silent. With a good imitation of embar-

The Famed Inhabitant of Kodiak Island

rassed modesty he resisted Esterley's urgings to describe how he had killed the "cub."

"Red's shy—guess he's afraid he'll be accused of bragging," Esterley explained to the visitor, "so I'll tell it."

And he was off in an avalanche of vivid narrative, filled with details that had his lordship bewildered. The bear, he declared, was not more than a month old (the paws had claws an inch thick and more than ten inches long) when Ellis had bagged him.

"It was like this," Esterley went on. "Red here was coming back from his mining claim just outside the town one afternoon two, three months ago, when he got this critter. Just as he reached the top of a steep hill—set me right, Red, if I ain't tellin' it just like it happened."

"Sure will," Ellis agreed.

"Well, as I was sayin', just as he got to the top of the hill, he sees this here cub amblin' up toward him. The cub was moseyin' along as though he hadn't seen him, but Red knew he had, all right, and that if he began to leg it the cub would leg it after him. And when a Kodiak, little or big, chases you there's only one way to stop him. But that was the trouble. Red was unarmed, not even a six-shooter, and for a moment he was scared stiff, in a panic—that right, Red?"

"You're damned tootin'," Red assured him.

"Well, he was sure in a sweat, fearin' certain death and not knowin' what to do. Then all of a sudden he notices a huge rock right there on the trail and he has an idea. With a mighty heave he pries the boulder loose, gives it a push and sends it rollin' down, hell for leather, straight at this here cub. Correct, Red?"

"Uh-huh. Kee-rect, Max," Ellis echoed.

"Well, the boulder is tobogganin' downhill and the cub

is amblin' up and Red here is awaitin' developments. Fortunately for him, the critter was too young and didn't
have sense enough to get out of the way. He just stops
dead in his tracks—petrified-like. And all the time this
here rock is gainin' momentum, unil it hits the cub with
terrific force smack between the eyes, knocks him bas-
sackward, and kills him deader'n all hell."

"And then I took out my jackknife and skun the
critter," Ellis added simply.

Lord Drumgoole was dazed between wonderment at
the evidence before his eyes of the cub's dimensions and
his admiration of Ellis' resourcefulness and phenomenal
luck. For a time he could make no comment.

"What would you have done, Red," Esterley asked, "if
you'd seen this fellow's mother comin' up that hill?"

"I'd have vamoosed like a bat outa hell, of course. You
don't catch me facin' no full-growed Kodiak bear, not
without a ten-inch cannon, you don't."

His lordship had now regained the power of speech.

"My word, what a country, what sport!" he commented.

His speech restored, his longing for a shot at such game
returned. Eagerly he begged his friends to lead him to the
den of a Kodiak bear, but they assured him that not for
all the gold in Alaska would they hunt Kodiak bear with
any weapon less powerful than field artillery. They told
him, too, that there were no hunting guides to be had in
Alaska, which was true at that time, although there are
plenty today. In every way they could they discouraged
him in his ambition to add this Alaska trophy to his toll
of jungle beasts.

When the *Excelsior* steamed away from Valdez next
day on her return voyage, Lord Drumgoole was aboard, all
designs on a Kodiak bear abandoned.

When I reproached Esterley for his yarning, which had been effective in marring the Englishman's plans for some good sport, he was unrepentant.

"Hell," he snorted, "if that guy ever bagged a Kodiak—and I believe he could at that, he's a bully sport—he'd have thought it wasn't no more than potting a measly lion or rhino. I did it for the honor of Alaska."

Of course, Esterley and Ellis were drawing the long bow in all this yarning about bears, but, probably, actuality was not so very far behind the spoofing. For Louis Lane, a colorful figure in the Far North of a quarter century ago, hailed as Stefansson's rescuer off Herschel Island, told me a couple of yarns about Arctic bears that seem to me almost to match that of Esterley's mythical "cub."

Lane, so he related, on one occasion observed a huge walrus sleeping near the edge of an ice floe. A great polar bear was creeping toward it. With a single blow of his paw on the walrus' head the bear swept him off the ice into the water. Then he stuck the paw into the water and in one mighty heave landed the walrus on the floe, ten feet back from the edge. As the bear was about to make a leisurely meal of walrus meat Lane killed him. He examined the walrus and saw that the head had been crushed by the single blow of the bear's paw. Later he had the walrus weighed. It weighed 3,700 pounds.

Lane, who was a miner, explorer, and adventurer, later joined up with Captain Kleinschmidt, a cameraman who was making motion pictures of walrus herds and Arctic game hunting for exhibition purposes. Lane had suggested a close-up of the killing of a polar bear and agreed to locate, engage at close quarters, and finish off the animal. He tracked a huge bear to an ice floe and, with the cameraman following, he maneuvered it into a position favorable to the range of his Colt .45, the only weapon he carried. It was ticklish business, but Lane, agile as a cat and utterly without fear, was upon the bear before he knew it, circling him for the best vantage point. The bear made for him, but not before Lane got into action and was pumping lead into him at close range. Two or three shots in the beast's heart finished him. As the huge creature collapsed on the ice, Lane, in triumph, but sweating at every pore from the tenseness of the situation, turned and shouted, "There, Cap, you've got a picture worth taking."

But all that he saw was Kleinschmidt's camera lying on the ice thirty feet away, and in the distance the cameraman legging it for dear life, doing a mile in nothing flat.

CHAPTER VIII

IT WAS ASTONISHING, WHENEVER I stopped to think of it, how quickly I had adapted myself to the shift in my life. I had not made many voyages before it seemed to me almost as though I had never known any existence, at least since my adult days, other than one aboard ship, and that in any other calling I would have felt alien and unaccustomed. My life in New York—then not more than a few years in the past—seemed to me as one known in some prior incarnation, as vaguely and mistily remembered as though it were a dream, or something I had read or heard about another person.

Even my more recent experiences as a gold hunter now seemed far in the past and not quite logical, as, indeed, they probably were not. I could, and often did, recall my days in the Klondike, prospecting, panning and digging for gold; mushing with dogs over the frozen trail; sleeping in the open with nothing in sight but a waste of snow; crossing mountain summits alone save for a team of Huskies; trudging through mud with a pack on my back and trailing clouds of mosquitoes swarming about my head. Or in my hours of ease and relaxation, loitering in saloons, dance halls, and gambling hells, drinking, watching the girls and their cadets and admirers as, in their own way, they relieved the tedium of long Arctic nights, I looked on while reckless men staked, won, and lost fortunes on the turn of a wheel or the flip of a card. All this now seemed unreal to me, and it was unregretted.

Yet there was no reason why that recent life of mine should not have remained fresh and vivid in my recollection. On every voyage there were aboard the living reminders of the life I had lived, men such as I had known and consorted with daily in the Klondike. Sourdoughs like the one I had been were constantly making the voyage to and from Skagway, their destination Dawson and the gold fields, or the States. However much I had changed in my attitude in the brief space since I had quit prospecting, they were unchanged. They were the same in their externals—their apparel, their speech, their eating, drinking, and play habits—and in the obsession that rode them like an Old Man of the Sea, their fevered lust for gold. And, too, those who were returning with full pokes were unchanged in their maniacal desire to spend their money in drink and at the gaming table, to shout and curse and fight, to do anything and everything that would give vent to the pent-up feelings of men who had spent many weary days in solitude, cold, ill-nourished, and sick with the sickness that comes of countless repetitions of hope deferred.

Some of these men, it is true, were counterfeits, show-offs who liked to justify the popular conception of a Klondike sourdough as it was later expressed by Robert W. Service in his heroic description, "Sired by a bulldog parent, tried in the furnace heat." But most of them were genuine hell-raisers, maybe not congenitally and consistently, but men who enthusiastically entered into the spirit of things when once they indulged themselves in a celebration.

As the Klondike stampede receded into history, class distinctions grew up among the men who had prospected in the Yukon. That is, the veterans who had "seen the Yukon freeze and thaw" contended that the proud term "sourdough" was properly applied only to them, and that anyone who had spent less time there was only a cheechako, a tenderfoot. Of course the term must have originated long before the Klondike strike, because prospectors on the trail had been substituting the fermented grain for yeast in their dough for many years—hence the expression.

But this was as good an occasion as any for drunken argument, and it was liberally invoked by the roisterers among the prospectors returning to the States.

I saw so much of this on every voyage—especially on the return voyages—that in time the uproar and commotion ceased to disturb me seriously. I think in this I reflected the attitude held by the ships' commanders. After all, there was nothing we could do about it. We could only hope that these outbursts of animal spirit would stop short of maiming or murder.

There were times, in fact, when a skipper allowed, or even encouraged a passenger to take the law in his own hands. One occasion of this kind I recall was on a southbound voyage of the *Jefferson,* Captain J. G. Nord, commander. There had been the usual drinking, carousing, and general high jinks aboard, and, of course, any amount of gambling. A few days out a sourdough went to the bridge and complained to the skipper that he had been cleaned out at black jack.

"Well, what do you think I can do about it?" the commander asked him coldly. "You know the risks of gambling."

"Yes, I know, but the game was crooked."

"How do you know that?"

"How do I know it? Hell, anyone with half an eye can see it. You can see for yourself if you go down to the smoking room and watch for a few minutes."

"All the more fool, you, for letting yourself get skinned in a game you knew was crooked."

Nord laughed heartily. Then, all trace of amusement gone from his features, he eyed the complainant sternly. The miner was a huge and powerful man, who could wrestle a grizzly to a fall, no holds barred.

When the skipper had measured the sourdough's physique with his gaze, he said, "You big stiff, if I were as husky as you and thought I was being robbed in a crooked game, I would never pull the baby act and complain to anyone. I'd kick the head off the guy I thought was cheating me and get my money back."

"Do you mean that, Captain?"

"Sure I do. I'd always get back my own in a crooked game. Now get the hell off the bridge, and don't ever again come to me with any such complaints."

The miner was off the bridge in a hurry, and making at top speed for the smoking room. In a minute there came from that direction sounds of the most gosh-awful rumpus in which shouts, curses, breaking furniture, heavy falls, and the noise of a general engagement smote the calm of the sea. The combat lasted for about ten minutes. At the end of that time the complaining miner reappeared on deck. His clothes were torn, his hair awry, his features battered and bloody, and he was panting hard, but there was a gleam of triumph in his eyes as he stood below the bridge and held aloft a hand in which were clutched many bills and gold pieces.

"You're all right, Cap. I got no kick comin' now. I got mine, and perhaps something more," he shouted.

Captain Nord grinned. "Well, if you ever travel with me again, I hope you know enough to keep out of crooked games."

While this type of passenger predominated on voyages in the days of the Klondike gold fever, there were others of a different and far worthier character. It was a relief to meet them and to realize that there were men and women purposed and actuated by motives higher than the acquisition of riches and the enjoyment of the dubious pleasures they made possible. One such man I met many times was the late Bishop Peter T. Rowe, head of the Episcopal Diocese of Alaska. He knew every mile of his vast territory, for he had traveled to every corner of it in his long ministry. I doubt if any man then living had covered more of the country, or knew it and its people better than he did. He was a godly man, very human, one who could make allowances for the faults and frailties of his fellows, who knew that many of the excesses in language and living indulged in by returning miners were to be accounted for as a sort of compensation for the hardships and rigors of the Arctic. These he knew at first hand, for he had experienced them himself.

The bishop admired the hardihood of sourdoughs; he liked their gusto and he liked their yarns, and he could tell many himself, and tell them well. One I heard him relate concerned a voyage he made from the Tanana Valley to Valdez, on the coast of Prince William Sound. He was headed for Seattle and, rather than wait two months for navigation to open on the Yukon, he had preferred to make the trip overland to the coast. To do it he had to cross three mountain ranges. With seven good dogs and a native boy, he set out from the Tanana, and for many days he was on the trail. As he neared the coast the thaws of the coming spring made the going harder. The dogs were weakening, the native boy was getting surly, and the struggle through mud and ooze was having its effect even on the rugged physique of the bishop.

After a particularly trying day, he was seeking a dry spot on which to camp for the night when he met an old prospector, traveling light toward the Tanana. Both men were clothed as are all on the trail—cap, canvas suits, boots, and the parka over all—and there was no purple and lawn to show the bishop's high ecclesiastic office. After the customary greetings the bishop was first to get in his question.

"How was the trail you came through, Pardner?"

The effect of the question was instantaneous and startling. The old prospector tore off his cap, threw it on the trail, spat on it, and then jumped on it, emitting howls of rage.

"Pardner, it's the golblamedest, meanest, blankety-blank trail that the Almighty ever created, if He did create it. In all my days I never saw such a ———— trail as that back yonder, and I'll be eternally ———— if I ever want to see it again."

And he began all over again, supplying oaths and combination of oaths he had omitted or forgotten in his first transport of rage. By the time he stopped, for want of breath, he had poured out such a wealth of heartfelt profanity as the bishop, in a long experience, had never before heard. When the prospector felt that he had done full justice to the subject and could again find voice, he remembered the amenities of Arctic travel.

"How'd you find the goin' on your trail, Pardner?" he asked.

The bishop pondered the question a moment.

"Well, I should say just about as you have described yours, only more so," he answered.

Years later, after "coming outside," I heard a yarn for which I believe the inspiration could have been the experience just related. It concerned a minister who, as he was driving over the desert in his Ford, came upon a motorist who had stopped to remove a flat tire. He was tugging vainly to detach the rim, sweating at every pore and cursing fervently and without ceasing. For a few minutes the minister in silence observed the traveler who was getting nowhere with his effort and whose profanity increased in an inverse ratio.

"How long have you been trying to get that thing off?" he asked the stranded one.

"For a mortal half hour," the other answered, and at the recollection of his woes and the fiendishness of inanimate things his curses increased in vigor and volume.

"And you've been cursing like that all the time?"

"Yes, you're damned right I have," and he resumed his tugging and swearing.

"Well, you see for yourself, it hasn't done any good. Why not try praying?"

"That's an idea," the other agreed in his desperation.

So, with the minister leading, they knelt in the sand and for three or four minutes tested the efficacy of prayer. Then the motorist arose, spat on his hands, gripped the stubborn rim and pulled. With almost no exertion on his part, it came off. The motorist was speechless with amazement; the minister was no less astonished.

"Well, I'll—be—damned," the reverend exclaimed as he viewed the result of their supplications.

Bishop Rowe's pastoral visits took him to all parts of Alaska and put him in the company of all sorts of men, with all of whom he was at ease because, while he had a natural dignity and a respect for his high office, he was a student of men and understood their diverse natures. On one occasion he called to pay his respects to the colonel in command of the military post at Fort William H. Seward, near Haines, twelve miles south of Skagway. It was a very hot day and the colonel was out inspecting the rifle range when the bishop arrived. When he returned to headquarters he was very warm and fatigued. After greeting the bishop and conversing with him a few minutes, he asked to be excused for a minute or so, explaining frankly that he felt the need of a drink badly.

"I'll be glad to excuse you," the bishop said, "but only on condition that you invite me to join you in a drink. Otherwise, I'll have to say good-by right now, and go down to the wharf and get a drink on the steamer."

CHAPTER IX

WHEN I WAS TRANSFERRED in 1910 to the *Jefferson*, as purser, I began to feel that I was getting along in the service. The *Jefferson* was then the crack ship of the fleet. Previously, I had never seen service aboard any vessel save the smaller, makeshift craft that were made to perform marvels of navigation in dangerous waters under able masters. The *Jefferson* had as skipper one of the best of them, Captain Nord, known throughout the Northwest as "Captain Gus."

Nord was of the breed of skippers who are never at home save with a ship under their feet, who will stay with their vessels as long as they are afloat, and who, when duty calls, know no rest or comfort until all dangers have passed. I have known Nord to remain on the bridge for seventy-two hours at a stretch, with no sleep except what he could snatch for perhaps five minutes at infrequent intervals. A native-born Swede, he had come to Seattle as a young man and shipped as a sailor before the mast. Within a year he had his first-mate's papers, and in his third year he possessed his master's papers. He was a pioneer skipper on the Inside Passage, safely navigating his vessels where no aids to navigation existed and where many rocks and reefs were as yet uncharted. A master navigator, he steered by his sheer local knowledge of the run. Of all the splendid skippers I have known in Alaskan waters I have never met one who was more conscientious, more unsparing of himself in stress or danger, or one who so readily assumed complete responsibility for the safety of his craft and those aboard her. At sea he was a martinet with strict discipline as his fetish, but no dour marine Praise-God Barebones, for he was beloved by his crew for his ability, fairness, and unselfishness, and esteemed by his passengers for his genial ways and his regard for their safety.

Coming to the *Jefferson* from the frail cockleshells I had known was like changing one's abode from a hovel to a palace. Just prior to my assignment to her I had been purser aboard the *Lydia Thompson*, of the Puget Sound Navigation line, a steamer of seven hundred tons making daily round trips between Seattle and Bellingham, Washington, via San Juan Island. On a dark night she had fetched up on Orcas Island, one of the San Juan group, but all of her thirty passengers were taken safely ashore at Orcas. She was a dingy little craft, and even an occasional piling up on shore did not greatly relieve the monotony of the run, so I was glad to be rid of her.

Aboard the *Jefferson* life was far pleasanter and, even though the purser's duties were more arduous, they were much more interesting. The character of the travelers was changing, too, and so were the ship's accommodations for them. De luxe suites were not uncommon, the cuisine was up to the best standards, and the tables gleamed with snowy napery, polished silver, sparkling crystal, and fine porcelain. While we still carried many brawling and lusty sourdoughs, and numerous hopeful prospectors on their way to the gold fields, these men no longer monopolized the passenger lists. Where Mackinaws and canvas suits had been *de rigueur*, dress clothes were beginning to be seen at the dinner tables and in the social hall in the evening, and even the dinner coat had made its tentative appearance. Many of the men who had been among the first in the Klondike stampede, and who had become wealthy, were, regularly, travelers on the Alaskan vessels. Others, who had vainly sought gold in the creeks and hillsides, had remained in Alaska, turned their thoughts to other pursuits, and had achieved note and some prosperity. And of these, too, I met many aboard Alaskan liners.

One of the latter, who has always seemed to me to be representative of the grit and character that will enable a man to triumph over what normally would be crushing misfortune, was Anthony J. Dimond, Alaska's delegate in Congress, serving since 1933, and one of the territory's most esteemed and useful citizens. "Tony" Dimond went to Alaska many years ago to prospect for gold in the mountains inland from Valdez. He experienced to the full all the hardships of the lone prospector on the trail, and knew his hopes and disappointments. He mucked like a galley slave, endured famine, fought scurvy, suffered frostbite in bitter cold, toiled wearily for miles under a backbreaking pack, and slept often beneath the snow.

Then one day while he was cleaning his gun in his camp high up on a mountain, there came the accident which put an end to his prospecting career. The gun was discharged, nearly blowing off his leg. He staunched the wound in time to keep from bleeding to death, crawled to the nearest point where he could obtain assistance, and was later taken by dog sled to Valdez, where he lay in the hospital, between life and death, for many weeks. When he had won this fight, he found himself crippled for life. His knee had stiffened so that, in walking, he dragged his leg. But he was not of a breed that is vanquished by adversity. Frustrated in his quest for gold, now disabled, he decided to study law. When he was admitted to the bar, he began to practice in Valdez, and afterward served several terms in the Alaska legislature. He is considered to possess one of the best legal minds in the territory, and certainly one incident of the practice, well known in Alaska, demonstrates that he is a shrewd and resourceful lawyer.

In Valdez Dimond's early practice consisted largely of the handling of damage suits brought against the Kennecott Copper Corporation by workmen injured while in their employ. Besides possessing a fine legal training, Dimond was a brilliant pleader whose power to sway a jury was known and feared by the opposing counsel. He was always careful about the selection of a jury. On the occasion of the trial of an important suit for damages involving a client who had been crippled, he was alert to have on the jury men who had lost a leg, an arm, a finger or fingers, an eye, or in some way had suffered maiming. In a mining community such as Valdez this was not a difficult matter. When the jury was completed nine of the twelve men had qualified to Tony's satisfaction in this respect. The trial judge himself was crippled.

When the time came to address the jury, Dimond arose laboriously, and, dragging his injured leg, strode back and forth in front of the jury box pleading the cause of his client in tones only less eloquent in their appeal than his own halting steps. He addressed them for only a brief time, but it was sufficient. When the judge's charge had been read, the jury returned a verdict without leaving their seats, finding for Dimond's client in a substantial amount.

The corporation's attorney, commenting on the verdict to a friend, remarked, "Justice is not only blind, but she's lame also, in Valdez anyhow. Next time I try a damage case against Dimond I'll take care to have every maimed man in Valdez kidnaped in advance of the trial."

Serving under Nord aboard the *Jefferson*, I came to appreciate that this skipper's solicitude for his passengers and his ship extended as well to the line's shippers and their property. A notable instance of this occurred on a voyage in 1911 when the *Jefferson* was making her way from Juneau to Skagway, 110 miles distant. We had aboard many passengers and a cargo of perhaps a hundred head of cattle. A gale of more than one hundred miles an hour had been blowing for a week in Lynn canal when the *Jefferson* entered it. Now Lynn Canal is a treacherous body of water, which at that time was almost wholly without lights or buoys. It was concerning this canal that a story, which may or may not have been true, was told with sardonic glee throughout Alaska.

A bill had been introduced in Congress, so ran the story, carrying an appropriation of $500,000 for lights at Eldred Rock and Sentinel Island, danger spots in the canal. When the bill reached the Committee on Waterways of the Senate for a hearing Senator Henry Cabot Lodge, chairman of the committee, demanded of one of the measure's proponents, "Who built this canal?"

The *Jefferson* steamed into the canal making twelve knots, and abeam Sentinel Island the gale struck her full force. For a time she seemed to be helpless and at the mercy of the wind and heavy seas, but by superb seamanship Nord worked her around into the lee of the island where he anchored and for five days rode out the storm. On the fourth day, the steamer *Sophia* of the Canadian Pacific line, also with a load of cattle aboard, passed her bound for Skagway. There the *Sophia's* captain rather deprecatingly reported that he had sighted "Gus Nord hugging the lee of Sentinel Island."

But Nord brought his ship into Skagway without the loss of a single head of cattle. When the *Sophia* reached there, sixty-five of the poor beasts in her cargo had been battered to pieces in the gale. And the *Jefferson* and the *Sophia* were to encounter each other again, with a more tragic sequel.

CHAPTER X

When Alaska became American territory in 1867, by purchase from Russia, a howl of derision resounded throughout the United States. "Seward's Folly" the purchase was called because the transaction had been negotiated by William H. Seward, Secretary of State, and because the purchase price was considered excessively high, $7,200,-000. This averaged less than two cents an acre for the 369,530,600 acres included in the area. Since that time the territory has yielded annually, from its fisheries and mineral products alone, several times the amount of the original cost. Since 1885 it has yielded millions of dollars in rare furs, more than a billion in fisheries and minerals combined. Of the more than half billion in minerals, more than half was gold—with the surface but scratched —and millions of acres of coal yet remain to be developed, and great iron deposits await the coming of those who will combine the two resources to create a new Gary or a new Birmingham.

Geologists assert that in Alaska there are greater mineral deposits than in any other place in the world. Besides gold, it has produced silver, copper, lead, and tin, but the rich strikes at Fortymile in 1887, at Rampart in 1893, in the Klondike in 1896, at Nome in 1898, and at Fairbanks in 1902, have made Alaska synonymous in the public mind with gold. And, indeed, since that metal has been the favorite quest of men, it has been mined in greater quantities than other minerals and has been the preferred means of accumulating fortunes.

Of all those hardy men who braved the Arctic for its wealth, one man, the late Stephen Birch, produced more gold from the hidden recesses of Alaska than any other person in the world.

Birch was not one of the original stakers in the Klondike, for he did not go to Alaska until about 1900. A graduate of the School of Mines of Columbia University, he brought to his prospecting activities a technical knowledge and engineering skill that were wanting in the sourdoughs of whose fraternity he became a member in good standing. For he had prospected and tested many creeks, gulches, hills, and mountains, mushed his Huskies over weary miles, broken trail on snowshoes, and felt the savage sting of Arctic blizzards, sleeping many times beneath the snow. He had dared the unknown, leading always, and was ever undismayed by the obstacles between him and what he sought. Unlike so many other brave spirits, he found it. He became president of one of the largest mining companies in the world, the Kennecott Copper Corporation, which he organized, a director in many banks and railroads, the head of an army of more than 300,000 persons employed in companies whose operations extend from the United States to the four quarters of the globe, to Canada, Central America, South America, South Africa, India, and China.

Of all the many sourdoughs I have met in my thirty years in the North, Birch was the most romantic and inscrutable figure. Thirty-odd years ago a prospector warming his beans in a skillet over a fire on the Arctic trail, he became a millionaire many times over, a power only less potent in the political world than in the mining world, and the most outstanding personality in all Alaska. Yet in New York, where he worked eighteen hours a day when not traveling over the country inspecting his vast properties, his name meant less to the general public than that of a fairly prosperous broker (if there are any now) in Wall Street. And that was as Stephen Birch would have it. Years ago Jack London and Rex Beach told me that, attracted by the glamor of his Alaskan exploits, they had asked Birch's permission to write his life. He refused them with so much finality that they did not insist.

I can well imagine the icy decisiveness of his tones as he refused, for there was something of the Arctic in the chill of his manner. That this was exterior I am convinced through my observations of him over the years, and in this opinion others, who knew him better than I, concur. George Esterley, who prospected with him in the early days, has often told me that Birch was the best fellow in the world as a companion when there were only the two of them, that he always rowed his weight, cheerfully did his share of the cooking, dishwashing, and the rustling and cutting of firewood. It was different, however, whenever a third person joined them. Then he would shut up like a clam, withdraw within himself, and maintain a cold and silent attitude.

Birch's great strike came when, on a prospecting trip with Jack Smith and Clarence Warner, he located the great Bonanza and Jumbo copper mines in the mountains at the source of the Copper River, five thousand feet above the level of the Kennicott Valley. The entire mountain was copper-bearing, the ore running 75 per cent pure metal. Birch saw that there were hundreds of thousands of tons of the rich ore, and believed he had found what would prove to be, as it has, the richest copper mine in the world. For other mines were operating at a profit with ore carrying only 2 per cent value in copper.

Then he got busy and enlisted capital from powerful financial interests for the development of the property. The Kennecott Copper Corporation was organized, a huge mill and concentrating plant were built near the foot of Kennicott Glacier, a dead, or inland glacier, and mining operations were begun. He bought steamships to carry the labor and supplies, built the Copper River and Northwestern Railway to transport the ore the two hundred miles from the mines to Valdez on the coast, acquired other vessels to carry the ore to Tacoma, where he had bought the great smelter owned and operated by William R. Rust.

Before a dollar in profits had been taken out of the mines he had expended for steamships, railroads, docks, smelter, trams, mills and the development of the mines, more than $100,000,000. During the first few years of operation Birch personally managed the mines. For years before the first World War, and for several years immediately thereafter, the mines shipped more than ten thousand tons of ore monthly, which for a long period sold at more than thirty cents a pound. The original investment long ago was returned many times over.

FROM THE *Jefferson*, ABOARD which I had made many voyages as purser, I went the rounds as purser on several vessels of the line before I was transferred to duty ashore as assistant in the city ticket office in Seattle. Prior to this assignment the old *Dirigo*, on which I had made my first voyage as chief steward, had met the fate that so often befalls a vessel that, through long years of service, has survived many perils. A year before, in the Gulf of Alaska, off Cordova, she had sunk when her machinery broke down as she was leaving that port with a cargo of copper ore. She was operating as a freighter in command of Captain Thomas Moore. Proceeding under a tow by the *Cordova*, Captain John Johnson, commanding, her hull opened up off Lituya Bay and she sank in half an hour, her crew of thirty-five being taken off by the *Cordova*. It was a sad end to the career of a gallant ship.

Shore duty was just that to me. I endured it because I had been assigned to it, but my preference was for service aboard ship. Not that the life at sea was one of ease, without its daily stint and responsibilities. In fact, the tasks on board ship were far more onerous, for, of course, there were no hard and fast office hours. Certainly my responsibilities as purser had been far more numerous and greater than those as an assistant ticket agent. It often amused me to think that I, who had for more than four years toilfully delved for gold, as purser had been the custodian of many millions of dollars in gold bullion, and more millions in currency. But it was not a matter for amusement to have the responsibility for this treasure in transit. I remember one occasion when for some harrowing hours I could not be certain that several millions in gold intrusted to my care had not been lost.

It was when I was purser aboard the *Northwestern*, under Captain Hunter, the same skipper who had engaged me as chief steward on the *Dirigo*. The steamer was lying at the dock at Skagway loading passengers and cargo for the homeward-bound voyage to Seattle. There was an express consignment of $2,500,000 in gold bullion which was in eight iron safes on the dock awaiting transfer to the vessel. I gave the mate the order for the transfer of the bullion aboard and obtained his acknowledgment of it. Then, as we had a heavy passenger list, I was extremely busy for the next hour. When I had completed my duties with the bookings, supposing the gold to be aboard, I sent up word to the skipper: "Sail when you like."

I went out on deck for a breath of air, and was horrified to observe the eight safes of bullion still on the dock. The ship was making ready to cast off, but her stern and bow-lines were still fast to the dock. I rushed to where the mate was giving orders to haul them in.

"You're leaving the gold behind," I told him.

"Captain's order," he answered.

I rushed to the bridge and told the skipper the gold was still on the dock.

"To hell with the gold. I can't wait for it. I've got to make the tide at Wrangell Narrows," he shouted as the vessel slid away from the dock.

Morgan Before Totem Pole at Wrangel

Alaskan Natives

Back to the rail, I shouted directions to the wharfinger to have the gold hauled back to the express company. Not until I reached Seattle and learned that the bullion was safe did I have an easy moment.

Although I was finding my duties as ticket agent not so congenial as service at sea, I was destined to have a few more years ashore before returning to sea duty. From the Seattle office I was transferred to Ketchikan as general agent in charge of southeastern Alaska. It was a promotion, of course, and that was gratifying to me, but still it was shore duty, with the difference, however, that it required that I make many trips into the interior, which theretofore had been terra incognita to me.

During the year and a half I made my headquarters at Ketchikan, which is the port of entry for all Alaska, I had exceptional opportunities to gain firsthand knowledge of the magnificent resources of our splendid Northwestern empire, sadly neglected by the government and contemptuously dismissed from consideration by the general public as "a land of ice and snow, walrus and bears, a forsaken region that God forgot." What I saw in those years of Alaska's matchless scenic splendors; her untouched resources of coal, oil, and minerals; the enormous latent power of her waterfalls; the wealth to be gathered in her timber, fisheries, and furs; her medicinal hot springs in the Valley of Ten Thousand Smokes; the richness of her soil for the fruits of the earth; and her potentialities as a paradise for sportsmen and tourists, so impressed me that I have never ceased to marvel that the territory to this day remains almost undiscovered.

In particular, the glaciers thrilled and awed me. There are thousands of them along the coast and in the mountain ranges for one hundred miles back from the sea in western

Alaska. It seemed to me as though they could supply to geologists the material for an important chapter in the history of our globe. Recently, I have been glad to see that the explorations and writings of the "Glacier Priest," Father Bernard R. Hubbard, S.J., have done much to arouse popular interest in these magnificent vestigia of the early age of the world. On my voyages through the Inside Passage I have never tired of viewing the splendors of the live glaciers, those huge bodies strung along the coast. Malaspina, the largest glacier in the world, covering an area greater than that of Switzerland, has a sea frontage on the southwestern coast of more than one hundred miles, and a width of one hundred and fifty miles. On a clear sunny day it is one of the most glorious sights one could hope to see, its crystal facets, castellated turrets, and spires reflecting all the colors of the spectrum against a background of mountains whose snow-crowned tops are gilded by the sun. I have also seen Malaspina on a clear moonlight night when the northern lights have added their harmony to a polychromatic symphony that is no less than appalling in its fearsome beauty.

Dead glaciers, or those which are inland, while they are awesome because of their vastness, have not the same quality of enchantment for the beholder as the live glaciers, which are continuously discharging thousands of tons of ice, presenting kaleidoscopic changes of form and color, and sending forth grinding, creaking, thunderous sounds which can be heard for miles.

Hardly less interesting to me than the resources and the scenic marvels of Alaska were the aborigines. The natives, as classified by the ethnologist, are of four strains, Eskimo, Athabascan, Thlingit, and Aleut, the last two named being indigenous to Alaska. But they have been pretty well commingled and to a sourdough like myself they were just Indians, without regard to tribal origins, although the Aleuts seemed to have a shade the best of it on the score of intelligence. While I cannot give them much on the score of pulchritude or cleanliness, they have one point of superiority over the Indians of the United States in that they are willing to work. Short, squat, and heavily built, they are active, strong, and vigorous, and can perform prodigies of labor, especially as fishermen, an avocation they prefer, relegating their women to work in the fish-packing canneries. In other respects they differ from the American Indian, their oblique oval eyes, wide cheek bones, and thick lips denoting a Mongol origin.

There are not many of the natives left, less than twenty-five thousand in all Alaska, and on the basis of the present birth and death rate among them it is estimated that the race will be extinct within a hundred years. One of the most informed students and best friends of the Alaskan native is William Duncan, known as Father Duncan and as the "Apostle of Alaska." For more than sixty years a missionary among the coast Indians, his settlement at Metlakatla was the physical embodiment of his ideas for native welfare. Here he has established a community with sawmills and other industries for the employment of the natives, as well as schools, hospitals, and churches. It is his theory that the native is not an object of charity, being able and willing to perform any manual work that a white man can. At the same time he is not in favor of higher education for them, because he believes that it is a positive detriment, causing them to adopt a superior attitude toward their kind and tending to fasten on them the vices and maladies of the white man.

The disintegrating processes of civilization upon Alaskan

natives began during Russian ownership of the territory, and they left a heritage of social diseases which have been supplemented by the strong liquor of the Americans. To these two evils have been added tuberculosis, whose ravages are abetted by whisky. Although the Federal laws are strict against the selling or giving of whisky to the natives, they get it and their fondness for it is constantly exploited by white men. The trade in this contraband stuff was active while I was in Alaska and despite the vigilance of Federal officers and the officials of the line the seamen were doing a thriving trade in supplying natives with whisky at $5.00 a bottle, which they had bought in Seattle at $8.00 or $9.00 the case. It was vile stuff, of course, but it satisfied the natives' craving for strong drink.

On a voyage aboard the *Northwestern* we had a steerage steward, Pat Kelly, a young Irishman who was eager to quit the sea, join his brother in Chicago, and settle down. He had it in mind to pool his savings with those of his brother and set up a saloon, but the obstacle was that he had no savings. For he could not resist the allures of life on shore leaves and as fast as he accumulated funds toward the realization of his ambition for a publican's life, they vanished in a wild spree ashore. When he was becoming discouraged and doubtful that he would ever amass the necessary capital for the venture, he had a bright idea.

He had been observing the ease with which bootlegging seamen disposed of their wares to Indians in the cannery towns, and he envied them their golden returns from the illicit trade. On a voyage when the trade had been unusually brisk he unfolded his idea to me. It was that on the next voyage he would bring a supply of bottled cold tea to sell to the natives as whisky at the standard bootleg prices.

"I won't be violatin' the law," he explained, "for the

stuff will be nothin' at all, at all, but cold tay. And there's no law against selling that stuff."

"Maybe not," I told him, "but I doubt if it would be very safe for you, even if you could get away with it, unless you never intended to return to the towns where you sold it."

"Of course not," he replied.

On the next voyage Kelly stocked up with eighty bottles of cold tea, representing a trifling investment for the tea and the glassware. When we arrived at Hoonah he caused word to be spread around among the native cannery workers that he had some choice stuff aboard which he would dispose of at $5.00 a bottle while it lasted. He stipulated that no sales would be made until a quarter of an hour before the ship was due to leave the dock and that intending buyers must present themselves with the exact change and leave the ship without sampling the contents of the bottles.

Kelly disposed of his entire stock with a margin of five minutes' time before the ship sailed. When the last Indian had laid down his $5.00 and departed with his tea, Kelly had in his jeans $400, almost all clear profit. He quit the sea upon the vessel's arrival at Seattle and I have no doubt amassed more profits from the sale in Chicago of potables more genuine than that which gave him his start in life.

On another voyage aboard the *Farallon* I myself just escaped arrest on a charge of bootlegging whisky to the Indians. The *Farallon*, Captain Nord commanding, was lying at Shakan loading salmon. We had been taking the cases aboard for hours, with some two score natives engaged as longshoremen. As usual, some of the crew had brought along liquor for sale to the Indians and, not having the same reason as Kelly for delay, had lost no time in selling their wares. I turned in at 10 o'clock that night while the loading was still going on. Always an early riser, I was up and dressed by six o'clock in the morning and was going ashore when I heard a frightful commotion forward. There, some thirty Indians, all fighting drunk, were milling around Martin Taft, the mate, who was trying to drive them off the ship. Before I could reach Taft's side he had escaped from them, speedily coupled the fire hose, and was directing a stream of hot water on the drunken group.

By this time I had joined Captain Nord on the bridge and we were viewing with some amusement the spectacle of the infuriated mate chasing the Indians in pell-mell flight from the avenging nozzle. Soon Taft had cleared the decks and we were twitting him on his encounter. While we were still laughing over the affair, a deputy United States Marshal came aboard escorting one of the drunken Indians. The marshal very evidently was wrathy.

"Show me the man who sold you the hooch," he demanded of the Indian.

The native blinked owlishly, and was silent.

"Point him out, I tell you, or you go to the skookum house yourself," the officer insisted.

The native hesitated no longer. Pointing directly at me, he said, "Him the man."

When I had recovered from my amazement at the unexpected and unmerited accusation, I made a lunge for the Indian. But the marshal pushed me away.

"Nothing doing, Morgan. I'll have to arrest you on this man's charge."

In vain I told him my purser's papers would account for every drop of liquor brought in the ship's supplies, of which only two or three bottles had been used. He would not even look at the papers. Nor would he heed Nord's objection that the testimony of the native was wholly un- reliable, that it was well known that an Indian, when drunk, would point to the first man his glance fell upon when asked to identify the purveyor of whisky. Perhaps the average white man would have done the same thing. The marshal was obdurate, but finally agreed to delay my incarceration until an appeal could be made to Federal Judge Royal A. Gunnison. Judge Gunnison promptly came down to the vessel, heard both sides of the story, looked steadily at the accusing Indian, and asked him, "Who did you say was the man that sold you the hooch?"

The Indian promptly pointed to Taft, the mate, who was directly in range of his vision. Fortunately, I was out of range.

"There, Marshal, you can see for yourself how reliable this man's identification is," Judge Gunnison smilingly told the officer. "He might have pointed to me as the one who sold him the stuff, if it had occurred to him."

The marshal agreed with him, and turned me loose. But he insisted on searching the ship and was rewarded by find- ing some half-dozen cases hidden in the fo'c'sle.

CHAPTER XII

Upon the termination of my duty ashore I was transferred to the *Northwestern,* "Dynamite Johnnie's" ship, aboard which I served as purser for a couple of years. Then I was transferred to the *Mariposa.* It was while aboard this ship that I experienced a trinity of wrecks as unusual as anything I have heard of in the annals of marine disasters.

The *Mariposa* was a ship of six thousand tons, carrying freight and passengers, and her skipper was Captain Charles O'Brien, in almost every way imaginable wholly unlike his namesake of the *Northwestern.* Although a capable master, he liked very much the social life aboard ship and would dance until far into the night—with a resultant hangover that made him cross and snappy the next day with officers, as well as with the crew. His short temper caused him to be feared by all under his command.

On this fateful voyage in November, 1918, bound from Skagway to Seattle, the *Mariposa* had aboard some 560 passengers, three hundred of whom were steerage, and she also had a cargo worth several million dollars in copper ore, salmon, and furs. More important, there was aboard an express shipment of more than two million dollars in gold bullion in bricks, packed in sealed wooden boxes, two hundred and forty thousand dollars in currency, and

The Wreck of the *Mariposa*

some valuable fur pelts. Gold, currency, and furs were consigned in the care of the purser.

Proceeding from Skagway, the *Mariposa,* on November 16, passed the *Alki,* a small, mail-carrying steamer which had been wrecked near Hooniah, near the north end of Chichagof Island, and abandoned by her crew. Prior to the *Mariposa's* coming up to the wrecked mail carrier, but unknown to us at that time, the *Manhattan,* a thousand-ton fishing steamer operated out of Ketchikan by the New England Fishing Company, had sighted the *Alki,* and her crew of seventy men had boarded and looted her. Among the spoils taken off her were sacks of mail.

Swift retribution overtook the pirates, for not long after the *Manhattan* had proceeded on her way, she had struck on Pinnacle Rock in the Gulf of Alaska, between Cape Spencer and Icy Point. Her crew had taken to the lifeboats and had spent more than twenty-four hours in the open when the *Mariposa,* on her homeward-bound voyage, picked them up about ten miles off Cape Spencer at daylight on November 18. They were clad only in oil-skins and were suffering frightfully from exposure.

It was not until the *Mariposa* called at Juneau that we learned that the men she had rescued were outlaws of the sea. Before the *Mariposa* had time to dock, United States Marshal Buford hailed us from the wharf and ordered that no one be allowed to land until he had boarded the vessel, demanding to know whether we had aboard the *Manhattan's* survivors who, he declared, had stolen mail from the wrecked *Alki.* The marshal and his deputies came aboard and for hours searched every nook and corner of the ship. The outlaws had heard his hail from the dock and had promptly scuttled away, hiding under boilers, in the coal, among the bales and boxes of the cargo—anywhere out of sight. They never were found by the marshals. Of course the engine crew knew where they could be found, but they would not inform on them. And when a sailor hides, it takes a special kind of knowledge to know where to ferret him out.

The next day the *Mariposa* came to grief, the third in an odd series of wrecks. From Juneau she had gone to Shakan, where she loaded thirty thousand cases of salmon. Proceeding at night with Henry Selness, a pilot, in charge, she came up to Strait Island in Sumner Strait. Selness, a conscientious young navigator who erred, perhaps, on the side of self-reliance, became confused as to the location of the island light. Mistrusting his own judgment, he requested the advice of the skipper in locating the north end of the island.

O'Brien had retired, was crusty and ill tempered, and replied in a manner to discomfit the diffident navigator. Selness, after his rebuff, attempted to find his way unaided, and presently informed the skipper he had located the island. It was not long after that the *Mariposa* piled up on a rock. Selness, had he been a more experienced and seasoned man, no doubt would have telegraphed the engine room to stop the ship dead and turned her over to her skipper, whose responsibility for her safety is never surrendered.

I was in my berth when the crash awakened me. Half asleep, I heard the shouts and confusion and immediately concluded that the ship had been scuttled for her treasure. We were in the first World War, the spy mania had spread even to the sub-Arctic, and I was romantically evolving a plot with a deep-sea setting. It was foolish, of course, but among our three hundred steerage passengers were many men from southeastern Europe of nationalities allied to our central European foes. They were returning from construction camps where they had been engaged in building the government railroad in Alaska, and it was known that some of them were intending to return to their own countries.

When I went on deck I saw that the *Mariposa* was in a bad wreck. My theory of a war plot, of course, was exploded, but my fears for the safety of the treasure in my care were not immediately quieted when I saw a milling throng of laborers, shouting and crying in a babel of foreign tongues. The first-class passengers, too, were in the greatest confusion while the lifeboats were being launched. I had gone out on deck in my sleeping clothes, but the bitter cold made me decide to return to my room for warmer garb.

Then I set about to save the bullion and currency in my charge. One glance at the heavy seas pounding the *Mariposa* told me it was out of the question to consider saving the furs, which were a bulky shipment. I decided not to attempt to take off the bullion in the boxes in which it was packed, for it was too evident what they contained. I still had visions of a war plot, and did not care to put temptation before the throng of steerage passengers just outside the purser's office.

Working frantically, with the assistance of freight clerks, the bullion and the currency were stuffed into empty mail sacks borrowed for the purpose from the United States mail clerk aboard. With the money, thus camouflaged, I felt easier, for there is something about a government mail sack that advises hands off to the average man bent on robbery. While some of the crew held back the jostling laborers, who, I am now convinced, had no designs on the treasure, we got the mail sacks ready for their transfer to the *Revilla*, a small freighter under command of Captain Bob McCluskey, which had come up to our rescue and was taking aboard the passengers from the lifeboats. Then as the *Mariposa* steadily pounded to pieces on the reef, the bullion and currency were transferred to the rescue ship.

At Wrangell the *Revilla* transferred the gold and most of the rescued passengers to the *Jefferson*, Captain Nord commanding, for the two-day run to Seattle. The balance of the *Mariposa's* passengers, with the exception of sixty steerage passengers who remained on the *Revilla*, were taken aboard at Ketchikan by a second relief steamer, the *Alameda*, with Captain Clinger in command.

To climax the series of mishaps that attended the last voyage of the *Mariposa*, the sixty steerage passengers who remained aboard the *Revilla* became obstreperous soon after that little vessel had left Wrangell. They demanded staterooms and all the accommodations of first-class passengers, although never in their lives had they experienced these soft delights. They became so threatening that Captain McCluskey put back to Wrangell and called on the United States Marshal to incarcerate them for mutiny. In the jail they were offered the alternative of returning peaceably to Seattle aboard the *Revilla* or facing prison terms for mutiny at sea. They chose the former.

I had been well satisfied to have saved the treasure in my care from the wreck of the *Mariposa*. My superiors of the steamship line also were pleased. But the officials of the express company were something less than satisfied. Six months after the wreck, when I was ashore in Seattle, I received word that the general manager of the express company, then in town on his annual trip, would like to see me in his office. There he greeted me politely, if not cordially, and after referring rather casually to the saving of the millions in bullion and currency from the *Mariposa,* he inquired, "But, Mr. Morgan, don't you think that with a little effort you might also have saved the sixty-thousand-dollar consignment of furs?"

I did not answer him. I could not trust myself to attempt to do so.

CHAPTER XIII

LESS THAN A YEAR AFTER the *Mariposa* piled up I was serving as purser aboard the *Alaska,* a sturdy vessel of six thousand tons in command of that equally sturdy mariner, Captain Nord. The *Alaska* had been operating as the *Colon* between New York and Panama, via the Canal. The Panama Steamship Company sold the boat to the Alaska Steamship Company, who then rebuilt and renamed her. When I began my duty with her I did not dream that I was destined to survive two wrecks aboard her, and to be in at the death on her second mishap.

On a return voyage from Seward to Seattle in mid-October, 1918, we had left Ketchikan with a capacity load of passengers, 350 first class and 400 steerage, and a cargo of 2,000 tons of high-grade copper ore in sack, 30,000 cases of salmon and 200 tons of general cargo. Also consigned to my care by the express company was $2,700,-000 in gold bullion, $250,000 in currency, and $150,000 in fine furs, marten, fox, ermine and mink.

In Hiekish Narrows, which flows between Sarah Island and the mainland, the rise and fall of the tides average about twenty-six feet. Entering the narrows on October 20 with a fair tide, the *Alaska* proceeded at a speed of twelve knots an hour, which, with a tide running at the rate of about sixteen knots, made her speed twenty-eight knots in all. She had traversed about half the length of the narrows at this smart gait when, at about half-past one o'clock in the afternoon, her steering gear parted and she took a sheer to port. Immediately the ship, her rudder useless, was swinging about aimlessly in the racing tide. Dead ahead of her was Bald Bluff, a perpendicular rock rising five hundred feet from the water.

Nord was on the bridge with Joe Dodge, a pilot, when the steering gear parted. This skipper in a tight place— and the narrows were that—always took the responsibility of navigating his ship, pilot or no pilot, and this occasion was no exception to his rule. When the *Alaska's* nose pointed straight at the bluff some one hundred feet ahead, he ordered the engines reversed. It was too late. There had not been a sufficient margin of time to back the ship away from ruin. The *Alaska* fetched up head-on into the huge rock.

The shock was terrific, but the staunch craft remained afloat. When the ship struck, her skipper telegraphed, "Full speed ahead."

It seemed like the order of a madman, but it was, in fact, the act of a consummate master of his calling and an extraordinarily quick thinker. For with her engines working full speed ahead the *Alaska* stood glued like a postage stamp to the sheer face of the rock, and that was what saved her. At the instant his vessel struck the rock Nord realized that the impact had stove in her bow, perhaps even to the collision bulkhead, and that if he could keep the smashed bow hard against the rock that had done the mischief, he had a chance to prevent the seas from pouring into her and to keep her afloat until he could stop up the hole with cargo.

With the *Alaska* jammed against the rock and still

afloat—but for how long he did not dare guess—Nord
next turned his attention to getting his passengers off the
threatened ship. For the next fifteen minutes, like Jim
Bludso, engineer of the *Prairie Belle,* who shouted over the
roar of the fire:

> "I'll hold her nozzle agin the bank
> Till the last galoot's ashore,"

Nord held the *Alaska's* nose fast against the bluff until the
last passenger and the treasure had been loaded into boats.

It was quick work, but not accomplished without danger
that at one time threatened the loss of a boatload of passengers. After the crash there was no panic, for Nord was
always cool and in perfect command of his ship in a crisis,
and his example inspired his voyagers. But on board there
were twelve insane patients, some of them violent, who
were being transferred to Seattle by United States Marshal
M. Irwin and twelve deputies. These men, some of them
in strait jackets, were brought out by their keepers to be
loaded into the last boat launched. While the boat was being swung out, the madmen became frantic, for they
were not so bereft of reason that they could not realize the
danger they were in. When they had all been loaded in
the boat, a frantic lunatic grabbed the sailor who was
assisting in lowering the craft and his action caused the
tackle to become unhooked. The bow of the boat dipped
suddenly, and all in it were spilled into the sea. The boat
was speedily righted and all the spilled passengers fished
from the water.

While the work of taking off the passengers was going
on, Nord was directing the crew in efforts to stop up the
hole in her bow. This was done by bringing up from the
hold sacks of copper ore, each weighing 160 pounds, which

were stacked up against the collision bulkhead. When all passengers had been taken off, I proceeded, at his direction, with the boats to Swanson Bay.

Swanson Bay was controlled by a British company operating wood-pulp and lumber mills, and they owned, as well, the only dock in the harbor. When we landed at the dock the wharfinger refused to allow us to proceed into the town proper, on the ground that there was influenza among our passengers. Nor would he permit any of us beyond the wharf, where the only shelter was drafty warehouses which freely admitted the cold and the rain that was coming down in torrents. He was very firm in his refusal, which extended even to the case of a woman more than eighty years old who was ill, and whom I desired to have placed in the hospital in the town. Of course, I was not surprised after this that he declined to allow me to take the bullion and currency to some safe place. Two freight clerks, the United States mail clerk, and I took turns guarding it that night.

In the morning the *Alaska* arrived, her bulkhead having held. But while Nord considered the vessel's condition not too risky for himself and the crew, he would not allow the passengers to remain aboard her except for meals and other necessary purposes. I had represented to him the hardships of the warehouses as shelter for women and children, but he regarded the vessel's situation as too precarious for them to sleep aboard her. Instead, he ran gangplanks ashore and fed them hot meals during the thirty-six hours that intervened before the *Jefferson* came up and took off the passengers and treasure.

While the *Alaska* was lying up at Swanson Bay, the steamer *Sophia*, northbound to Skagway, came up and her skipper demanded that Nord pull out and let him dock there. He was insistent about it, as he declared Nord's ship was occupying his berth. But Nord was equally emphatic that he would not leave the dock until the temporary repairs to his smashed bow had been completed. So the *Sophia's* captain could do nothing about it except lighter his cargo. This he did, and proceeded to Skagway.

Two days later the *Sophia* sailed from Skagway for Vancouver with 347 passengers and crew aboard. At midnight on her first day out, in a dense snowstorm in Lynn Canal, she fetched up on Vanderbilt Reef near Sentinel Island. For hours the *Sophia* lay on the reef, but there was no thought of danger among her officers or her passengers. While they awaited the coming of the *Princess Alice,* of the Canadian Pacific, which had been summoned to her assistance, the passengers danced and sang and made merry. During that time fifteen or sixteen American vessels passed the *Sophia* and offered their assistance, but to each her captain replied that the *Princess Alice* was coming up and would take off her passengers. The *Princess Alice* was owned by the Canadian Pacific, which also owned the *Sophia,* and using her instead of foreign vessels would mean the avoidance of payment for the passengers' fares.

At five o'clock the following morning when most of her passengers were in their berths a heavy sea lifted the *Sophia* off the reef, crushed in her double bottom, and she sank immediately in one hundred fathoms. All aboard were lost. It was the worst wreck in the history of Alaskan waters.

At about the hour the *Sophia* went down in Lynn Canal the *Alaska* steamed slowly into her dock at Seattle. Nord once again had saved his ship, his passengers, and his cargo.

An amusing, but irritating, sequel to the *Alaska's* mishap occurred after I reached Seattle aboard the *Jefferson*, which had taken off the *Alaska's* passengers. Mindful of the express company's reproach of me for not having saved its consignment of furs from the wreck of the *Mariposa*, I had caused the transfer to the *Jefferson* of the company's consignment of $150,000 in furs. Some of the *Jefferson's* crew had broached the fur shipment and more than half the pelts were stolen. I was tartly criticized by the express company officials for having transferred the furs to the *Jefferson*.

CHAPTER XIV

THE GREAT STRIKE OF THE seamen's union that, in 1922, tied up all shipping along both coasts for months, and paralyzed much of the nation's commerce while it lasted, found the *Alaska* fast to Pier 39 in San Francisco harbor. I was again her purser. Since she had struck on Bald Bluff in 1918 I had served as purser aboard various other ships of the line, alternating for the most part between the *Northwestern* and the *Alameda*. At the time of the seamen's strike the *Alaska* was operating under charter to the Union Pacific Railroad, making three trips a month between Portland, Oregon, and San Francisco. Under the terms of the charter the Alaska Steamship Company supplied the crew for the vessel, but as the company was unable to obtain men for her operation, she had remained idle for six weeks at her pier in San Francisco.

Eventually, early in August, she signed on a scratch crew and proceeded to Portland with three hundred passengers. Sometime during the three days she lay up at Portland, her commander, Captain Nord, a sincere supporter of the union demands, had wired to the company's offices in Seattle asking to be relieved of his command. His request was complied with and Captain Harry Hobey was sent from Seattle to take over the vessel.

Prior to his assignment to the *Alaska*, Hobey had completed a voyage to Alaska on the *Northwestern* with a non-union crew. It was the first vessel to leave any Pacific port during the strike. There were no mishaps on that voyage, but from then on Hobey was a marked man. After his completion of that voyage, he had received many letters denouncing him as an enemy of the union and threatening him with death if he did not quit the sea. Hobey was an upright and fearless skipper, and although the letters did not intimidate him in the least, he took their threats seriously. He had shown me several of them prior to our sailing.

The strike had been settled before the *Alaska* was due to sail for San Francisco and she left Portland with a crew of 125 men, of whom 90 per cent were union members, the balance men long in the service of the Alaska Steamship Company who had not joined the strike. There were aboard 240 passengers, among them women and children. We had good weather on the voyage until within one hundred miles of San Francisco, when the *Alaska* ran into a heavy fog such as is prevalent along the California coast at that season. Hobey, a splendid mariner, at all times alert and cautious at the least sign of danger, immediately changed his course and proceeded warily at half speed.

He was in the purser's office at nine o'clock the night before the *Alaska* was due to make port and mentioned to me that he had thought it expedient, because of the fog, to change her course and to reduce her speed, adding that it would mean a delay of not more than half an hour in her scheduled time of arrival. After chatting with me for half an hour or so, he went up on the bridge, and later retired some time before eleven o'clock.

I turned in a short time after completing the day's

routine, and to the accompaniment of the measured and mournful sounding of the foghorn I soon fell asleep.

I was only half awake at five o'clock—my usual rising time—when I heard a rending, grinding crash. Immediately a long shudder passed through the vessel as she came to a lurching stop and listed to starboard. The sound and the shock could mean only one thing. The ship had struck something. I hurried out on deck. The fog was still dense; I could see no other vessel near by. I could make out the figure of the skipper on the bridge, cool, alert, issuing his orders calmly and unhesitatingly. The *Alaska* had struck on Blunts Reef about ten miles off Cape Mendocino, and it was evident that she was in a bad way. I hurried back to the purser's office, donned my overcoat, and with a safety pin secured in its inside breast pocket the ship's currency and lists of her passengers and crew. Then I returned to the deck.

The skipper's first order, when he realized what had happened, was to the wireless operator to send out S O S signals. His next was to launch the boats. There was perfect discipline among the crew and little alarm among the passengers, and as the sea was calm, with only a long, heavy swell with no wind, the boats were swung out speedily and without difficulty. But after they were launched the crew left the vessel and gave no assistance in loading the passengers into them. Hobey, John Calpas, Chief Engineer, and I were the only ones to do this. In the meantime the wireless had given the *Alaska's* position to the *Comax*, of the British Colonial Salvage Company, and she had replied that she was only ten miles distant and would come up to our assistance.

While we engaged in getting off the passengers, the *Alaska* took another bad list to starboard and lay at an angle of forty-five degrees. As she listed many of the passengers, for the most part women and children, ran to starboard and clung to the life lines. The skipper, Calpas, and I had great difficulty in persuading them to let go the life lines and slide into the boats, which they could easily have done, for they were now almost level with the saloon deck. In some cases we had forcibly to loosen their grip on the lines and push them into the boats. I had passed several children over the rail to a boat when the *Alaska* took another heavy list, which brought the rail but a few feet above the water. Hobey came up to me and we climbed the sloping deck to the portside rail where we hung on. We looked about but could see no one else on the deck except Calpas, who had gone to the stern to look for any passengers who might have been left behind.

"Jump, Calpas," the skipper ordered.

The chief engineer hesitated a moment, then dropped overboard. Hobey turned to me.

"You'd better do the same, Morgan. There isn't much time. She's going down fast."

I poised myself on the rail. I knew that Hobey, in compliance with tradition, wanted to be the last to abandon his sinking ship. Then I jumped.

As I did so I heard a shot. It seemed to have come from one of the boats. I hit the water at the moment the crest of a wave neared the vessel and as I went through it I held my breath and struck out vigorously away from the vessel to avoid being engulfed by the suction when she should sink, which I expected to happen at any moment. After a minute or so I came up just as a mass of wreckage hurtled through the air and hit the water not a foot away from me. There was no sign of the *Alaska* or her skipper, but a churning disturbance of the water marked where the ship had gone down.

In drawing my breath upon emerging from the wave I had sucked in large quantities of the oil which coated the water. Almost immediately I became violently nauseated, retching and vomiting, and in the act shipping yet more oil-smeared sea water. The vomiting was making me weak, I was cold and numb, and the weight of my overcoat and my life belts impeded me in my attempts to paddle away from the oil patches on the water. I was suffering excruciating pain from cuts caused by splinters of wreckage, and I was reconciling myself to the fate that was inevitable when I could no longer hold my head up. I was trying, with not too much success, to remember prayers appropriate to the occasion, when just ahead of me I saw a mattress floating on the water, and made for it. I got aboard with great difficulty, and promptly my position on it was endangered by a renewed spell of vomiting. When I had thrown up—as I hoped—all the oil I had swallowed, I observed that my mattress raft was sagging badly at one end. It was becoming waterlogged and could not remain afloat much longer.

Providentially, a piece of hatch floated by just then and after much effort I maneuvered to get it under the mattress, and transferred myself to the upholstered raft. Then, weak from my vomiting, smarting from the pain of the cuts on my legs, and numb from the cold, I fainted. How long I remained unconscious I do not know, but when I came to I was still on my raft. The fog had lifted a little and in the water all about me were people, afloat because of their life belts, but terrified and suffering from exposure, and crying piteously for help. The only aid I could give them now was counsel. I called to those who could hear me that the *Comax* was coming up, that she was only a short distance away, that she ought to arrive at any moment, and that they should not exhaust their energy by crying out.

I had another vomiting attack which left me weaker than ever and just barely able to keep myself on the raft. I drifted around on it for hours—about four hours, I later calculated—and as the fog steadily lifted I noted that there were fewer persons to be seen in the water. Also, the cries for help had stopped. Presently I could discern the misty outlines of a lifeboat not a dozen feet away from me. Using my hands for sweeps, I paddled furiously toward it and in another minute it was drifting alongside. A sailor was in the bow, and there were about a dozen passengers in the boat. I recognized the seaman as John Desmond, a quartermaster on the *Alaska*. Promptly I slipped off the raft and gripped the gunnel of the boat forward. I was too weak to get myself into it.

"Give us a hand and pull me in," I ordered. I could see that Desmond did not recognize me.

"No, there's no room in this boat," he answered gruffly.

I held on and renewed my demand to be taken aboard, telling him that there was plenty of room in the boat.

"No, damn you, I tell you there's no room. Let go, or I'll smash your hand."

He raised an oar threateningly. I let go, paddled back to the stern and with a painful effort hooked a leg over the side. A sad-faced boy, one of the passengers, sat in the stern.

"Here, Son, for God's sake help me over," I begged him.

Without a word or a change of expression he grabbed my shoulders and tugged with all his might until

I fell into the boat. There I lay on the bottom, exhausted but conscious, for several minutes. When I had recovered my breath and a little strength I sat up.

"I'll take charge of this boat, quartermaster," I called to Desmond. "Look sharp now and take an oar."

Now for the first time he recognized me, but he said nothing, only gave me a surly nod as he obeyed the order. When I had come up to the boat no one was making an effort to row. In addition to Desmond and myself there were four men, the rest women. I ordered the men to take oars and row, and for all in the boat to be on the watch for persons in the water. For two hours we cruised about in a search for survivors. They were fewer now, for some of them had been picked up by other boats; some had been drowned. We saw many bodies afloat, but we did not bother with the dead. However, we had rescued four women by the time the *Comax* came up six hours after the *Alaska* had sunk. Although she was only ten miles distant when she got our wireless signal, she had been slow in coming up because, at the time, she was towing a barge loaded with a thousand tons of coal, and this she had had to turn over to another vessel before proceeding to our relief.

When it came our turn to be taken aboard the *Comax* I mistrusted my ability to make it. I was so weak from my incessant vomiting, the loss of blood from the gashes in my legs, and my long immersion, that I was afraid to climb the Jacob's ladder for fear I would fall back into the lifeboat and break some bones. I insisted on everyone else taking precedence over me, which they did without protest, so that, as the last one out of the boat, I could kick it away as I mounted the ladder. Then, if I fell, it would be in the water. I got aboard without incident.

Once on the *Comax* I crawled to her fireroom for

warmth. There I was delighted to see John Calpas drying himself. I had last seen his heels going over the *Alaska's* stern and I had not been sure that he had survived. At sight of me Calpas, in spite of the seriousness of the occasion, burst out laughing. I believed that it must be hysterics, for I could see no occasion for levity and, most assuredly, I was not in the mood for it.

"If you could see your face, Morgan, you'd laugh too," the chief told me, noting my grimness.

"What's wrong with my face?"

"Nothing, only it's as black as a nigger's, but not so uniformly so. It's streaked like a Zulu on the warpath."

Then, while we dried our clothes and warmed ourselves, I told him about my oil baths. It was days and days before frequent bathings removed all traces of it from my face and body.

CHAPTER XV

IN THE LITTLE DINING ROOM of the *Comax,* her skipper,
Captain Snoddy, checked from the lists I gave him the
names of passengers and crew who had been rescued.
When he had rechecked against the total of the survivors
the names of those missing—120 were lost—he again
silently scanned the lists.

Then, "Where is Captain Hobey?" he asked gravely.

No one answered. Where was Hobey? Where, indeed,
would he be save where a gallant skipper such as he would
prefer to be—with his ship at the bottom of the sea, there
to remain, his bones picked clean by vulture fish, in
sepulcher until the last trumpet shall summon land and
sea to yield up their immemorial dead.

The *Comax* landed the *Alaska's* survivors at Eureka,
California, early in the evening. Those among them who
were in good shape were lodged in hotels, the others in
hospitals. I was among the latter, for I was suffering
greatly from the cuts on my legs, my vomiting, and exposure. At the Sisters' Hospital I was X-rayed, and when
it was found my bones were intact, my wounds were
dressed and I was put to bed for a rest. But I could not
rest. The gashes on my legs, scars of which I bear to this
day, pained me frightfully. Quite as intolerable was the
agony in my midriff, caused by the retching and vomiting

of the bilge and oil I had swallowed. It seemed to me that never in my life had I experienced such pain and weariness; that the only thing that would assuage the torture was a copious draught of whisky. Yet all I was offered was a cup of thin broth. I pushed it aside impatiently and demanded whisky. The nurse soothingly tried to insist upon my drinking the broth, but when I again refused and persisted in my demand for whisky she left the room, saying she would ask the doctor.

In a moment she returned with one of the Sisters, an elderly woman, kindly and understanding, to whom I renewed my pleading for whisky. She smiled, but there was no hint of acquiescence in the smile.

"Of course, I can't give you that," she said. "Drink the broth; it's much better for you."

"I don't want the stuff. I need whisky more than broth. I'm chilled through, and weak. These bandages are too tight and they are torturing me. Why can't I have a drink?"

"Because the doctor's directions said nothing about whisky, and I wouldn't take the responsibility of giving it to you without his order."

"When will he be around again?"

"Oh, he's gone for the night. He won't call again until morning."

"Telephone him, then," I demanded. "I must have some whisky and I can't wait until morning."

"Now, you know I can't do that," she said. "Anyhow, I'm sure he doesn't want you to have it, for he did not leave word to let you have any. Now, please, drink the broth and go to sleep. You need rest more than anything else and you are not doing yourself any good by getting excited."

But I was quite as determined to have the whisky as she was that I should not have it. I made one more effort.

"Unless you do what I ask, Sister, I tell you—and I'm in dead earnest—I'll leave the hospital at once and go where I can get the whisky."

I think the good woman saw I was in earnest, but hoped by her patience to overcome my stubbornness. I am sure that she did not realize, any more than I myself did, that she had to deal with a half-delirious man.

"But you can't go without your clothes," she told me smilingly, "and where would you go?"

"To a hotel—anywhere that I can get a drink. And I'll go just the way I am if you refuse to give me my clothes."

I half rose from the bed as if to put my threat into action.

"Very well, if you are determined," she said, and I knew I had won. "But the responsibility is yours. If you'll be patient for a minute or two, I'll phone for a taxicab for you and bring you your clothes."

She was back presently with my clothes. I dressed hurriedly and as I was shucking into my overcoat someone knocked on the door. It was the Sister to announce that the taxicab had arrived. I went out, thanking her as she stood at the door, a worried expression on her countenance.

At the hotel the clerk told me they were full up. I examined the register, saw Calpas' name on it, and went up to his room. There I found Calpas beset by reporters who were plying him with questions about the wreck, how and where and when it had occurred, how many had been lost, how many rescued, his own experience in the water, when he had last seen Captain Hobey. At sight of my oil-begrimed features and wrinkled and tattered uniform, about which clung the rank odors of brine and iodoform, they sensed I was another survivor and pounced on me. As I sank wearily into a chair, however, they seemed to have a momentary feeling of compassion for me, and one of them offered me my pick of several suits of clothing which they had brought along for survivors. None of them was anywhere near my size, and in their eagerness to be of help they next offered me food, coffee, cigarettes, all of which I declined.

"You fellows suggest everything but the one thing I want," I told them.

"A drink of course," one said, and as I nodded he went to the telephone and gave an order. Five minutes later a bellboy arrived with three quart bottles of whisky and glasses.

I poured myself a jolt, the size of which awed even the two-fisted drinkers of the press, and gulped it down. Oh, that was recompense for the bilge and vile oil I had swallowed after my plunge. Almost immediately I felt a tingle and warm glow in my veins. The weariness that oppressed me was dropping off like a discarded cloak, the smart of my wounded legs and the soreness of over-strained stomach muscles were soothed. Whisky! Thank God for this life-giving liquid, the nonpareil among all restoratives! I poured myself another drink, of the same generous proportions as the first, and drank it down at a single toss. Its effect was even more beneficent. Presently I grew sleepy and the reporters' questions came to my ears as though spoken far away.

The drowsiness was delicious. I ceased to attempt any replies to the reporters' questions. I was completely in-different to them. To hell with them! Let them get their story without me as best they could. What was there to tell anyway? Except that the *Alaska* had struck on a reef in the fog, had sunk, so many saved, so many drowned. Hadn't I heard the shot that put an end to the skipper's gallant life? I poured myself another drink and once again fell into a doze. When I was aroused by Calpas gently shaking my shoulder, the reporters had gone.

Then came the reaction. I was not drunk, I assured myself, but I would not heed Calpas' suggestion that I turn in and get some sleep and rest. How could I sleep, with the mournful sound of the *Alaska's* foghorn, the rending crash of her hull on the reef, the cries of her drowning passengers, the shot that cut down her skipper still sounding in my ears?

No more could I dismiss from my vision the sight of drowning men and women and children, the ghostly wraiths evoked by the fog, and the figure of the skipper as I had last seen him clutching the port rail as his ship went down under his feet.

The recollection of what I had heard and seen and undergone since the moment the *Alaska* struck was so poignant that I poured myself another drink, and another. Thoroughly drunk by now, I pressed drinks upon poor Calpas, who was saner than I and craved only rest. He did not need whisky, did not want it, but drank it only to still the clamor of my urgings. In a frenzy I tore the bandages from my legs and laughed drunkenly at my wounds and the bloodstained lint on the floor. Then I sang, or tried to sing sailors' chanteys, ribald songs of the sea, but the discord brought the hotel manager to the door. Seeing my condition, he sympathetically urged that I get some sleep and let my fellow survivors, of whom there were many in the hotel, get some also. But I only laughed and offered him a drink, and, when he would not accept it, cursed him, bade him "get the hell out of here," and slammed the door in his face.

When he had gone I progressed to a phase of my inebriation in which my voice became muted, my mood grave, almost to tearfulness. From noisy outburst, I subsided into a great calm in which, in tones subdued but charged with drunken feeling, I apostrophized persons and things. With glass raised in an unsteady hand which spilled its contents over me and the floor, I toasted the sea. The sea—more than wife to a man, far more than mistress! The sea, best of mothers, who takes to her bosom her weary children! The sea, God bless her! No, God damn her! She's a slut, a vile strumpet who takes all, gives nothing, who destroys men in her embrace! A loathsome spider, who devours men even as they woo her. The sea, the sea is a, is a —— I had run out of invectives.

"What is the sea, John?"

But Calpas did not answer. He had fallen crosswise on the bed, not to awaken until he had slept the clock around.

I forced myself to drink again, toasting perdition to the seamen's union; to Desmond, the heartless quartermaster who would have let me die in the water; to the doctor who had sought to withhold whisky from me. But most fervently I drank death and damnation to the coward whose bullet had killed Hobey, kindly, gallant Hobey.

And then I drank to the skipper, "To Hobey, brave soul, wherever you are——"

I remember no more of that drunken night.

CHAPTER XVI

I HAD MADE MY LAST VOYAGE as an officer aboard a ship at sea. Six years after the *Alaska* had gone down I was a passenger on board the *Aleutian,* bound from Seattle to Seward, the commander Captain Nord, a skipper whom I had always admired and under whom I had been proud to serve. After the wreck of the *Alaska,* there had been an inquiry which came to nothing. There had been ugly rumors that the ship had come to her tragic end as the result of foul play at the hands of some of her crew, that her compass had been tampered with, that her skipper had not been drowned but had been assassinated just before his vessel sank. Divers had been sent to the scene of the wreck to bring up her instruments if possible, to find Hobey's body and establish proof or disproof of the rumors as to the cause of his death.

Nothing had been found, nothing had been proved, and the mystery was unsolved—except for me. I did not need the production of his poor, sea-bleached corpse to satisfy me as to the manner of his death. I had heard the shot that killed him. I was convinced, and to this day I remain unshaken in my belief, that the bullet that ended his gallant career was not fired by his own hand. For I knew the man, knew him as a kindly, clean-living, God-fearing

sailor, too high-minded and too brave to have done himself to death. And I knew he was no quitter.

In the interval between the sinking of the *Alaska* and
my final voyage as a ship's officer I had been shifted from
pillar to post, serving as purser on various ships of the line
until I began to consider myself a marine Wandering Jew.
My last transfer had been to the *Victoria*, which formerly
operated in the Cunard transatlantic service as the *Pathia*.
I made several voyages aboard her, and it was on one of
them that I decided to quit the sea for good.

My decision was not made impulsively. I long had been
considering this step, not because I was tiring of the sea,
or because I regarded its hazards as too great. There was no
life so alluring, so fascinating, so altogether congenial to
me as that of a mariner, and it was only because of its
attraction that I had been so long in coming to a decision.
But I had finally convinced myself that I could no longer
afford to indulge myself in this preference. I was getting
on in years, and soon I would be in the sere and yellow.
Whether I wanted to or not, I would have to quit the sea
when the time of superannuation overtook me. Better to
anticipate that time while there yet remained to me
strength and vigor to engage in some occupation which
would return to me, in greater measure than marine service,
something of the worldly goods I had all my adult life been
seeking with indifferent success.

I owed it to myself, as well as to my patient, helpful
wife, to accumulate a competence for our old age while
there was yet time. She was a good sport—none better—
who had never complained at the frequent long separations
entailed by my service at sea, but I knew that she would
welcome my decision to quit, however calmly she might
accept any decision to the contrary I might make. I had

had a glorious time indulging my bent for freedom of movement, for change, for adventure—first in the Yukon, next upon the sea. It had been fun, but not very profitable. Perhaps I had had as much enjoyment out of my avocations as anyone could reasonably expect who had to live by his own efforts. Decidedly it was time to think of something besides enjoyment in life. "Gold is where you find it." So far, I had not found it. Perhaps, by persisting, I might yet find it.

So I had said my farewell to a mariner's occupation, had invested my life savings of $35,000 in a cannery that promised generous returns on my capital investment, and now, aboard the *Aleutian*, I was on my way to take over the ownership of the plant I had bought.

The cannery plant was off Latouche, on Hobo Island, the name of which subsequently was more happily changed to Evans Island. Hobo Island's meteorological eccentricities were perhaps the most diabolical of any spot of land on the globe. Daily on the island it blew a gale of such intensity that one, literally, could lean against it, and the wind was of such strength that buildings had to be anchored against flight into the Gulf of Alaska. Stout cables were passed over them and secured to near-by rocks, of which there was an oversupply. When it wasn't raining on Hobo Island it was snowing. Often it was doing both. Almost daily there were temblors, subterranean rumblings that threatened to, and sometimes did, topple over buildings the gale had spared.

Decidedly Hobo Island was no paradise for weather. The island had so bad a name in this respect that it was the subject of a popular explanation as to how the whale, a mammal, had become permanently a denizen of the sea. The whale, the story went, originated on Hobo Island,

Dock at Valdez

but after less than a year's experience with its meteorological vagaries, the original settlers decided they had had enough of a land existence and took permanently to the water.

Aboard the *Aleutian,* Nord twitted me on my abandonment of a seafaring life and my choice of locale for my commercial efforts. He was one of the most genial and likable, as well as capable, sea captains I had ever known and it was a pleasure to be aboard his ship. There were only about thirty passengers aboard on this voyage and I spent a great deal of time with him, almost to the hour we reached Valdez, where I was to land before going on to Hobo Island.

At Valdez, just before I went ashore, Nord came to me and gripped me cordially by the hand.

"Sorry you're quitting the sea for a landlubber's life, Morgan," he said, "but I wish you the best of luck."

I thanked him. "When are you going to quit yourself, Gus?"

I knew that he had been thrifty and, on that score, could retire at any time he was so inclined.

"Me? Never," he answered. "Why, what would I do if I quit? I'd have to keep busy somehow, and the only thing left for me would be to become a damned pilot."

The *Aleutian* proceeded on to Seward. A few days later she fetched up at midday, in broad daylight, on an uncharted reef off Kodiak Island in Uyak Bay, and sank in less than ten minutes. All of her crew of 190, and the passengers were saved. It was an inexplicable mishap for a navigator so skilled and cautious as Nord, who for thirty-five years had sailed these waters without losing a vessel. Nevertheless, he was set down for two years. It broke his spirit. He never again got a command. When

I last heard of him he was a pilot on ships navigating the waters he knew so well.

Two years later I myself suffered the shipwreck of my venture. I invested my modest fortune in the cannery almost at the peak of the late lamented boom. For a time the business prospered; then came the crash. Prices dropped, and my little craft began to sink. I clung to her rigging desperately, but as she foundered, I let go. I was a survivor—with an empty poke.

POSTSCRIPT

Edward Morgan died on May 17, 1939, in Meadowbrook Hospital, Hempstead, New York, in his sixty-ninth year. For several years after his return from Alaska, and until a short time before his death, he had lived in a bungalow on the shores of Long Island Sound, just outside the quaint little town of Stony Brook. His death occurred not long after the completion of this narrative of his adventurous life in the territory.

H. F. W.

Jackson Heights, N. Y.
June, 1947.